Alice Jovy

English Correspondence and Report Writing for Real Estate Professionals

2. Auflage Juli 2012

© 2012 IZ Immobilien Zeitung Verlagsgesellschaft, Luisenstraße 24, 65185 Wiesbaden

Alle Rechte, insbesondere das Recht der Vervielfältigung und der Verbreitung sowie der Übersetzung, vorbehalten. Kein Teil des Werkes darf in irgendeiner Form (durch Fotokopie, Mikrofilm oder ein anderes Verfahren) ohne schriftliche Genehmigung des Verlages reproduziert oder unter Verwendung elektronischer Systeme gespeichert, verarbeitet, vervielfältigt oder verbreitet werden.

Lektorat: Thomas Hilsheimer
Umschlagsgestaltung: epiphan, Wiesbaden
Satz: s.tietze@medien-frankfurt.com
Druck: Beltz Druckpartner GmbH, Hemsbach

ISBN 978-3-940219-16-9

Alice Jovy

English Correspondence and Report Writing for Real Estate Professionals

Anleitung, Mustersätze und -formulierungen, Briefe und Fachvokabular zur professionellen englischen Kommunikation in der Immobilienwirtschaft

2., überarbeitete und erweiterte Auflage

Table of Contents

Preface 7

Acknowledgements 8

Introduction 9

1. Language, Grammar
   and Style 11

2. General
   Correspondence 25

3. Office Property 49

4. Retail Property 65

5. Industrial and
   Logistics Property 83

6. Managing Properties 91

7. Acquisitions & Sales 139

8. Due Diligence 169

9. Property Development 195

10. Invitations and
    Seasons Greetings 227

11. Job Applications 237

Glossary 269

 Ausführliche Inhaltsverzeichnisse zu den einzelnen Kapitel jeweils am Kapitelanfang

Preface

When visiting the offices of many real estate professionals in Germany, one cannot help but notice a copy of the Immobilien Zeitung Real Estate Dictionary propped up on a shelf or desk. This dictionary has become an essential reference tool for professionals and students alike, particularly as almost every sector of the real estate business has experienced the effect of increasing globalisation and the need to communicate with colleagues, clients and business partners in English.

Many of my students have commented that it would be useful to have examples of how individual words are used in context in the form of ready-made phrases and how they may be adapted to everyday situations. This is of course beyond the scope of a dictionary and so this book was conceived as a practical guide and reference to correspondence for professionals in the real estate business.

A high standard of correspondence suggests a high standard in business. It reflects the competence and professionalism of the person who has written it and the company they work for. This book aims to provide guidance and ready-to-use phrases for effective real estate correspondence in English. It is hoped this will enable readers to improve their writing skills so that they can approach business writing tasks with increased confidence. Examples are provided for situations commonly encountered by real estate professionals in many fields of work. The real estate business encompasses a wide range of different professions and areas of work. Therefore the focus of this book is assigned to commercial property as this is considered to be the sector where most correspondence is undertaken in English.

Interviews and research were conducted with professionals in the UK in order to capture the authenticity of language used by native professionals. The correspondence and documents used reflect authentic information in real estate practice.

Preface

A common criticism of model phrases is that the user may copy them for inappropriate situations. The user is not relieved of the necessity of understanding the context or making decisions regarding the context of the letters and to make whatever amendments seem fit in the circumstances. Having said that, there is no doubt that model phrases, sensibly used, are a useful tool to the busy professional.

Although every possible care and attention has been taken to ensure that all definitions and translations are accurate, no responsibility can be accepted for inadvertent errors or omissions. The information in this book is not designed to provide legal or specific advice in managing or in the transaction of property. Decisions made in any given circumstances or for any given property are subject to many factors. In all cases the information provided in this book serve only as an example and should not be used or relied upon for legal purposes or be considered as the only way of approaching business situations.

It is of course an impossible task to include all aspects of correspondence encountered in the real estate business and inevitably some situations will not be covered. I should be grateful to receive any suggestions for standard phrases or letters for inclusion in a further edition.

Acknowledgements

I am very grateful to all those who have made this book possible. Comments, suggestions and criticism have provided valuable insights and contributions. First and foremost I wish to acknowledge the patience of my husband, Kurt Jovy. I also wish to express my gratitude to my father, John Waldron for the proofreading and professional input he has provided. I am most grateful to the editor, Thomas Hilsheimer and graphic designer Sybille Tietze, who through their expertise have added so much in creating the final product. Finally, I thank my students, who are a constant source of inspiration and knowledge. Through my teaching, I am always learning and as my students share their knowledge with me, I hope to share it with my readers.

Furthermore, I would like to thank the following people for their professional input: Alan Mitchell, Anja Schäfer, Anke Haverkamp, Annette Kaiser, Antje Haas, Beatrix Kersten, Dagmar Marx, Elif Ebeci, Erika Schröder-Eisenach, Irina Hinz, Karsten Kujus, Katrin Gibbons, Dipl-Ing. Maja Procz, Marta Kosilo, Oliver Schmitt, Peter Cairns MRICS VOB, Managing Partner Gleeds Germany GbR, Regina Andreas, Robert Renner, Ruth Laxton, Semir Selcukoglu, Tina Reuter.

Bad Soden a. Ts., Juli 2012

Alice Jovy

Introduction

The contents of this book are arranged into key real estate activities encountered by professionals in their work. Each unit offers vocabulary and phrases that deal with situations specific to these individual areas. It is possible to access the book at any stage, however, vocabulary and phrases examined in earlier units are not necessarily repeated where an overlap in activities exist.

In addition to specific real estate activities, three further units address common correspondence issues.

Unit 1 introduces the issues of grammar and style and examines the way English is used as a global language. The use of modern business English is discussed and guidance is given on when it is appropriate to use formal and informal language as well as the etiquette of using first names. An overview of key grammar issues is provided and a glossary of common British and American spelling and grammar differences. Finally common abbreviations and acronyms are listed.

Unit 2 deals with general correspondence for everyday situations – arranging a meeting, beginning and ending emails, requests, complaints and many other common phrases. A glossary of phrases for everyday business situations is provided with illustrations of both formal and informal examples. In addition, example emails and letters are provided.

Units 3 to 9 cover real estate specific topics starting with descriptions of office, retail and industrial/logistic properties and moving on to examine the areas of managing the property, acquisitions and sales, due diligence, and property development.

Unit 10 provides examples of social business correspondence with illustrations of greetings, invitations and other personal matters.

Unit 11 examines the language, content and format of job applications. This unit explains the many differences between German, British and

Introduction

American applications as well as common real estate jobs and provides useful tips. Example CVs are provided for students and experienced applicants alike, with a glossary of phrases for describing different professional activities.

For the purposes of this book, British English is used, however North American differences are provided where possible. Correspondence examples are shown in fully blocked format, which is the style most commonly used in modern business correspondence. Fully blocked text is aligned to the left margin and no punctuation is used in the address or following the salutation or complimentary close (Dear and Yours sincerely/faithfully). Other layouts are also perfectly acceptable and individual companies may have their own preferred style of correspondence.

Explanations, tips and translations are provided in the margins along with space for the reader to make their own notes.

This book is primarily written in the English language for German native speakers and assumes some previous knowledge / linguistic proficiency. German translations have been provided for some correspondence examples and have been kept as close as possible to the original English meaning in order to aid understanding of the vocabulary used. The German text therefore, does not necessarily represent authentic German correspondence.

Throughout the book the following symbols highlight important issues:

TIP! Useful tips on style, tone and intercultural issues.

✗ Mistake! Common language traps and grammatical errors.

✓ Correct! Examples of correct language.

Where appropriate differences in British and North American terminology are highlighted.

 Formal language

 Informal language

The words from the individual units can be found in alphabetical order in the glossary at the end of the book.

Language, Grammar & Style

1

Intercultural Communication 12
International English 13
Formal and informal language 13
Gender neutrality 14

Grammar 15
Capital letters 15
Punctuation 16
Street Names... 16
Numbers 18

Differences between British and American English 18

Abbreviations and Acronyms 22

States in the Federal Republic of Germany 23

Test your Grammar and Style 24

1 Language, Grammar & Style

Intercultural Communication

To use language effectively and to understand the real meaning of messages it is important to be aware of the cultural context, the personality of the communication partner and to choose a style that is appropriate to the given situation. Researchers have found distinctly different communication styles between different cultures, indeed even the English language varies according to the culture in which it is spoken.

Linguistic and intercultural experts have identified tendencies or averages in the value system that makes up a culture and while this is not an exact science, the framework provides interesting insights into the tendencies within different cultures.

In German culture, truth and directness have been found to be key values which often come before diplomacy. Researchers have identified that Germans use more absolutes to intensify their language (**auf keinen Fall, bestimmt, völlig, absolut**) and more frequently use the modal verb **müssen** as well as the imperative. This usage when translated directly into English can appear overly strong and unfriendly. While Germans, Americans and Australians use direct language, the perceptions of directness differ. Germans are often more direct than Americans particularly when talking about facts or giving criticism.

In American culture direct language is more commonly used when communicating positive issues e.g. when giving a compliment. Being liked by others is considered to be a key value in American culture. When communicating issues such as criticism, Americans will therefore use more indirect language.

In Australia openness is highly valued and the style of communication is often considered to be very direct by cultures that do not speak in such a straightforward manner. At the same time Australians are considered to be informal and relaxed and distrust self-promotion. First names are used in almost all situations and academic titles have little relevance in business situations.

British and Asian cultures are almost similar in the use of diplomatic language. Diplomacy is put strongly before directness in communication. Directness is often associated with open confrontation and rudeness. Negative matters or disagreement are often expressed in a coded way:

> "**I disagree**" could be expressed "**I see your point, however …**"

To avoid misunderstanding, consideration should be given to language style and how it will appear to the recipient, especially when writing to important business partners and dealing with sensitive issues.

TIP!

Certain words can be used to "soften" sentences:

- **Unfortunately**, the meeting has been cancelled.
  (before giving "bad" news)

- **I am afraid** I can't agree to your offer.
  (before giving "bad" news)

- I **just** wanted to remind you about the deadline tomorrow.

- We have a **slight** problem.

- "**Could**" and "**would**" are used to make questions or statements less direct.

1 Language, Grammar & Style

International English

In the field of sociolinguistics, international English is a comparatively recent topic which describes the movement towards a global English standard as a lingua franca. It is acknowledged that the majority of English spoken in the world is by non-natives and the international variation of English promotes vocabulary that is easier to understand in the international context. American grammar and spelling is often used because it is normally simpler. The concept is difficult to define, particularly as it is not controlled by a specific institute or organisation, but rather by consensus.

Formal and informal language

Formal language is used in letters, reports and emails with a serious content. There are many fixed phrases with standard salutations and closes and the language is impersonal and polite. Contractions (**I've** for **I have**) are not used.

When the writer and reader have a more informal relationship language is closer to speech. It is simpler and more direct, with the use of contractions and its use is especially common in emails.

Below is a list of informal and formal words. Longer words of Latin origin tend to sound more formal and shorter words more informal.

Formal	Informal
enquire / request	ask
due to	because of
purchase	buy
verify	check
receive	get
contact	get in touch
assistance	help
postpone	move, put off (a meeting)
require	need
arrange	set up
regret / apologise	sorry
inform	tell

1 Language, Grammar & Style

Using first names in English is very common with business partners. Here are some tips to help you:

- If it is the first time you write to an important contact and are unsure how to address them, you should use their last name. Often you will receive a response with your first name.
- Use first names if you have had previous contact.
- Do what the other person does. If you are addressed by your first name, respond by using the other person's first name. If, however, the other person has a much higher status you may want to use their last name to show respect.
- Use last names for official correspondence such as important letters.

Academic titles play little part in business situations and are used mainly by medical doctors or by academic professionals.

Gender neutrality

In English there is no singular pronoun that can be used for both genders ("it" can only be used for objects, not for people). In modern language it has become increasingly inappropriate to use the personal pronouns he or his in correspondence when referring to a person whose sex might be either male or female.

There is no real satisfactory solution to this problem. However "them" and "their" are increasingly being accepted as singular pronouns.

"If anybody calls while I am out, tell him I will be back in an hour."

"If anybody calls while I am out, tell **them** I will be back in an hour."

Other options include:

- Using both pronouns together: he or she or he/she or s/he
- Rephrase the sentence to avoid the need of a pronoun.

1 Language, Grammar & Style

Grammar

Capital letters

- **Beginning sentences:**
  Dear Alan
  Please find attached the agenda for tomorrow's meeting.
- **Names of people, places and buildings:**
  Michael, Manchester, King's Road, Fiveways House
- **Authorities and organisations:**
  The Royal Institution of Chartered Surveyors
- **Acronyms:**
  BCSC (British Council of Shopping Centres)
- **A person's job title:**
  John Hall, Head of Sales & Acquisition
- **For nationalities and languages:**
  She is from France and speaks French.
- **Days, months, holidays:**
  Monday, January, Christmas
- **For countries, regions and defined areas:**
  The Hague, Germany, The West End
- **For undefined but recognisable political or geographical areas:**
  The Middle East, North Atlantic
- **To improve the layout and understanding of documents some words, such as in titles or table headings, may have capital letters:**
  Management Report, Tenancy Schedule, First Floor

Capitals are **not** used for ...

- **Nouns:**
  property, real estate, building
- **Seasons:**
  spring, summer, autumn, winter
- **Compass points:**
  north, south, east, west (except as in above)

Unlike in German, the first letter after the greeting is always a capital:

~~Dear Alan
please find ...~~

Dear Alan
Please find ... ✓

1 Language, Grammar & Style

> **Capital Letters in Contracts**
>
> English contracts usually start with a preamble which is similar to an introduction. The preamble defines the parties and the terms which are used in the main body of the contract in order to avoid repetition. Each time the party or definition is mentioned in the contract this is a reference to the corresponding long definition. Capital letters are used for these terms to indicate to the reader that they should refer to this definition section. For example, the main body of the contract does not mention the name of the company or individual; it simply refers to the Vendor, the Purchaser, or items important to the contract may be referred to as the Property, or the Lease.

Unlike German, commas are not used before "that" clauses:

I think, that the rents will increase.

I think that the rents will increase. ✓

Punctuation

Commas are not as common in English as in German and the rules are not as widely applied. As a general rule, commas are used in English to reflect pauses in speech.

- **After an initial phrase or clause:**
  Following some negotiation, we managed to come to an agreement.

- **To separate words in a list:**
  I am responsible for the Austrian, French, Dutch and Polish markets.

- **After writing a phrase or clause in the middle of a sentence:**
  Tom Martin, the Construction Engineer, will write the report.

- **After many linking words at the beginning of a sentence:**
  However, …   Unfortunately, …   Although, …

Street names

Definite articles are not used for streets in English: Regent Street (rather than The Regent Street).

1 Language, Grammar & Style

 In the UK it is now common not to use punctuation after the title, the opening and the closing greeting:

Dear Mr Collins
Sincerely

 In North America it is common to put a full stop after the title and commas after the opening and closing greeting:

Dear Mr. Collins,
Sincerely,

Apostrophes

- **Apostrophes show possession.**
  The apostrophe comes before the 's' when the noun is singular:
  My colleague's work (one colleague)
- **The apostrophe comes after the 's' when the noun is plural:**
  My colleagues' work (several colleagues)
- **If the singular form ends in an 's' the apostrophe can be used alone or after another 's':**
  Mr Collins' assistant will contact you.
  or Mr Collins's assistant will contact you.
- **Apostrophes show where letters are missing in contractions:**
  I'll, he's, we'd, we're

 Be careful not to confuse **it's** which means it is, with the possessive form **its**

The consultancy raised it's fee. ~~

The consultancy raised **its** fee. ✓

Colons and semi-colons

Colons are used to introduce lists:

The floor covering is available in the following colours: brown, grey and black.

Semicolons are used to link two clauses, which could stand alone but are closely related. Semicolons can be difficult to use. If you are unsure of their use, start a new sentence instead.

The office has a good staff canteen; other facilities could be improved.

Quotation marks

In English quotation marks are placed at the top of the word.

30 St Mary Axe is known as „the Gherkin". ~~

30 St Mary Axe is known as "the Gherkin". ✓

1 Language, Grammar & Style

Numbers

In English a comma is used to mark thousands and a point is used to show decimals. The currency is placed before the number.

English	German
0.1	0,1
1.1	1,1
Euro 100	100 Euro
Euro 1,000	1.000 Euro
Euro 10,000	10.000 Euro
Euro 1,000,000 (one million) 1m	1.000.000 Euro (eine Million) 1 Mio.
Euro 1,000,000,000 (one billion) 1bn	1.000.000.000 Euro (eine Milliarde) 1 Mrd.
one trillion	eine Billion

Million is abbreviated with 'm' in English, not with 'Mio'. Confusingly, so are minute and metre!

1 Mio ~~1 Mio~~
1m ✓

Differences between British and American English

Dates

 In the UK the date is shown in the order of day/month/year without commas.

15 August 2012

 In North America the date is shown in the order of month/day/year with commas.

August 15, 2012

In modern business correspondence the date is not written in full.

~~10th October 2012~~
or
~~Tuesday, 3rd of July 2012~~

10 October 2012 ✓
or
Tuesday 3 July 2012 ✓

Time

The 24-hour clock is rarely used in English except for travel documents. The Latin **ante meridiem** (a.m.) is used for morning and **post meridiem** (p.m.) for afternoon. The following written forms are also common:

am and pm, AM and PM, A.M. and P.M.

The meeting is scheduled for 2pm.

1 Language, Grammar & Style

Vocabulary

British English	American English
autumn	fall
block of flats	apartment building
car park	parking lot
cinema	movie theatre
crossroads	intersection
curriculum vitae (CV)	résumé
diary (appointments)	calendar
engaged (phone)	busy (phone)
first floor	second floor
flat	apartment
ground floor	first floor
holiday	vacation
let	lease
lift	elevator
main road, motorway	highway, freeway
mobile phone	cell phone
pavement	sidewalk
postal code	zip code
property	real estate
quote	quotation, estimate
rubbish	garbage, trash
shop	store
solicitor	lawyer, attorney
toilet	bathroom, restroom
transport	transportation
turnover	revenue
(the) Underground	subway

1 Language, Grammar & Style

Spelling

Some words are spelt differently in British and American English. American English is more phonetic than British English as the words tend to be spelt as they are pronounced.

The main differences are listed below:

Endings

British English	American English
- re (centre)	- er (center)
- our (colour)	- or (color)
- ise (organise)	- ize (organize)
- ence (defence)	- ense (defense)

The double use of the letter 'l' is normally not used in American English when modifying a noun or a verb:

British English	American English
traveller	traveler
cancelled	canceled

Spelling

British English	American English
aluminium	aluminum
apologise	apologize
centre	center
colour	color
enquiry	inquiry
fulfil	fulfill
grey	gray
harbour	harbor
litre	liter
mould	mold
neighbour	neighbor
programme	program
realise	realize
storey	story
theatre	theater
through	thru
travelling	traveling

1 Language, Grammar & Style

Grammar

British and American English have some grammatical differences. The main differences are summarised below.

Prepositions

Some prepositions are used differently in British and American English:

British English	American English
at the weekend	**on** the weekend
at Christmas/Easter	**on** Christmas/Easter
Please contact me **on** extension 338	Please contact me **at** extension 338

The present perfect tense

The present perfect tense is used less in American English than in British English. The simple past tense is often used as an alternative in sentences where an action has taken place in an unspecified time in the past and is linked to a present situation

British English	American English
I **have given** your report to the Head of Sales.	I **gave** your report to the Head of Sales.
They **haven't paid** their rent.	They **didn't pay** their rent.
Have you seen our presentation?	**Did you see** our presentation?

American English uses **the simple past** in sentences which contain the words **already**, **just** and **yet**:

British English	American English
The CEO **has just left** the office.	The CEO **just left** the office.
He **has just gone** home.	He **just went** home.
I **haven't read** the article yet.	I **didn't read** the article yet.

Some verbs have different simple past and past participle forms in British and American English:

British English	American English
I **learnt** a lot on the seminar.	I **learned** a lot on the seminar.
We have **got** a new heating system.	We have **gotten** a new heating system.

1 Language, Grammar & Style

Abbreviations and Acronyms

The following abbreviations and acronyms are often found in correspondence.

English		German	
#	Number / hash key / pound sign	Nummer / Rautetaste	
a.m.	before noon (ante meridiem)	morgens / vormittags	
AGM	Annual General Meeting	Jahreshauptversammlung	
asap	as soon as possible	baldmöglichst	
Attn.	attention	z.Hd. / zu Händen	
cc	copy/copies circulated to	in Kopie an	
CEO	Chief Executive Officer	(Haupt-) Geschäftsführer/in	
CET	Central European Time	Mitteleuropäische Zeit (MEZ)	
doc	document	Dokument	
e.g.	for example (exempli gratia)	zum Beispiel (z.B.)	
enc	enclosed	beiliegend	
etc.	and so on (et cetera)	und so weiter (usw.)	
FAQ	frequently asked questions	häufig gestellte Fragen	
Fwd	forwarded	weitergeleitet	
FYI	for your information	zu Ihrer Kenntnisnahme	
GMT	Greenwich Mean Time	Mittlere Greenwich-Zeit (UK-Zeit)	
i.e.	that is (id est)	das heißt (d.h.)	
N/A	not applicable	keine Angabe / nicht zutreffend	
NB	take note (nota bene)	mit der Bitte um Kenntnisnahme	
No.	number	Nummer (Nr.)	
p.a.	per annum	pro Jahr, jährlich	
p.m.	afternoon (post meridiem)	nachmittags / abends	
Pls	please	bitte	
p.p.	on behalf of (per procurationem)	im Auftrag (i.A.)	
PTO	please turn over	bitte wenden (b.w.)	
Re	with reference to, regarding	betreffend, mit Bezug auf	
rgds	regards	mit freundlichen Grüßen (mfg)	
RSVP	répondez s'il vous plait	um Antwort wird gebeten	
TBA	to be announced	wird noch angekündigt	
TBC	to be confirmed	(noch) zu bestätigen	
TBD	to be decided	noch zu entscheiden / noch festzulegen	
VAT	Value Added Tax	Mehrwertsteuer (MwSt.)	
PS	Postscript (post scriptum)	Nachschrift	

p.p. is often misinterpreted. It is used when someone is authorised to sign a letter on behalf of somebody else.

1 Language, Grammar & Style

States in the Federal Republic of Germany

Baden-Württemberg	Bavaria
Berlin	Brandenburg
Bremen	Hamburg
Hesse (Hessen)	Lower Saxony
Mecklenburg-West Pomerania	North Rhine-Westphalia
Rhineland-Palatinate	Saarland
Saxony	Saxony-Anhalt
Schleswig-Holstein	Thuringia

TIP!

In the UK the word county is used instead of state.

In the United States there are counties and states. A county is a local level of government below the state.

Test your Grammar and Style

Test your knowledge gained in this unit by identifying these common language mistakes. Underline the correct word or phrase.

1. The rent is *249,500 € / € 249,500* per annum.
2. The rent is € *1.080 / 1,080* per sq m.
3. The service charge is an additional € *3,90 / 3.90* per sq m.
4. Mutual House is a prime property at the corner of *the Bond Street / Bond Street*.
5. Please could you send the *German / german* version of the document.
6. Take-up in the *west end / West End* office sector increased last quarter.
7. The premises are located to the *north / North* of Frankfurt.
8. The meeting is scheduled for *17 pm / 5 pm* on Wednesday.
9. The tenant will take possession of the property on *it's / its* completion.
10. The current investment volume is *25m / 25 mio*.
11. *I think, that / I think that* we need to offer further incentives.
12. The *Winter / winter* weather has caused delays to the construction works.

# General Correspondence — 2

Useful Expressions 26
Salutation 26
Opening: Referring
to previous contact 26
Reason for contact 28
Requests 28
Requesting information 28
Responding to requests 30
Giving information 30
Arranging a meeting 30
Accepting / Declining a meeting 32
Rescheduling a meeting 32
Confirmations 32
Following up on meetings 34
Promising action 34
offering help 34
Attachments / Enclosures 34
Thanking 36
Recommendations / Suggestions .. 36
Status reports 36
Complaints /
Showing dissatisfaction 38
Apologising 38
Giving difficult news 38

Expressing opinions 40
Agreeing 40
Disagreeing 40
Closing sentences 40
Complementary closing 42
Colloquial expressions 43

Example Correspondence 44
Arranging a meeting 44
Confirming a meeting 44
Cancelling a meeting 44
Rescheduling a meeting 45
Requesting action 45
Thanking 45
Out-of-office replies 46
Payment reminders 46
 First reminder 46
 Second reminder 47
 Final reminder 47

Avoid the general language mistake and improve your style 48

2 General Correspondence

Useful Expressions

The following unit provides a glossary of useful expressions for general correspondence. Examples of formal and informal expressions are given, however deciding which style is appropriate depends on the context and the personal style of writing.

Formal

Salutation

Dear Sir
Dear Madam
Dear Sir or Madam
Dear Sirs
Dear Mr/Mrs/Ms

~~Miss~~

Ms ✓

Miss is not used in business correspondence. Mrs is used for married women, if this information is known.

Opening: Referring to previous contact

I refer to our recent conversation/telephone conversation regarding …
I refer to your letter/email of 25 March concerning/regarding …
Thank you for your letter of 10 January concerning/regarding …
Further to our meeting on 3 April, …
Further to your last email, …
Further to our telephone conversation of 14 August, …
Thank you for calling this morning regarding …
I apologise for the delay in replying.
I apologise for not replying sooner to your letter of 15 April regarding …
We met last month at the Expo Real in Munich.
Thank you for your email.

2 General Correspondence

Informal

Salutation

Hallo Mary

Mary

Opening: Referring to previous contact

Thanks for your email of 15 July.

Re your email, ...

Sorry for not getting in touch sooner.

It was good to meet you again last week.

Thanks for contacting me about ...

Following our telephone conversation last Tuesday, ...

Following our discussion/meeting last week, ...

Thanks for your email.

Many thanks for contacting me.

TIP!

"**Re**" is short for "with reference to" or "regarding"

2 GENERAL CORRESPONDENCE

Formal

_ Reason for contact

I am writing with regard to/with reference to ...

I am writing in connection with ...

I am writing to you regarding/concerning ...

I am contacting you regarding ...

Your name was given to me by ...

I am writing to advise you that ...

request
Anfrage

TIP!
"**I wonder if you could**" is a polite and cautious way to ask somebody for something.

_ Requests

I would be grateful if you could ...

I wonder if you could ...

I have a couple of questions regarding ...

Your help would be appreciated.

I would be grateful if you could contact me as a matter of **urgency** in order to ...

I understand that you are very busy, but I would very much appreciate any assistance you can offer and will, of course, reciprocate as and when the opportunity arises.

I would be most grateful if you could help me in this matter.

Please contact me as soon as possible to discuss this.

urgency
Dringlichkeit

_ Requesting information

I would be grateful if you could send me/forward me details regarding ...

I would appreciate it if you could send me a copy of ...

Could you please send me further/additional information about ...

Please provide details of ...

I am interested in receiving information about ...

We require the document by ...

asap
as soon as possible

I would appreciate a reply **asap**.

2 GENERAL CORRESPONDENCE

Informal

Reason for contact

Just **a short note** about …

Just a note to say …

I am writing about …

Just a short message to let you know / to confirm / …

Please note that …

Just wanted to let you know that …

a short note
ein kurzer Hinweis

Requests

Please could you …

Could you …?

Can you do me a **favour** and find out …?

Would you check to see if …?

Could you take a look at these documents and send me your comments before the end of the week?

Can I have …?

Could you clarify …?

I hope you can help.

Please get in touch to discuss.

favour
Gefallen

Requesting information

We need the document by …

I'd like to know …

Please send me …

2 GENERAL CORRESPONDENCE

Formal

Responding to requests

Thank you for your enquiry dated 2 October regarding …

Thank you for your request for information.

Further to your request …

Attached is a PDF file that explains …

I apologise for not replying sooner.

The person you want to speak to is ….

I have tried to respond to your questions below. Please let me know if you need any further clarification.

Giving information

I am writing to let you know that …

We are able to confirm that …

Please be advised that …

We regret to inform you that …

Please find enclosed/attached …

Please find below information regarding the…

Arranging a meeting

I am writing to arrange a meeting regarding …

Could we schedule a time to meet next week?

I would like to schedule a meeting as soon as possible.

Please let me know your availability.

Please let us know a date and time that would be convenient.

I am arranging a meeting with … and I should be grateful if you could let me have some dates on which you would be able to attend.

I would like to discuss a couple of **items/issues** with you.

Perhaps we could meet and go over the details together.

I don't think I will need more than 10 minutes of your time.

Would Wednesday at 11 am be **convenient**?

Would Thursday at 5.30 suit you?

I have attached a map with directions to our office.

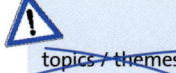

See page 44 for example correspondence

topics / themes ~~ ~~
items / issues ✓

convenient
passend, genehm

2 GENERAL CORRESPONDENCE

Informal

Responding to requests

Great to hear from you.
Here is the **information** you asked for.
Sorry for not getting back sooner.
Let me know if you need anything else.
See my responses below: ...

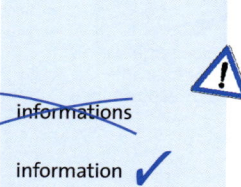

informations
information ✓

Giving information

Just to let you know that ...
We are sorry to tell you that ...
Attached/enclosed is ...
Below is the information about the ...

Arranging a meeting

We need to set up a meeting regarding ...
Just writing to arrange a meeting to discuss the schedule for the new project.
Could we meet next week?
Could we meet on ... to discuss this issue?
How about next week?
What about Wednesday at 9?
Can we meet and go over the details together?
If you're free later today or tomorrow, I'd like to get together to discuss this.

2 General Correspondence

Formal

_ Confirming/Declining a meeting

I/We look forward to seeing you on Thursday at 10 am.
Monday 20 March at 5.30 is fine.
Unfortunately, I already have an appointment **scheduled** for Wednesday morning. Would Thursday be possible?
Unfortunately, I will not be in the office on Wednesday. Would it be possible to meet on Thursday?

See page 44 for example correspondence

to reschedule
neu ansetzen, verlegen

_ Rescheduling a meeting

Unfortunately, I will not be able to attend the meeting next Friday.
I wonder if we could move our meeting to Monday.
Can we reschedule for Friday?
I apologise for any inconvenience caused.

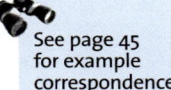

See page 45 for example correspondence

_ Confirmations

This is to confirm that …
We are able to confirm that …
I would like to confirm …
Please let me know if you …
I would like to confirm next week's meeting …
This is to confirm that the next meeting concerning 6 Charleston Avenue will take place on 5 May at 10 a.m.
Thursday is fine.

2 GENERAL CORRESPONDENCE

Informal

Comfirming/Declining a meeting

Yes, that works for me.

Yes, that's fine.

Ok, see you on Monday at 2.

Look forward to seeing you then.

Rescheduling a meeting

Re our meeting next week, I'm afraid I can't make Friday. How about Monday instead?

Unfortunately, something urgent has come up and I will have to reschedule our meeting tomorrow.

It looks like I won't be able to make Tuesday. Can we move our meeting to …

Sorry for the inconvenience.

Confirmations

Just checking to see if …

Just to confirm that …

I/We can confirm that …

Thursday is good for me.

Thursday works well.

That should be ok. I'll get back to you if there's a problem.

Could you confirm the meeting on Friday 20 in London?

2 GENERAL CORRESPONDENCE

It was a pleasure to meet you yesterday
jmdn. kennenlernen

It was a pleasure to see you yesterday
jmdn. wiedersehen

Formal

Following up on meetings

It was a pleasure to **meet** you / **see** you yesterday.

Following our meeting on Monday, please find attached the minutes.

Further to our meeting on 6 June I thought it would be useful to confirm the decisions reached as follows: ...

I refer to our meeting of 10 March regarding ... and I confirm the following: ...

It was a pleasure meeting/seeing/talking with you last week. As promised I am sending you ...

As promised at our meeting yesterday, please find attached the following documents: ...

I have considered the minutes of the meeting held on 4 May and have the following comments: ...

Promising action

I will ...

I will investigate the matter.

I will contact you again shortly.

As soon as I have further information, I will be in contact.

Offering help

Would you like me to ...?

Let me know whether you would like me to ...?

If you need any assistance, please do not hesitate to contact me.

Attachments / Enclosures

> **TIP!**
> - **attachment** only used for emails
> - **enclosure** only used in letters
> - **a copy** ein Exemplar

Please find attached a copy of the ...

I attach a copy of the ...

Please see the **attachment** for full details of the ...

Enclosed is a **copy** of the ...

Please find enclosed the ...

2 GENERAL CORRESPONDENCE

Informal

Following up on meetings

It was good to see you yesterday.
As promised yesterday, here are the documents.
As mentioned in the meeting on Wednesday …
Please include the following comments in the **minutes**: …

(meeting) minutes
Besprechungs-
protokoll

Promising action

I'll look into it.
I'll get back to you soon.
I'll let you know asap.
I'll be in touch again soon with more details.
Let's talk next week and see how things are going.

Offering help

Shall I …?
Let me know if I should …
Let me know if you need any help.

Attachments / Enclosures

I've attached …
Here is the … you wanted.
I'm sending you the …

2 GENERAL CORRESPONDENCE

Formal

_ Thanking

Thank you for taking the time to ...

Many thanks for the ...

Thank you for your assistance.

Thank you for your kind help.

_ Recommendations / Suggestions

Our recommendation is to ...

I/We suggest holding a meeting on Thursday to resolve these issues.

to propose
vorschlagen

May I **propose** that we ...

Another option would be to ...

I think this could work as long as ....

I would strongly recommend that you .....

I strongly advise you not to follow this course of action because ...

Please let me know what you think of this idea.

_ Status reports

I am pleased to report that ...

I am writing to bring you up to date on the status of our project.

I recommend that ...

At the close of this quarter/phase ...

Indications are that ...

We are making progress with ...

We expect to complete ... by ...

We are within budget.

We are slightly over budget.

We are over budget by ...

I am optimistic that ...

2 GENERAL CORRESPONDENCE

Informal

Thanking

Thanks.
That's great, thanks.
Thanks for your help.
Thanks again for looking into this for me.
Cheers. (UK)

Recommendations / Suggestions

Why don't you …
What about if we …
Perhaps we should …
Tell me what you think of this idea.
What do you think about …
How about …

Status reports

Just to let you know the status of …
Just to update you on …
We are now …
We should be finished by…

2 GENERAL CORRESPONDENCE

Formal

Complaints / Showing dissatisfaction

complaints	I wish to draw your attention to the ...
Beschwerden	I wish to inform you that ...
	I am writing to inform you that ...
	I am writing to express my dissatisfaction with ...
concerned	We are very **concerned** about the way that ... is being handled.
besorgt	I was surprised to hear that ...
to trust	I/We **trust** you will deal with this issue as a matter of urgency.
annehmen, davon ausgehen	I look forward to your assistance in resolving this matter.
matter	I would be most grateful if you would look into this **matter** as soon as possible.
Angelegenheit	I appreciate your attention to this matter.
	Please let me know as soon as possible what action you propose to take.

Apologising

to apologise, apology (apologies)	Please accept our sincere **apologies** for ...
sich entschuldigen, Entschuldigung(en)	I/We apologise for any **inconvenience** this may have caused.
	The matter is receiving our full attention.
inconvenience	We are making every effort to resolve this issue.
Unannehmlichkeit	**You have my assurance** that we are working to resolve this issue.
You have my assurance	Again we apologise and thank you for your understanding.
Seien Sie versichert	Once again we would like to apologise for ...

Giving difficult news

	As you will appreciate, ...
to regret	I **regret** to inform you that ...
bedauern	Unfortunately, we are unable to offer ... at this time.
	As you will understand, ...
	We hope this is satisfactory.
	I am sure you understand that ...

2 GENERAL CORRESPONDENCE

Informal

Complaints / Showing dissatisfaction

I am concerned about ...
My expectation was ...
Please look into this asap.

Apologising

I'm very sorry that I didn't ...
Sorry about that.

Giving difficult news

Unfortunately, we won't be able to ...
We are sorry, but we're not able to ...
I am afraid that ...

2 General Correspondence

Formal

_ Expressing opinions

I strongly believe that …
There is no question that …
As I see it …
My understanding is …
It seems/appears to me that …
It is my opinion that …

_ Agreeing

I agree to your proposal.
I fully agree with your comments.
That seems fine to me.
I generally agree, however I have the following reservations …

_ Disagreeing

I can't agree with …
As I see it …
I feel that …
I am afraid I cannot agree because …
I can see your point, but …
I am afraid I see some negative consequences which are …

⚠ Care should be taken with the tone of emails when disagreeing. See page 12 in Unit 1 on style.

_ Closing sentences

I look forward to hearing from you (soon).
I am looking forward to meeting you next week.
I look forward to seeing you next week.
I hope to hear from you soon.
I look forward to hearing your response.
Please let me know if I can provide any further help.
Please let me know if you need any further details.
Should you have any further questions, please do not hesitate to contact me.
If you need any further information please give me a call on +49 713 310.
Thank you in advance for your help in this matter.
Thank you for your help.
We look forward to working with you.

2 General Correspondence

Informal

Expressing opinions

I really believe that …
I feel that …
I think that …

Agreeing

I agree.
That's fine.
Yes, I agree.

Disagreeing

I can't agree with …
As I see it …
I feel that …
I am afraid I can't agree because …
I can see your point, but …
I am afraid I see some negative consequences which are …

Closing sentences

If you have any other questions, please let me know.
Let me know if you need anything else.
Just give me a call if you have any questions.
Give me a call if anything changes.
Can you get back to me today?
Look forward to seeing you next week.
Look forward to hearing from you soon.
Speak soon.

2 GENERAL CORRESPONDENCE

complementary close
Briefabschluss, Grußformel

Complementary closing

Formal Letters

The complementary close in a formal letter differs in British English depending on the name

🇬🇧	name of recipient known: Dear Mr Knight	Yours sincerely
	name not known: Dear Sir/Madam	Yours faithfully
🇺🇸		Yours truly, Truly yours, Sincerely yours,

Formal

Informal

Emails
Formal
Regards
Kind regards
Best Regards

in addition, the following can be used for **informal**:
All the best
Talk/Speak soon

2 GENERAL CORRESPONDENCE

Colloquial expressions

The following colloquial expressions are often used in emails.

Colloquial expression	Explanation
ball park figure	a rough estimate or approximate number
to check something out	to find out or try to get something
to chase something up (US down)	to find someone or something (that is missing)
to touch base	to talk with someone
to be out of the loop	not part of a group that is up-to-date with information about something
to put something on hold	to postpone / to leave something until a later time
to be in touch	to communicate with someone by phone, email etc.
to be up to speed	to have the latest information
the bottom line	the final result or basic meaning
to draw a line in the sand	to make final conditions that cannot be changed
a back-of-the-envelope calculation	a quick, informal calculation
to get all our ducks in a row	to get organised/prepared
to drop someone a line	to communicate in writing
to catch up on/with	to bring up to date

2 GENERAL CORRESPONDENCE

Example Correspondence

Arranging a meeting (formal)

> Dear John
>
> I am writing to arrange a meeting in order to discuss the status of the fit-out works to 56 Alton Place.
>
> I suggest Wednesday 18 February at 9.00 in our London office. Alternatively, I could also do the morning of Thursday 19 February.
>
> Would either of these be convenient for you?
>
> I look forward to hearing from you.
>
> Regards
>
> Anna Gibbons

Confirming a meeting

> Simon has asked me to confirm the appointment you made to see him at our Frankfurt office at 10.30 a.m. on Thursday 5 June. Please find attached directions.
>
> He looks forward to meeting you.
>
> Best wishes
>
> Lucy Edwards
> Executive Assistant to Simon Goodwood

Cancelling a meeting

> Dear Paul
>
> Unfortunately, I will not be able to keep our appointment tomorrow as an urgent matter **has come up** which needs my immediate attention.
>
> I sincerely apologise for the inconvenience. I will contact you next week.
>
> Kate

---

something has come up
es ist etwas dazwischen-
gekommen.

2 GENERAL CORRESPONDENCE

Rescheduling a meeting (informal)

Christine

I am afraid **I can't make the meeting** on Tuesday as I will be travelling with James to meet clients.

Sorry about this, but things are very busy here right now. Would it be ok if we **postponed** our meeting until the week after next? I should have time on 12 or 14 September.

Please let me know if either of these days is convenient.

Have a nice weekend.

Andy

I can't make the meeting
Ich kann den Termin nicht einhalten

to postpone
auf einen späteren Zeitpunkt verlegen

Requesting action

Subject: Agenda

Please find attached the Agenda for next week's management meeting. If you have any comments to add please send them to Laura by Thursday. She will **circulate** these to everyone prior to the meeting.

Mary

to circulate an agenda
eine Tagesordnung an die Teilnehmer versenden

Thanking

Dear Bob

It was a pleasure meeting you in Washington last week. I would like to thank you for your hospitality on our trip. We really appreciated the time you took to show us the Brentwood development as well as the wonderful meal afterwards.

Both Alan and I felt the meetings were very productive.

Should you ever be in Frankfurt it would be my pleasure to return your kindness.

Best regards

Miranda Houghton

2 General Correspondence

Out-of-office replies

Thank you for your message.

I am currently out of the office and will be back on Monday, 23 August 2012. I will reply to your e-mail as soon as possible when I return.

In the meantime, if your message is urgent, please contact my colleague, Gary Phillips on +44 (0) 20 7877 6579 or at g.phillips@jonesmay.com

Kind regards
Susan Reynolds
Senior Consultant Investment
Jones & May Property Consultants Ltd.

Tel: +44 (0) 20 7877 6578
Fax: +44 (0) 20 7877 4424
Mobile: +44 (0) 172 228 8989

Payment reminders
First reminder

Dear Mr Smithson

Invoice no. 321J0810

We refer to our invoice for the sum of € 10,500 a copy of which is enclosed. It appears that this invoice has not yet been settled.

You will appreciate that we rely on clients **to settle accounts** *promptly. No doubt the matter has escaped your attention, however we would appreciate payment.*

Yours sincerely

Enc.

---

to settle an account
eine Rechnung begleichen

Second reminder

Dear Mr Smithson

Invoice no. 321J0810

We refer to our invoice for the sum of € 10,500 and our letter of July 15. We **regret to note** that we have **not yet** received payment.

We are concerned that we have neither received your payment nor any explanation as to why **the balance** of € 10,500 has not been **cleared**.

Would you please give this matter your attention within the next seven days?

Yours sincerely

we regret to note
wir bedauern feststellen zu müssen

not yet
noch nicht

to clear a balance
einen Saldo ausgleichen

Final reminder

Dear Mr Smithson

Payment of invoice no. 321J0810

We refer to our invoice for the sum of € 10,500 which has not been paid despite reminders dated 15 July and 15 August.

Unfortunately, we have received no reply to explain why the balance has not been cleared, or a remittance.

We are **reluctant** to take legal action to recover the amount, but you leave us no alternative. Unless we receive your payment within the next seven days, we will instruct our **solicitors** to start proceedings.

Yours sincerely

to be reluctant to do sth.
damit zögern, etwas zu tun, etwas nur ungerne tun wollen

solicitor
Anwalt

Avoid the general language mistake

Test your knowledge gained in this unit by identifying these common language mistakes.

Underline the correct word or phrase.

2
1. Please reply *until / by* the end of the week.
2. We have a lot of *topics / themes / items* to discuss in the meeting today.
3. Could we *meet / meet us* next Thursday at 2pm?
4. Please could you send me all *informations / information* on the property.
5. I have considered the *meeting minutes / protocol* and have the following comments: …
6. Dear *Ms Smith / Miss Smith*

Improve your style

Exchange the word/phrase in brackets with a more formal option from the unit.

7. I refer to your letter of 10 January (about) _____
8. Would Thursday at 5.30 (be ok with you)? _____
9. Unfortunately, I will not be able to (come to) the meeting. _____
10. I would like to (tell) you that _____
11. Please let me know if you (need) any more information. _____
12. Would it be possible to (move) _____ our meeting to next week?

1. by | 2. items | 3. meet | 4. information | 5. meeting minutes | 6. Ms | 7. concerning/regarding | 8. be convenient/suit you | 9. attend | 10. inform | 11. require | 12. postpone

Office Property

3

| Describing Office Space .... 50 | General Description of Office Space .... 55 |

Main useable area /
Ancillary space 51
Circulation areas 51
Building services 51
Structural elements 51

Reception area 58
Façades 59
Partition walls 59
Heating, ventilation and
air conditioning (HVAC) 59
Floors, ceilings & cables 60
Types of raised floors 61
Lighting 61
Lifts 61
Security 62
External grounds 62
Parking 62

Useful Office Terms 52

Types of
Office Buildings 53

Location 54

Avoid the real estate mistake, improve your style and test your real estate vocabulary 63

3 Office Property

Describing Office Space

In historical terms, the office is a relatively new type of building. Its physical presence represents the large changes in working environments that have taken place during the last century. The office building as we know it today, in particular high-rise office architecture, dominates skylines all over the world. Offices are a diverse class of building, varying both externally and internally, in shape, size, fit-out and facilities. Differences exist particularly between the northern European office model and the North American model. **Statutory protection** is stronger in Northern European countries. In Germany, tight regulations protect the interests of workers and ensure that they are provided with, among many other criteria, adequate natural day light and work space. A typical London office worker may occupy far less space than a European counterpart. In order to comply with regulations, German offices tend to have narrower **footprints**, whereas in North America and some parts of the UK, where issues such as natural daylight are not as strictly regulated, offices tend to have larger and deeper **floorplates**.

In order to meet the specific space needs of the tenant and respond to changing business demands, office buildings must provide flexible working environments that allow for future reorganisation. Issues that are important to the tenant include their desired image, operating hours, security and technology requirements such as easy access to cabling and power distribution. Nothing can be taken for granted for very long in the office world as changes in occupational trends and the search for increased business efficiency and optimisation of real estate assets continues.

---

statutory protection
gesetzliche Vorschriften

footprint
the outline of a building at ground level

floorplate
the size and shape of a single floor of a building

3 Office Property

Main useable area / Ancillary space

English	German
office space	Bürofläche
archive space	Archivraum
sanitary areas	Sanitärräume
cleaner's room	Putzraum
pantry / kitchenette	Teeküche
shower and changing room facilities	Dusch- und Umkleideräume
canteen facility	Kantine
conference room	Konferenzraum

ancillary space
Nebennutzfläche

TIP!

useable und **usable**: both spellings are possible

Circulation areas

English	German
corridors / hallways	Flure / Gänge
lobby	Eingangshalle
reception	Empfangsbereich
elevator/lift lobby	Aufzugsvorraum
staircase	Treppenhaus
emergency/fire exits	Notausgänge

circulation areas
Verkehrsflächen

Building services

English	German
service core	Gebäudekern
plant rooms	Haustechnikräume
shafts / service risers	Schächte / Versorgungsschächte

building services
Gebäudetechnik / Haustechnik

Structural elements

English	German
structural walls / load bearing walls	Konstruktionswände / tragende Wände
columns	Säulen / Stützen

3 Office Property

Useful Office Terms

English	German
accommodation	Räumlichkeiten
break out areas/zones	Rückzugsräume
cellular office	Einzel-/Zellenbüro
common areas	Gemeinschaftsflächen
floor box	Fußbodentank
floor depth/height	Raumtiefe/-höhe
floor plan	Grundriss / Raumaufteilung
floor plate	Geschossgrundriss / Etagengrundriss / Geschossfläche
footprint	Grundfläche
high specification (high spec.)	hochwertige Ausstattung
grid - column grid - planning grid - structural grid	Raster - Stützenraster - Ausbauraster - Gebäuderaster
layout	Flächenaufteilung / Raumplan
live load	Nutzlast
open-plan office	Großraumbüro
partition walls	Trennwände
raised floor	Doppelboden / Hohlraumboden
refurbishment - complete refurbishment / major refurbishment	Renovierung - Grundsanierung
signage	Beschilderung (z.B. Firmenlogo)
site boundary	Grundstücksgrenze
solar shading - external sun shading	Sonnenschutz - außenliegender Sonnenschutz
specification	Spezifikation / Leistungsbeschreibung / Baubeschreibung
suspended ceiling	abgehängte Decke
tenanted areas / tenant demise	Mietfläche
workstations / work spaces	Arbeitsplätze

floor plan
a drawing showing the layout of a building or section and the arrangement of the interior space

⚠️
~~open-space office~~

open-plan office ✓

3 Office Property

Types of office buildings

English	German
administrative building	Verwaltungsgebäude
business park	Gewerbepark
city centre office	innerstädtisches Büro
headquarters building	Firmenzentrale
low-rise	Gebäude mit nur wenigen Stockwerken
mid-rise	mittelhohes Gebäude, kleiner als ein Hochhaus
high-rise	Hochhaus
new-build	Neubau
new-build behind a retained façade	Neubau hinter einer erhaltenen Fassade
office suite/unit	Büro, Büroeinheit

Grade A office opace

In the UK and North America office buildings are often graded into A, B and C specifications. There are no exact criteria for grading offices as the characteristics of local markets differ and a certain amount of judgement is always involved. However the following location and quality factors provide a guide:

Grade A office space (US: Class A) usually refers to new buildings of the highest quality, featuring significant architectural detailing. These buildings are in **sought-after locations** and obtain the highest rents.

Grade B office space may be modern but not new, is in a less **sought-after location**, of lower quality with fewer architectural details.

Grade C office space is older and of poorer quality in poorer locations. Rents are low and leases are often short.

sought-after location
gefragter Standort

3 Office Property

> **TIP!**
> The word **communications** or **transport communications** is often used to describe **Verkehrsanbindungen** in letting and sales details.

> ⚠
> 'nearby' does not mean the same as 'near'.
> Nearby cannot be used as a preposition.
>
> my flat is nearby the station ✗
>
> my flat is near the station ✓
>
> 'nearby' can however be used as an adjective or an adverb:
> I work in a nearby town.
> Is there a bank nearby?

> ⚠
> ein repräsentatives Büro:
>
> a representative office ✗
>
> a prestigious office ✓
>
> "A representative office" is an office set up by a company in a foreign country to conduct marketing and other non-transactional activities.

Location

- central business district (CBD)
  Hauptgeschäftsviertel

- panoramic views over the city centre
  Panoramablick über die Innenstadt

- city centre location
  Innenstadtlage

- an established office location
  eine etablierte Bürolage

- high profile corner site
  markante Ecklage

- (Name of station) and (name of station) stations are within easy walking distance.
  Die Haltestellen (Name der Haltestelle) und (Name der Haltestelle) sind fußläufig zu erreichen.

- The development benefits from excellent **communications** via nearby (name of station) and (name of station) stations.
  Das Bauvorhaben verfügt über direkte Anbindung an die (Haltestelle / U-Bahn-Station) und (Name der Haltestelle).

- The property is **near** the main rail station; which is within a 5-10 minute walk.
  Das Objekt befindet sich in der Nähe des Hauptbahnhofs in nur fünf bis zehn Gehminuten Entfernung.

- The area is well served by hotel, leisure and retail facilities with the (name of hotel) adjacent to the property as well as a wide range of bars, restaurants and cafés such as Pizza Express, My Thai, and Starbucks.
  Die Gegend bietet zahlreiche Übernachtungs- und Einkaufsmöglichkeiten sowie Freizeitangebote. Das (Name des Hotels) grenzt direkt an die Immobilie an. In direkter Nachbarschaft finden sich Bars, Restaurants und Cafés wie Pizza Express, My Thai und Starbucks.

- A catchment population of approximately 850,000 within 40 km of the city centre provides a highly skilled labour force. Large employers include the financial services and insurance sector as well as major government bodies.
  Das Einzugsgebiet umfasst 850.000 Einwohner innerhalb eines Radius von 40 km rund um die Innenstadt. Es verfügt über eine überdurchschnittlich gut ausgebildete Bevölkerung. Die Hauptarbeitgeber kommen aus der Finanz- und Versicherungswirtschaft sowie dem öffentlichen Sektor.

3 Office Property

- Neighbouring occupiers include (name of company), (name of company) and (name of company).
  In der Nachbarschaft befinden sich (Name der Firma), (Name der Firma) und (Name der Firma).
- There are many **local amenities** such as restaurants and shops in close proximity to the property.
  Es gibt zahlreiche Möglichkeiten zur Deckung des täglichen Bedarfs wie Restaurants und Einzelhandel in der direkten Umgebung der Immobilie.

local amenities
Nahversorgung (Dienstleistungen und Anlagen, die das Leben der Einwohner Mieter angenehmer machen, wie Geschäfte, Restaurants usw.)

General Description of Office Space

- high profile trophy office
  sehr hochwertige und bekannte Büroadresse
- a landmark office building
  eine Landmarke
- standalone **headquarters** building
  frei stehende Firmenzentrale

The noun headquarters always has an -s at the end

- The property is a prominently located headquarters building arranged over basement, ground and seven upper floors.
  Das hervorstechende Hauptverwaltungsgebäude ist aufgeteilt in ein Untergeschoss, ein **Erdgeschoss** und sieben Obergeschosse.
- (Name of property) comprises a self contained modern four storey building, within a landscaped setting and with spectacular views of the city.
  (Name der Immobilie) ist ein frei stehendes, modernes, vierstöckiges Gebäude inmitten einer Grünanlage mit spektakulärer Aussicht über die Stadt.
- The building is located at the rear of a well established industrial estate.
  Das Gebäude befindet sich im rückwärtigen Bereich eines etablierten Gewerbegebietes.
- The accommodation is arranged over ground and three upper floors and can be split into single floors.
  Die Gesamtfläche erstreckt sich vom Erdgeschoss bis in den dritten Stock und kann etagenweise abgetrennt werden.
- The building was completely refurbished in 2009.
  Das Gebäude wurde 2009 komplett saniert.

Erdgeschoss
In North America and some other countries the Erdgeschoss is the first floor!

In the UK, as in Germany and most of Europe, the Erdgeschoss is the ground floor and the first floor is a level higher.

Untergeschoss
The Untergeschoss is the basement or lower ground floor in both British and American English.

55

3 Office Property

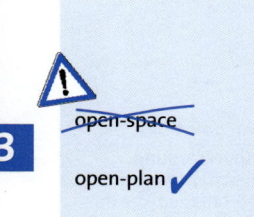

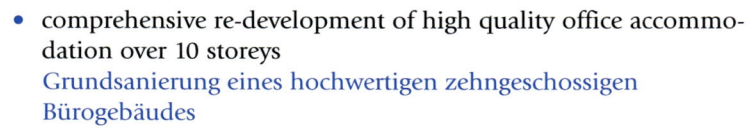

⚠️ ~~open-space~~
open-plan ✓

- comprehensive re-development of high quality office accommodation over 10 storeys
  Grundsanierung eines hochwertigen zehngeschossigen Bürogebäudes

- The floors are fully flexible for layout as cellular or **open-plan** offices.
  Die hochflexiblen Flächen ermöglichen eine Aufteilung als Einzel- oder Großraumbüro.

- highly efficient space capable of cellular and open plan accommodation
  hocheffiziente Flächen, geeignet für Einzel- sowie Großraumbüros

- Offices may be laid out as **open-plan** or cellular units or a combination of office layouts and meeting rooms.
  Die Büros können als Großraumbüros, Einzelbüros oder auch Kombibüros mit Besprechungsräumen angelegt werden.

- The building has been designed to a modern Grade A specification.
  Das Gebäude verfügt über eine sehr hochwertige Ausstattung.

- The property is designed to provide ultimate leasing flexibility on a floor by floor basis.
  Die Immobilie wurde so konzipiert, dass sie etagenweise flexibel vermietet werden kann.

- The office accommodation of 16,240 sq m is of a high specification with large floorplates of 2,030 sq m.
  Das hochwertig ausgestattete Bürogebäude umfasst insgesamt 16.240 qm und bietet großzügige Etagengrundrisse von je 2.030 qm.

- The office floors comprise a highly efficient floorplate with **perimeter** office suites surrounding the central service core.
  Die Büroflächen bieten effiziente Etagengrundrisse für Büroeinheiten rund um den zentralen Versorgungskern.

perimeter
Umkreis

3   Office Property

- an impressive working environment satisfying all the operational requirements of modern business
  ein eindrucksvolles Arbeitsumfeld, das alle Anforderungen an den modernen Geschäftsbetrieb erfüllt

- (Name of property) has been extensively refurbished and extended to provide contemporary, Grade A offices in a commanding West End location.
  (Name des Gebäudes) wurde umfassend saniert und erweitert und verfügt nach heutigem Stand über erstklassige Büroflächen in einer sehr prominenten Westend-Lage.

- (Name of property) has undergone a major refurbishment which includes remodelling of the reception area and high quality finishes in the common area.
  (Name des Gebäudes) wurde umfassend saniert. Dies beinhaltet auch eine Neugestaltung des Empfangsbereichs sowie hochwertig gestaltete Gemeinschaftsflächen.

- high quality **fit-out** and finishes throughout
  durchgehend hochwertiger Ausbau

- flexible layout
  flexible Flächenaufteilung

- male and female WCs on all floors
  Damen- und Herren-WCs auf allen Etagen

- open-plan office with 52 workstations
  Großraumbüro mit 52 Arbeitsplätzen

- cellular office with 24 workstations
  Einzelbüros für 24 Arbeitsplätze

- combination of cellular und open-plan offices providing 44 workstations
  Kombibüro mit 44 Arbeitsplätzen

Ausbau
fit-out / (US) build-out

~~equipment~~
fit-out ✓

3 Office Property

English	German
reception area	Empfangsbereich
façade	Fassade
partition wall	Trennwand
floors, ceilings & cables	Boden, Decken & Kabel
lighting	Beleuchtung
lifts / elevators	Aufzüge
security	Sicherheit
external grounds	Außenanlagen

Reception area

- Access to the offices is provided by a well proportioned reception area from (name of street).
  Der Zugang zu den Büroflächen von der (Name der Straße) aus erfolgt durch einen wohlproportionierten Empfangsbereich.
- an impressive two-storey entrance hallway with full height glass façade, which is manned 24/7
  ein imposanter, zweigeschossiger Eingangsbereich mit einer Glassfassade über die gesamte Höhe, der 24 Stunden an 7 Tagen der Woche besetzt ist.
- generous reception
  großzügiger Empfangsbereich
- double height reception
  sich über zwei Geschosse erstreckender Empfangsbereich
- **prestigious** entrance
  repräsentativer Eingangsbereich
- impressive feature entrance
  sehr beeindruckend gestalteter Empfangsbereich
- bespoke reception desk
  maßgefertigte Rezeption
- manned reception with 24 hour security
  besetzter Empfang mit 24-Std.-Sicherheitsdienst

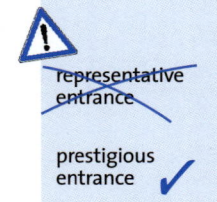

representative entrance ~~✗~~

prestigious entrance ✓

Façades

- electric external solar shading
  außenliegender elektrischer Sonnenschutz
- internal sun blinds
  innenliegender Sonnenschutz
- curtain wall glazing
  vorgehängte Glasfassade
- granite façade / granite wall cladding
  granitverkleidete Fassade
- openable windows
  öffenbare Fenster
- solar and sound insulating glazing
  Sonnen-/Schallschutzverglasung

Partition walls

- 1.5m planning grid
  1,5 m Ausbauraster
- 15 m column-free floor plates
  15 m stützenfreier Grundriss
- demountable partition wall
  bewegliche/mobile Trennwand
- moveable partition wall system
  flexible Trennwände
- glass partition walls
  Trennwände aus Glas
- metal stud partitions
  Metallskelettwand

Heating, ventilation and air conditioning (HVAC)

- air conditioning
  Klimatisierung / Klimaanlage
- fully air conditioned / partially air conditioned
  vollklimatisiert / teilklimatisiert
- natural ventilation / mechanical ventilation
  natürliche Belüftung mit unterstützender Kühlung
- chilled ceiling
  Kühldecke

HVAC refers to the technical installations that provide climate control in buildings (with the exception of plumbing).

3 Office Property

- chilled beam cooling system
  Kühlbalken
- maximum load/peak load cooling
  Spitzenlastkühlung
- heat recovery
  Wärmerückgewinnung
- heating via underfloor convectors
  Heizung über Unterflurkonvektoren
- district heating distributed via radiators
  Fernwärme über Heizkörper verteilt
- Building Management System (BMS)
  Gebäudemanagementsystem

Floors, ceilings and cables

- fully accessible raised floors (or raised access floor)
  flexibel zugänglicher Doppelboden
- **raised floors** incorporating cable trunking throughout
  durchgängiger Doppelboden mit eingebauten Kabelkanälen
- perimeter trunking
  Fensterbankkabelkanäle
- natural stone flooring
  Natursteinboden
- carpeting
  Teppichfliesen
- carpet tiles / ceramic floor tiles
  flexible Teppichelemente / Keramikfliesen
- clear floor to ceiling height of 2.85 m
  lichte Höhe von 2,85 m
- fully accessible suspended ceiling system
  flexibel zugängliche abgehängte Decke
- suspended ceiling with integrated lighting
  abgehängte Decke mit integrierter Beleuchtung
- metal tile suspended ceiling
  abgehängte Metallpaneldecken
- mineral fibre tiles / metal tiles / perforated metal tiles
  Mineralfaser-/ Metall-/ perforierte Metall-Deckenelemente

⚠️ ~~double floor~~
raised floor ✓

3 Office Property

Types of raised floors

> A **raised floor** is a general term used to describe all types of floor construction which provide space for cabling underneath. If the system can be accessed this is described as a (fully) accessible raised floor.
>
> The two most common types of raised floor in offices are described in technical terms as:
>
> **deep void raised floor**
> Installationsdoppelboden auf Stützenkonstruktion mit höherer Installationshöhe
>
> **shallow void battened floor**
> Doppelboden auf Lattenkonstruktion mit geringer Installationshöhe
>
> The *Hohlraumboden* construction is less common. It can best be described as a: jointless raised floor or a raised and screeded floor system.

Lighting

- recessed light fittings
  innenliegende Einbauleuchten
- suspended ceiling with modular recessed **luminaires**
  abgehängte Decken mit Rastereinbauleuchten
- suspended / recessed / surface mounted **luminaires**
  Pendel- / eingelassene / Aufbauleuchten
- individually controllable uplighters with motion sensors
  individuell regelbare Stehleuchten mit Bewegungsmeldern
- downlighters / spotlights
  Decken-Einbauleuchten
- fluorescent lamps
  Neonleuchten

Luminaires are also known as light fittings.

Lifts

- 2 x passenger lifts (13 person)
  zwei Personenaufzüge (für 13 Personen)
- goods lift
  Lastenaufzug

3 Office Property

Security

- individual access control to office suites with video monitoring
  individuelle Zugangskontrolle der Büroräume mit Videoüberwachung
- CCTV (closed circuit television)
  Videoüberwachung
- access control system
  Zugangskontrollsystem
- access control turnstiles
  Drehsperre

External grounds

- high quality landscaping
  hochwertige Landschaftsarchitektur
- landscaped site
  begrüntes Gelände
- landscaped courtyard
  begrünter Innenhof
- bicycle storage
  Fahrradständer
- stand-by generators
  Notgeneratoren

Parking

- 1 **parking space** per 30 sq m
  1 Parkplatz pro 30 m²
- 47 on-site car parking spaces
  47 Parkplätze auf dem Firmengelände
- ample on-site car parking
  ausreichende Parkmöglichkeiten auf dem Gelände
- 120 underground parking spaces
  120 Tiefgaragenstellplätze
- 275 car parking spaces (1:80 sq m)
  275 Parkplätze (1:80 qm)
- 2 public car parks within close proximity
  2 öffentliche Parkhäuser in nächster Umgebung

parking place (crossed out)
parking space ✓

Avoid the real estate mistake

Test your knowledge gained in this unit by identifying these common mistakes. Underline the correct word or phrase.

1. The office is *nearby / near / in the near of* the station.
2. The tenant has taken an additional 3 parking *places / spaces*.
3. The office has high quality *equipment / fit-out*.
4. The property was completely *renovated / refurbished* in 2010.
5. The building features a *representative / prestigious* area in the entrance.
6. The *headquarter / headquarters* building is in a prime location.

Improve your style

Exchange the word/phrase in brackets with a more appropriate expression from this unit.

7. The refurbishment was (done) in 2009 _____.
8. The office floors (have) highly efficient floorplates _____.
9. The property is designed to (give) ultimate leasing flexibility _____.

Test you real estate vocabulary

10. There are many local *(Nahversorgung / Dinge des täglichen Bedarfs)* _____ such as restaurants and shops.
11. The office benefits from *(Doppelböden)* _____.
12. The floors are suitable for layout as cellular or *(Großraum)* _____.

1. near | 2. spaces | 3. fit-out | 4. refurbished | 5. prestigious | 6. headquarters | 7. undertaken | 8. comprise | 9. provide | 10. amenities | 11. raised floors | 12. open plan

Retail Property

4

General Terms 66

**Key Types of
Retail Property** 67

Retailer Types 67
General 67
Clothing 68
Food / Grocery 68
Homeware 68
Other.. 69
Food and beverage 70

**Describing
Retail Areas** 70
Zoning and ITZA 70

Shopper Demographics 71

**Describing
Retail Properties** 71
General 71
Location and communications 72
Demographics 75
Accommodation 75
Fit-out 77
Shopping centres / Malls 77
Retail park / Trade park 79
Retail park location 80
Retail park car parking facilities 80

**Avoid the real estate
mistake, improve your
style and test your real
estate vocabulary** 81

4 Retail Property

Retail properties and their usage differ between countries perhaps more than other commercial property. These differences reflect national and local cultures, consumer attitudes and shopping preferences as well as town planning policy. For this reason, translating retail characteristics directly is not always possible. This unit looks at the different types of retail property, their location and the retailers who operate them. Descriptions are given where differences exist and no direct translation is possible.

General Terms

English	German
anchor store / magnet store	Anker / Magnetbetrieb
anchor tenant	Ankermieter
arcade	Passage
checkout	Kasse
major shop/store unit (**MSU**)	großflächiger Einzelhandel
multiple (national multiple / regional multiple)	Filialist
pitch (The relative position of a retail property with regard to potential business and profitability)	Einschätzung der Lage einer Einzelhandelsimmobilie im Bezug auf potenziellen Umsatz und Gewinn
point of sale (POS)	Verkaufsort
point of sale terminal	POS-Kassensystem
prime trading location / prime pitch	1a-Handelslage
product range	Sortiment
retail chain	Einzelhandelskette
shopping basket	Warenkorb
shopping trolley (US: shopping cart)	Einkaufswagen
standard shop unit (SSU)	Standard-Ladenlokal

TIP!
MSU: also known as major space unit or major space user

The **point of sale** is the location where the sale transaction takes place (often the checkout).

⚠️ sortiment
product range ✓

4 Retail Property

Key Types of Retail Property

English	German
cash and carry / wholesale	Abholgroßhandelsmarkt
department store	Warenhaus, Kaufhaus
factory outlet centre	Fabrikverkaufszentrum
high street shop / town centre (in-town sector)	Geschäft in der Fußgängerzone/ Innenstadt
local/neighbourhood shopping centre	Nahversorgungszentrum
local shopping parade	Haupteinkaufsstraße in einem kleineren Ort / vorgelagerte Ladenzeile
out-of-town shopping centre/mall	Einkaufszentrum auf der grünen Wiese
regional town / city centre scheme	regionales Einkaufszentrum
retail warehouse / **solus unit** (also: big-box store)	Fachmarkt
retail warehouse centre/park	Fachmarktzentrum
speciality retailer	Fachgeschäft

Solus unit is often used to describe a retail warehouse that stands alone and is not part of a retail warehouse park/centre.

Speciality Retailer
The word speciality retailer is not an exact definition and can refer to different types of retailers. Sometimes the term is used to describe a store that sells a similar group of items, e.g. different brands of shoes. A speciality store can also refer to an independent local shop that is not part of a chain. In the US a speciality apparel retailer could include a clothing chain whose products are manufactured only for that particular store and its brand.

Retailer Types

General terms

English	German
independent retailer	privat oder familiengeführtes Geschäft (nicht einer Kette angehörend)
international brands pan-European retailers	internationale Markenshops europäische Einzelhändler
luxury **retailer**	Einzelhändler im Luxussegment
high-end retailer	Einzelhändler im Nobelsegment
upmarket brand	gehobene Marke
mid-market retailer	Anbieter im mittleren Segment
value retailer, discount retailer	Discounter

TIP!

The word **retailer** can usually be interchanged with shop (UK) or store (US).

4 Retail Property

Clothing

English	German
children's clothes	Kinderbekleidung
fashion retailer	Modegeschäft, Modeboutique
men's **clothing** / men's fashion	Herrenbekleidung, Herrenmode
premium clothing retailer	Modegeschäft im oberen Preissegment
shoe shop (footwear)	Schuhgeschäft
value clothing / fashion discounter	Textildiscounter
women's clothing / women's fashion	Damenbekleidung / Damenmode
young fashion	junge Mode

⚠ **clothing = Textilien**
The meaning of "texile" in English refers to material (Stoff) rather than clothes. In US English the word apparel is often used in retail instead of clothing.

grocery
Lebensmittel

Food / Grocery

English	German
convenience store	kleiner Lebensmittelladen / Tante-Emma-Laden
food discounter	Lebensmitteldiscounter
supermarket	Supermarkt
superstore (hypermarket)	Verbrauchermarkt

homeware
Haushaltswaren

Homeware

English	German
carpet retailer	Teppichgeschäft
DIY (Do It Yourself) store / (US) home improvement center	Baumarkt
electronics retailer (electricals)	Elektrohandel, Elektrofachhandel
home furnishing, furniture retailer	Möbelgeschäft, Möbelmarkt

Other

English	German
antique shop	Antiquitätengeschäft
bank	Bank
beauty salon	Kosmetikstudio
betting shop	Wettbüro
bookseller / bookshop	Buchhandlung
bridal wear	Brautmode
cleaners	Reinigung
florist	Blumenhändler / Florist
gift shop	Geschenkartikelladen
health & beauty retailer / (US) drugstore	Drogeriemarkt
health food shop	Reformhaus
jewellery shop	Juwelier
mobile telephone shop / telecommunications	Handyladen / Mobilfunkgeschäft
newsagent	Zeitungsladen, Kiosk
optician	Optiker
pharmacy	Apotheke
shoe repair	Schuhreparatur
sports shop	Sportgeschäft
toy shop	Spielwarenhandlung
travel agent	Reisebüro
video store	Videothek

4 Retail Property

> **TIP!**
> **Gastronomy** in English refers to the art of fine dining. To describe the German word Gastronomie the following words can be used for the sector:
> food & beverage
> catering
> restaurants and coffee shops
> food courts

> **TIP!**
> **takeaway**: a shop or restaurant that sells meals that are taken away from the premises on which they are prepared and eaten elsewhere (US: takeout)

Food and beverage

English	German
kiosk	Kiosk
bar	Bar
public house	Kneipe, Gaststätte, Wirtshaus
restaurants: - high-class restaurant - full table-service restaurant - restaurant chain - franchise restaurant - **takeaway** - fast food chain	Restaurants: - Nobelrestaurant - gehobene Küche - Systemgastronomie - Franchiserestaurant - Schnellrestaurant / Imbissbude - Fastfoodkette

Describing Retail Areas

English	German
retail area	Verkaufsfläche / Einzelhandelsfläche
frontage	Schaufensterfront Schaufensteranlage Länge der Straßenfront
return frontage	eine Schaufensterfront auf der Seite oder Rückseite des Gebäudes
shop width	Breite des Geschäfts
shop depth	Ladentiefe
ancillary areas: staff rooms, kitchens, offices etc.	Nebenflächen: Sozialräume, Küchen, Büros usw.
storage areas	Lagerfläche
display window	Schaufenster

Zoning and ITZA

Some countries such as the UK and Ireland use zoning, which is a sliding scale of rental values for the floor area within a retail unit. The front of the retail unit is worth more than the rear and is known as Zone A. This is not a method of valuation but a means of comparing the value of one shop with another "in terms of zone A" (ITZA).

Shopper Demographics

English	German
catchment area	Einzugsgebiet
- core catchment area	- unmittelbares Einzugsgebiet
- secondary catchment area	- sekundäres Einzugsgebiet
- tertiary catchment area	- tertiäres Einzugsgebiet
centrality index	Zentralitätskennziffer
consumer spending	Verbraucherausgaben
conversion of footfall to spend	Anteil der Kunden am Passantenstrom
customer profile	Kundenprofil
disposable income	verfügbares Einkommen
drive time	Fahrzeit
dwell times	Verweildauer
employment structure	Beschäftigungsstruktur
footfall	Passantenfrequenz
pedestrian flow / shopper flow	Passantenströme
population	Einwohnerzahl
purchasing power	Kaufkraft
retail turnover	Einzelhandelsumsatz
shopping centre visitors	Kundenfrequenz in einem Einkaufzentrum
socio-economic profile	soziökonomisches Profil
unemployment rate	Arbeitslosenquote

Describing Retail Properties

General

- retail unit to let
  Einzelhandelsfläche zu vermieten

- The retail premises are let on a ten year lease from 2nd October 2009 at a current rent of € 100,000 per annum.
  Die Ladenflächen sind mit einer 10-jährigen Laufzeit ab dem 2. Oktober 2009 zu einer Jahresmiete von 100.000 € vermietet.

- corner shop
  Eckladen

4 Retail Property

- ground floor fast food restaurant
  Fast-Food-Restaurant im Erdgeschoss
- prime retail unit to let within newly built major mixed use development
  erstklassige Einzelhandelsflächen in einem neu entwickelten, größeren, gemischt genutzten Geschäftshaus zu vermieten

communications
Verkehrsanbindungen

Location and communications

- prime retail location / prime pitch
  Ia-Einzelhandelslage
- The property occupies a prominent position in the (name of town area) area, adjacent to (name of retailer next door e.g. H&M), with other retailers nearby including (name of retailer) and (name of retailer).
  Das Gebäude besitzt eine ausgezeichnete Lage in (Name des Stadtteils), direkt an (Name des Einzelhändlers nebenan, z.B. H&M) angrenzend, mit (Name des Einzelhändlers) und (Name des Einzelhändlers) in der unmittelbaren Nachbarschaft.
- The property is located on (name of road) in an area that benefits from a high footfall.
  Das Objekt befindet sich in der (Name der Straße), an einem Standort, der sich durch eine hohe Passentenfrequenz auszeichnet.
- The property is situated fronting (name of road) in the heart of the city with return frontage onto (name of road). There are numerous offices and headquarters buildings in the immediate vicinity. Nearby occupiers include (Corporations Bank), (ABC International Bank) and (Starlight Coffee).
  Das Gebäude liegt an der (Name der Straße), im Herzen der Stadt, mit einem weiteren Eingangsbereich auf der Rückseite zur (Name der Straße). Es gibt eine Vielzahl von Bürogebäuden und Hauptniederlassungen in der unmittelbaren Nachbarschaft. Zu den Nachbarn gehören die (Corporations Bank), (ABC International Bank) und (Starlight Coffee).
- The property occupies a prime retail location on the south of (name of city area), adjacent to the (name of shopping centre) shopping centre.
  Das Gebäude belegt einen erstklassigen Einzelhandelsstandort im Süden von (Name des Stadtteils), angrenzend an das Einkaufszentrum (Name des Einkaufszentrums).

4 Retail Property

- (Name of road) is one of the premier retailing locations in (name of city) and is anchored by the renowned department store, (name of department store). There are a number of well-known national and international retailers represented on the thoroughfare including (name or retailer 1), (name or retailer 2), (name or retailer 3).
Die (Name der Straße) ist einer der besten Einzelhandelsstandorte in (Name der Stadt). Als wichtigster Frequenzbringer fungiert das Kaufhaus (Name des Kaufhauses). Mehrere bekannte nationale und internationale Einzelhändler sind mit Läden direkt an der Hauptverkehrsstraße vertreten, darunter (Name des Einzelhändlers 1), (Name des Einzelhändlers 2) und (Name des Einzelhändlers 3).

- (54 Goethe Strasse) occupies an extremely prominent corner position opposite (name of retailer) and one of the entrances to (name of U/S-Bahn) station. In 2009 the station recorded over 2 million passengers.
(Goethestraße 54) belegt eine sehr prominente Ecklage gegenüber (Name des Einzelhändlers); einer der Eingänge grenzt an die (Name der U/S-Bahn) Station an. Im Jahr 2009 wurden mehr als 2 Millionen Fahrgäste an dieser Haltestelle gezählt.

- (Name of town) high street is a popular retailing destination benefiting from excellent public transport links. Recent additions to the street include (name of retailer) and (name of retailer).
Die Fußgängerzone von (Name der Stadt) ist ein beliebter Einzelhandelsstandort und zeichnet sich durch sehr gute öffentliche Nahverkehrsverbindungen aus. Jüngste Zugänge in der Straße sind (Name des Einzelhändlers) und (Name des Einzelhändlers).

- The subject property occupies an extremely prominent corner location within the (name of development) development.
Das Gebäude belegt eine sehr prominente Ecklage auf dem Gelände von der/dem (Name der Entwicklung).

- Retailers in the immediate vicinity include (name of retailer), (name of retailer), (name of retailer) and (name of retailer).
Unter den Einzelhändlern in der unmittelbaren Nachbarschaft befinden sich (Name des Einzelhändlers), (Name des Einzelhändlers) und (Name des Einzelhändlers).

- The premises are located on the eastern side of (name of road).
Die Liegenschaft befindet sich auf der Ostseite der (Name der Straße).

- There is a moderate/good/high level of footfall.
Die Passantenfrequenz ist mäßig/gut/hoch.

⚠ **Definite articles are almost never used for street or road names in English.**

~~On the Salisbury Road~~

On Salisbury Road ✓

4 Retail Property

~~parking house~~

multi-storey car park ✓

- Multiple retailers within the High Street include (name of retailer), (name of retailer), (name of retailer) and (name of retailer).
  In der Haupteinkaufsstraße befinden sich mehrere Filialisten wie (Name des Einzelhändlers), (Name des Einzelhändlers), (Name des Einzelhändlers) und (Name des Einzelhändlers).

- There is a public **multi-storey car park** to the rear of the premises in (name of street).
  Ein öffentliches Parkhaus befindet sich auf der Rückseite des Gebäudes in der (Name der Straße).

- The premises occupy a prominent corner position on the south-west side of (name of street) at its junction with (name of street).
  Das Gebäude belegt eine prominente Ecklage auf der Südwestseite der (Name der Straße), an der Kreuzung zur (Name der Straße).

- The premises are well located on (name of road) adjacent to (name of retailer) and (name of retailer) and close to (name of retailer) and (name of retailer). (Name of underground/bus station) is within easy walking distance.
  Das Gebäude ist gut gelegen an der (Name der Straße), direkt neben (Name des Einzelhändlers) und (Name des Einzelhändlers) sowie nicht weit von (Name des Einzelhändlers) entfernt. (Die U-Bahn/Busstation) ist innerhalb weniger Gehminuten zu erreichen.

"downtown" is used in US English to describe the lower part of a city or the business centre. This does not always work as a translation for Stadtzentrum, particularly not in British English.

~~The shopping centre is downtown~~

The shopping centre is in the city centre ✓

- This prime retail unit is ideally located in the centre of (name of town) on the primary throughway.
  Diese erstklassige Einzelhandelsfläche ist ideal im Zentrum von (Name der Stadt) gelegen, direkt an der Hauptverkehrsstraße.

- The property is located on the west side of (name of street) and is approximately 40 metres south of (name of underground station) station. Immediate occupiers include (name of retailer), (name of retailer) and (name of retailer)
  Das Objekt befindet sich auf der Westseite der (Name der Straße), ca. 40 m südlich der (Name der U-Bahn-Station). Zu den Nachbarn zählen (Name des Einzelhändlers), (Name des Einzelhändlers) und (Name des Einzelhändlers).

- Nearby retailers include (name of retailer), (name of retailer) and (name of retailer).
  Unter den benachbarten Einzelhändlern sind (Name des Einzelhändlers) und (Name des Einzelhändlers).

- The high street includes a mix of independent and corporate operators including (name of fast food chain), (name of large retail chain), and (name of large retail chain).

4 Retail Property

Die Haupteinkaufstraße weist eine Mischung aus unabhängigen Einzelhändlern sowie Filialisten auf, darunter (Name der Fastfood-Kette), (Name der großen Einzelhandelskette) und (Name der großen Einzelhandelskette).

Demographics

- (Name of part of town) is a densely populated suburb of (name of town) with a largely residential community.
  (Name des Stadtteils) ist ein dicht besiedelter Vorort von (Name der Stadt), der überwiegend aus Wohngebieten besteht.

- The primary catchment area is within a 10 minute driving radius of the centre and has a resident population of 118,035 people based on data from the Office of Statistics.
  Innerhalb des primären Einzugsgebiets in einem Radius von 10 Autofahrminuten leben laut Einwohnerstatistik 118.035 Personen.

- (Name of city) has a resident population in the order of 480,000. The wider conurbation has a population in the order of 1.4 million persons. In comparison with other cities in the region, the population has a higher proportion of young adults (age 20-39) and a fewer number of residents in the age group between 40 and retirement. It is anticipated that the city's population will increase slightly over the next decade.
  Die Stadt (Name der Stadt) hat rund 480.000 Einwohner. Der Ballungsraum umfasst 1,4 Millionen Einwohner. Im Vergleich zu anderen Städten in der Region wohnen hier verhältnismäßig mehr junge Erwachsene (im Alter von 20 bis 39 Jahren) als Erwachsene der Altersgruppe 40 bis Rentenalter. Es wird erwartet, dass die Einwohnerzahl der Stadt in den nächsten 10 Jahren leicht ansteigen wird.

Accommodation

- The property comprises a new development, the retail element of which is arranged over basement, ground and first floor.
  Die Neuentwicklung bietet Einzelhandelsflächen im Untergeschoss, im Erdgeschoss sowie auf der ersten Etage.

- The premises benefit from over 8 m of double height glazed frontage.
  Die Liegenschaft zeichnet sich durch eine gut 8 m lange, zweigeschossige Glasfassade aus.

4 Retail Property

accommodation
Räumlichkeiten

- The store will be handed over in developer's shell finish.
  Die Einzelhandelsflächen werden im veredelten Rohbau an den Mieter übergeben.

- The **accommodation** comprises ground floor sales area of 215 sq m and ancillary space at basement level of 54 sq m and benefits from a gross frontage of 30 sq m
  Die Ladenfläche umfasst 215 m² Verkaufsfläche im Erdgeschoss und 54 m² Nebenraum im Untergeschoss und verfügt über eine Schaufensterfront von 30 qm.

- The unit provides an open and efficiently shaped retail area.
  Die Einheit bietet einen offenen und effizient geplanten Einzelhandelsbereich.

- The accommodation forms part of a new mixed use development, providing 200 residential apartments and 1,000 sq m of office space.
  Die Flächen sind Bestandteil einer neuen, gemischt genutzten Immobilienentwicklung mit 200 Wohneinheiten und 1.000 m² Bürofläche.

- The premises comprise one ground floor retail unit with storage to the rear.
  Das Objekt bietet eine Einzelhandelsfläche im Erdgeschoss mit Lagerräumen auf der Rückseite.

- The ground floor provides good retailing space with storage and staff accommodation on the first floor.
  Das Erdgeschoss bietet gute Einzelhandelsflächen mit Lager und Personalräumen im 1. OG.

- ability to combine two units
  die Möglichkeit, zwei Einheiten zusammenzulegen

- flexibility to split if required
  flexible Aufteilung bei Bedarf möglich

- The two units can be taken together as one single unit or let as individual units.
  Die zwei Einheiten können als Ganzes oder einzeln vermietet werden.

- units available from 189 sq m to 811 sq m
  verfügbare Flächen von 189 m² bis 811 m²

- The space benefits from over 5 m of double height glazed frontage.
  Die Flächen verfügen über eine 5 m hohe Schaufensterfront, die sich über zwei Etagen erstreckt.

Fit-out

- The unit is currently fitted out to a high standard and ready for immediate occupation.
  Die Flächen sind qualitativ hochwertig ausgestattet und können umgehend belegt werden.
- The premises have been fitted out to a high standard.
  Die Räume sind hochwertig ausgestattet.
- The two retail units are constructed to a shell specification on the ground floor of a residential apartment scheme.
  Die zwei im Erdgeschoss befindlichen Einzelhandelsflächen wurden im veredelten Rohbau eines Apartmenthauses erstellt.
- Newly built ground floor retail unit to let comprising of 2,500 sq m of space in shell condition.
  Neu errichtete, 2.500 m² große Erdgeschoss-Einzelhandelsfläche im Edelrohbau zu vermieten.
- The sales area features a suspended ceiling with fluorescent lighting, air conditioning and wood flooring.
  Die Verkaufsflächen zeichnen sich durch Besonderheiten wie abgehängte Decke mit eingebautem Neonlicht, Klimaanlage und Holzfußboden aus.
- good service access and parking to rear
  gute Anlieferung- und Parkmöglichkeiten auf der Rückseite
- The generous retail frontage ensures prominence along the street.
  Die großzügige Ladenfront garantiert einen hohe Sichtbarkeit entlang der Straße.

Shopping centres / Malls

- (Name of shopping centre) consists of 43,000 sq m of retail space with 30,000 sq m hotel, residential and office space. The scheme also contains 3 underground parking levels for 2,000 cars. Pedestrian flow is organised around a generous interior street. The project has been carefully masterplanned to provide civic spaces that allow for a greater sense of place.
  Das (Name des Einkaufszentrums) umfasst 43.000 qm Einzelhandelsfläche sowie 30.000 qm für Hotel, Wohnungen und Büros. Der Gebäudekomplex verfügt ebenfalls über eine Tiefgarage mit 3 Untergeschossen für 2.000 Fahrzeuge. Der Passantenstrom wird durch eine großzügige, innenliegende Passage geleitet. Durch die sorgfältige Planung wurde reichlich öffentlicher Raum geschaffen, der dem ganzen Ensemble eine gewisse Großzügigkeit verleiht.

4 Retail Property

- The centre is anchored by (name of anchor tenant) and a 12 screen cinema. The subject unit is located immediately adjacent to (name of retailer to left) and (name of retailer to right) and opposite (name of retailer opposite). Other neighbouring operators include (name of retailer), (name of retailer) and (name of retailer).
  Das Einkaufszentrum hat (Name des Hauptmieters) als Ankermieter und verfügt über ein Kino mit zwölf Sälen. Die zu vermietende Einheit liegt gleich neben (Name des Einzelhändlers zur linken Seite) und (Name des Einzelhändlers zur rechten Seite) und gegenüber von (Name des Einzelhändlers gegenüber). Weitere Betreiber in der Nachbarschaft sind …

- The premises comprise a self-contained retail unit benefiting from a wide frontage onto the (name of shopping centre) and a return frontage onto the high street. The premises have first floor storage which can be accessed either from the shop or the delivery deck.
  Das Gebäude verfügt über eine eigenständige Einzelhandelseinheit, die sich durch eine große Schaufensterfront hin zum (Name des Einkaufszentrums) auszeichnet und über einen rückseitigen Eingang zur Haupteinkaufstraße verfügt. Die Lagerräume im ersten Obergeschoss des Gebäudes können entweder über das Geschäft oder durch die Wareneingangskontrolle erreicht werden.

- Large shop occupying a very prominent location on the lower floor of the shopping centre adjacent to (name of retailer) and close to a number of multiple retailers including (name of retailer), (name of retailer) and (name of retailer).
  Große Einzelhandelseinheit in einer gut sichtbaren Lage im Untergeschoss des Shoppingcenters, direkt angrenzend an (Name des Einzelhändlers) und in der Nähe der Ladenlokale von (Name des Einzelhändlers), (Name des Einzelhändlers) und (Name des Einzelhändlers).

- The possibility exists to extend the ground floor area to include the 2 units adjacent, taking the area to 3,000 sq m.
  Es besteht die Möglichkeit einer Flächenerweiterung im Erdgeschoss durch Zusammenlegung der angrenzenden zwei Flächeneinheiten zu einer Gesamtfläche von 3.000 m².

- The (name of shopping centre) which has a footfall of approximately 65,000 per week is situated in the heart of (name of city/town) and tenants include (name of retailer), (name of retailer) and (name of retailer).

Das (Name des Einkaufszentrums) mit einer wöchentlichen Passantenfrequenz von ca. 65.000 ist im Herzen von (Name der Stadt) gelegen. Unter den Mietern befinden sich u.a. (Name des Einzelhändlers), (Name des Einzelhändlers) und (Name des Einzelhändlers).

- The unit is located on the ground floor of the centre situated close to the entrance/exit to the pedestrian area and close to the (name of car park) car park.
  Die Geschäftseinheit befindet sich im Erdgeschoss des Einkaufszentrums, direkt am Ausgang des Centers zur Fußgängerzone sowie in der Nähe zum (Name des Parkhauses) Parkhaus.

Retail park / Trade park

- an attractive, modern retail unit situated on a pleasant, well-laid-out park available for immediate occupation
  eine ansprechende, moderne Einzelhandelsfläche innerhalb eines sehr gut konzipierten Fachmarktzentrums, die umgehend bezogen werden kann
- (Name of retail park) is a high quality retail park designed to a high standard using quality materials.
  (Name des Einkaufszentrums) ist ein hochwertiges Fachmarktzentrum, das sich durch hohe Qualität der Baumaterialien auszeichnet.
- The retail park has covered pedestrian walkways and excellent car parking.
  Das Einkaufszentrum verfügt über überdachte Gehwege und hervorragende Parkmöglichkeiten.
- newly refurbished units to let from 340 sq m available from winter 2012
  kürzlich renovierte Geschäftseinheiten ab 340 m² zu vermieten, verfügbar ab Winter 2012
- Trade units range from 2,700 sq m to 5,400 sq m in size. All adjoining units can be combined to meet individual operators' requirements.
  Die Gewerbeeinheiten sind in Größen von 2.700 m² bis 5.400 m² verfügbar. Alle angrenzenden Einheiten können bei Bedarf miteinander verbunden werden.
- roller shutter door to rear accessing service yard
  Anlieferbereich mit Rolltür/Sektionaltor auf der Rückseite

4 Retail Property

Retail park location

- located 4 km north of the city centre fronting the B8
  4 km nördlich des Stadtzentrums an der B8 gelegen
- The retail park is located 2 km south of (name of city/town) city centre in a prominent position just off the (name of motorway/main road).
  Das Fachmarktzentrum liegt 2 km südlich der Innenstadt von (Name der Stadt) in einer hervorragenden Lage unmittelbar an der (Name der Autobahn/Hauptstraße).
- The site can be accessed directly from the (name of motorway/main road) from (name of road).
  Das Grundstück ist direkt von der (Name der Autobahn/Hauptstraße) über die (Name der Straße) zu erreichen.
- prominent retail warehouse premises on corner position within the (name of development) development overlooking (main road) close to (name of town/city centre)
  weithin bekannter Fachmarkt in Ecklage des Bauprojekts (Name der Entwicklung) mit Blick auf die (Hauptstraße), nahe der Stadt (Name der Stadt/ Innenstadt)
- prominently positioned at junction between (name of road) and (name of road) approximately 2 km west of (name of town) centre
  hervorragend gelegen an der Kreuzung (Name der Straße) / (Name der Straße), etwa 2 km westlich des Stadtzentrums von (Name der Stadt)
- Adjoining occupiers include (name of retailer), (name of retailer), (name of retailer) and (name of retailer).
  Unter den benachbarten Einzelhändlern finden sich (Name des Einzelhändlers), (Name des Einzelhändlers), (Name des Einzelhändlers) und (Name des Einzelhändlers).

Retail park car parking facilities

- ample customer parking
  ausreichend Kunden-Parkplätze vorhanden
- car parking to the front of the property for 282 vehicles shared with the adjoining occupiers
  282 Pkw-Parkplätze vor dem Gebäude, die mit den benachbarten Nutzern geteilt werden
- 225 surface car parking spaces
  225 Außenstellplätze
- designated parking with each unit
  separat ausgewiesene Parkplätze für jede Einheit

Avoid the real estate mistake

Test your knowledge gained in this unit by identifying these common language mistakes. Underline the correct word or phrase.

1. *The Regent Street / Regent Street* connects Oxford Circus and Piccadilly Circus.
2. The property benefits from high *customer frequency / footfall*.
3. The high-street has many retail chains in the *textile / fashion* sector.
4. 30 % of the shopping centre units are let to *gastronomy / food and beverage* tenants.
5. The *parking house / multi-storey car park* is conveniently located.
6. The property is located *in the city centre / downtown*.

Improve your style

Exchange the word/phrase in brackets with a more appropriate expression from this unit.

7. The property is (next) to a number of other well-known retailers. _____
8. The (property in question) occupies a prominent corner location. _____
9. The property (has got) one ground floor retail unit with storage to the rear.
 _____

Test you real estate vocabulary

10. Two retail units constructed to a (veredelter Rohbau) _____ specification on the ground floor.
11. The generous (Ladenfront) _____ ensures prominence along the street.
12. The primary (Einzugsgebiet) _____ is within a 10 minute driving radius of the shopping centre.

1. Regent Street (without „the") | 2. footfall | 3. fashion | 4. food and beverage | 5. multi-storey car park | 6. in the city centre | 7. adjacent | 8. subject property | 9. comprises | 10. shell / shell and core | 11. frontage | 12. catchment area

Industrial & Logistic Property

5

Useful Industrial and Logistic terms 84

Describing Logistics Properties 85
Location 85
General Description 86
Construction and Specification 87
Heating, Ventilation and Air Conditioning (HVAC) 87

Floors 88
Docking Area and Doors 88
Site and External Areas 89
Service Yard 89

Avoid the real estate mistake, improve your style and test your real estate vocabulary 90

5 Industrial & Logistics Property

The Industrial & Logistics sector is sometimes referred to as the "Shed" sector by property professionals working in the market. The properties can be divided into different types and sub-markets such as:

- industrial units / light industrial units
- warehouses
- distribution centres

Properties in this sector fulfil a variety of functions within the supply chain from the receiving, assembly, storage, consolidation, sorting and distribution of goods through to accommodating the needs of the operating personnel. These functional properties must often convey a corporate image; therefore the aesthetics of the buildings and quality of landscaping also play an important role in competitive markets.

Useful Industrial & Logistics Terms

English	German
Automated Storage and Retrieval System (AS/RS)	automatisches Hochregallagersystem
assembly	Zusammenbau / Montage
consolidating	Konsolidierung
conveyor belt	Förderband
cross docking	„Direktumschlag" oder „Kreuzverkupplung"
distribution centre	Verteilzentrum, Verteilerzentrum
docking area	Ladebereich
forklift truck	Gabelstapler
handling equipment	Hebetechnik
high-bay warehouse	Hochregallager
incoming shipments	Wareneingang
kitting	Bereitstellung, Konfektionierung
manufacturing	Fertigung, Produktion
materials handling	Materialfluss
order picking	das Kommissionieren, die Kommissionierung
outgoing shipments	Warenausgang
pallet	Palette
racks	Regale
service yard	Andienungszone
sorting	Sortierung
staging area	Bereitstellungszone
warehousing	Lagerung, Einlagerung

5 Industrial & Logistics Property

Describing Logistics Properties

Location

- high profile location
  hervorragende Lage, erstklassige Lage

- well positioned distribution facility in established warehouse location
  günstig gelegenes Verteilzentrum (oder Distributionszentrum) an einem etablierten Logistikstandort

- an established industrial/warehouse location which is home to numerous businesses including (name of company), (name of company) and (name of company)
  ein etablierter Industrie-/ Logistikstandort, an dem zahlreiche Unternehmen, darunter (Namen der Unternehmen), ansässig sind

- The scheme is prominently located fronting the A5.
  Das Objekt grenzt direkt an die A5 und ist von der Autobahn aus gut sichtbar.

- strategically located on the A3
  strategisch günstig an der A3 gelegen

- a proven distribution location with a number of well-known occupiers
  ein bewährter Standort, an dem bereits namhafte Firmen/ Logistikdienstleister ansässig sind

- excellent communications
  hervorragende Verkehrsanbindungen

- easy access/direct access to **junction** 12 of the A1
  einfache/direkte Anbindung an die Autobahn A1, Abfahrt Köln-Lövenich

- within 5 minutes drive time of junction 12 of the A1
  5 Fahrminuten von der A1, Autobahnabfahrt Köln-Lövenich, entfernt

- The property is visible from the A3, although access is from (name of road).
  Das Objekt ist von der A3 aus sichtbar, wird aber über die (Straßenname) angefahren/erreicht.

- Alpha Park is situated approximately 40 km from Frankfurt am Main.
  Der Alpha Park ist ca. 40 km von Frankfurt am Main entfernt.

- The development is approached via (name of road).
  Die Entwicklung ist über die (Straßenname) anfahrbar.

Logistikhalle
logistic unit/facility/building

~~logistic hall~~

logistic facility/building ✓

UK motorway **junctions** are normally referred to by their number rather than the city/direction to which they lead.

5 Industrial & Logistics Property

HGV = heavy goods vehicle

- The property is situated to the western end of the (name) industrial estate.
  Das Objekt ist am westlichen Ende des Gewerbegebiets (Name) gelegen.

- **HGV** drive times
  Lkw-Fahrzeiten

- large local workforce available
  großes Angebot an lokalen Arbeitskräften vorhanden

- access to a skilled and flexible local workforce
  gut ausgebildete und flexible lokale Arbeitskräfte verfügbar

General description

- high-bay distribution unit
  Logistikimmobilie mit Hochregallager

- modern high-bay distribution centre
  modernes Hochregal-Distributionszentrum

- refurbished industrial/warehouse unit
  modernisierte Industrie-/Hallenflächen

- 26,538 pallet capacity (narrow aisle / wide aisle)
  Palettenkapazität: 26.538 (Schmalgang / Breitgang)

⚠ The word **detached** is used in English to show that a property is not just part of a complex but is a free standing building (Solitär).

- A modern **detached** industrial/warehouse building
  ein modernes, frei stehendes Industrie-/Logistikgebäude

- The premises comprise industrial/warehouse units.
  Die Liegenschaft verfügt über Industrie-/Hallenflächen.

- The property comprises a modern production/warehouse facility together with offices, generous loading facilities and parking.
  Das Objekt verfügt über moderne Produktions-, Lager- und Büroflächen, eine großzügige Andienungszone sowie ausreichend Parkplätze.

- flexibility in unit sizes
  flexible Flächengrundrisse

- consent for production, services and logistic use, 24 hours/7 days a week
  Nutzung für Produktion, Service und Logistik im 24h-Betrieb an 7 Tagen die Woche möglich

Construction and specification

- steel portal frame construction
  Stahlskelettbau
- reinforced concrete frame construction
  Stahlbetonskelett
- hybrid construction
  gemischte Bauweise
- wide column spacing
  breites Stützenraster
- clear span, column free
  stützenfrei
- **clear height** 10 m
  lichte Höhe 10 m
- Roof lights create a bright atmosphere and provide ventilation.
  Lichtkuppeln im Dach sorgen für beste Lichtverhältnisse und ausreichende Belüftung.

Heating, ventilation and air conditioning (HVAC)

- sprinkler system
  Sprinkleranlage
- radiant tube heater
  Dunkelstrahler
- radiant ceiling heater
  Deckenstrahlheizer
- warm-air heater
  Lufterhitzer
- temperature and humidity controlled stores
  Lager mit kontrollierter Temperatur und Luftfeuchtigkeit
- evaporative cooling system
  Verdampfungskühlungssystem
- cold store
  Kühllager
- deep freeze store
  Tiefkühllager
- separate metering of gas, water and electricity
  separate Zählung von Gas, Wasser und Strom

---

specification
Baubeschreibung, Spezifikation

clear height:
Two other phrases are also used for expressing the height between the floor surface and the underside of the roof covering in a warehouse:

eaves height 10 m
Traufhöhe von 10 m

haunch height 10 m
lichte Höhe bis Unterkante Binder: 10 m

5 INDUSTRIAL & LOGISTICS PROPERTY

Floors
- 50 kN/m² floor loading
  50 kN/m² Bodenbelastbarkeit
- high tolerance floor
  hochbelastbarer Boden
- Steel Fibre Reinforced Concrete (SFRC), suitable for forklift trucks
  verstärkter Stahlfaserbeton, gabelstaplergeeignet
- few flooring joints / jointless flooring
  fugenarm / fugenlos
- floor flatness / levelness
  Bodenebenheit

Docking area and doors
- 12 roller shutter doors
  12 Rolltore
- sectional overhead doors
  Sektionaltore
- dock levellers
  Überladebrücken, Rampen-Ladetor, Laderampen
- mechanical dock leveller
  mechanische Überladebrücke
- electro-hydraulic dock leveller
  elektro-hydraulische Überladebrücke
- surface level loading doors / ground level loading doors / level access doors
  ebenerdige Hallentore
- loading docks/doors 4.04 m wide x 4.98 m high
  Ladetüren von 4,04 m Breite x 4,98 m Höhe
- Each property has a separate pedestrian entrance to the offices.
  Jedes Gebäude hat einen separaten Personeneingang zu den Büros.
- Loading canopies are provided at each end of the building.
  Das Gebäude ist an allen Seiten mit Vordächern ausgestattet.
- reinforced concrete external slabs to dock areas
  Laderampen mit außenliegendem Stahlbeton-Rammschutz

5 INDUSTRIAL & LOGISTICS PROPERTY

Site and external areas

- secure site with electronic access
  elektronisch gesicherte Toranlage
- landscaped environment
  gepflegte Außenanlagen
- The building sits on a **self-contained site** with security fencing and gatehouse.
  Das Gebäude befindet sich auf einem eingezäunten Grundstück mit Pförtnerhaus.
- fully fenced
  vollständig umzäunt
- The property occupies an area at the front boundary of the site with land for expansion to the **rear**.
  Das Objekt liegt an der vorderen Grundstückfront und bietet Erweiterungsflächen nach hinten.
- CCTV (closed circuit television)
  Videoüberwachung
- 24 hour CCTV coverage
  24-Stunden-Videoüberwachung
- security lighting
  Sicherungsbeleuchtung
- expansion land
  Erweiterungsflächen

> ⚠️ The phrase **self-contained site** is often used to emphasise that the property is separated and fenced off from any other neighbouring buildings.
>
> ⚠️ ~~rearside / backside~~
> rear / back ✓

Service yard

- yard depth 35 m
  Hoffläche 35 m tief
- generous manoeuvring area
  großzügige Rangierflächen
- 132 car parking spaces
  132 Pkw-Stellplätze
- 18 HGV/trailer parking spaces
  18 Lkw-Stellplätze
- ample parking for both visitors and employees
  ausreichende Pkw-Stellplätze für Mitarbeiter und Besucher
- concrete yard / concrete plates / asphalt / brick/clinker paving
  Andienungszone aus Beton / Betonflächen / Asphalt / schwerlastgeeigneten Pflastersteinen

Avoid the real estate mistake

Test your knowledge gained in this unit by identifying these common language mistakes. Underline the correct word or phrase.

1. A well positioned distribution *hall / facility* in an established logistics location.
2. Separate *counters / meters* for gas, water and electricity.
3. The *clear height / light height* is 10 meters.
4. There is land for expansion to the *rear side / rear* of the site.

Improve your style

Exchange the word/phrase in brackets with a more appropriate expression from this unit.

5. (Lots of) _____ parking for both visitors and employees.
6. The property (is on) _____ an area at the front boundary of the site.
7. A proven distribution location with a number of (famous) _____ occupiers.

Test your real estate vocabulary

8. The property is (sichtbar) _____ from the A3.
9. The property has 50 kN/sq m (Bodenbelastbarkeit) _____ capacity.
10. A modern (Hochregallager) _____ .
11. Access is provided via 12 (Rolltüre) _____ .
12. The site benefits from a generous (Rangierflächen) _____ .

---

1. facility | 2. meters | 3. clear height | 4. rear | 5. ample | 6. occupies | 7. well-known | 8. visible | 9. floor loading | 10. high-bay warehouse | 11. roller shutter doors | 12. manoeuvring area

Managing the Property

6

Tenant Correspondence 92
Examples
   Letter of introduction from new
   property manager to tenants 93
   Letter from property manager
   to tenant regarding prospective
   new tenant viewing 94
   Letter from property manager
   to tenant regarding repair/
   maintenance contractor visit 95
   Letter from property manager
   to tenant regarding inspection
   contractor visit 96

Requests for Payment 97
Payment phrases 97
Examples
   Rent demand 1 98
   Rent demand 2 99
   Rent demand 3 100

**Operating Costs and
Service Charges** 101
Service charge items 101
Example
   Letter from property manager to
   tenant regarding service charge
   budget 103

Service charge budget 104
Example
   Letter from property manager
   to tenant regarding outstanding
   service charge payment 105

Reporting 106
Example
   Quarterly management report 106
   Letter from property manager
   to owner regarding
   management meeting minutes 109

Meeting Minutes 110

**General Property
Management Activities** 111
Tenant concerns 111
Issues with tenants 112
Tradespersons and
contractors 113

Technical Issues and Works 114
Common defects in existing
buildings 114
Repair and maintenance 119
Repair works 119
Maintenance and inspections 121
Facility management issues 121
Installations and alterations 123
Landlord consent 123

Letting and Leases 124
Tenancy schedule 126
Letting activity 128
Tenant's credit standing and
payments 130
Examples
   Email from letting agent
   to client confirming instruction 131
Negotiating a lease contract 131
Asset management strategy 132

**Avoid the real estate
mistake, improve your
style and test your real
estate vocabulary** 138

6 Managing the Property

This unit provides vocabulary and phrases for many aspects of managing property, including facility, property and asset management activities. It features examples of correspondence with tenants for issues regarding collecting rent, arranging inspections, repair work and service charges, as well as management reports to owners regarding the status of their investment.

Tenant Correspondence

Whether you are a property owner or you are representing one, communicating effectively with tenants is an important part of your role. Regardless of the information contained in the letter, it is important to maintain a polite and friendly tone in order to promote goodwill.

English	German
contractor	Auftragnehmer
issues with tenants	Probleme/Angelegenheiten mit Mietern
landlord consent	Einverständnis des Vermieters
maintenance	Instandhaltung
meeting minutes	Besprechungsprotokoll
operating costs	Betriebskosten
rent demand	Mahnung/Zahlungserinnerung bezügl. der Miete
repairs	Instandsetzung
reporting	Berichtswesen
request for payments	Zahlungsaufforderung
service charges	Nebenkosten
tenant concerns	Anliegen / Beschwerden von Mietern
tenant's credit standing	Mieterbonität
tradesperson / craftsperson	Handwerker

6 Managing the Property

Letter of introduction from new property manager to tenants

CURATE
Property Management

15 October 2012

Mr David Newman
6 St Mary's Square
London
SW2 4HT

Dear Mr Newman

A warm welcome from (name of new property manager)

We are pleased to announce that we have recently been appointed Managing Agents for (name of property). Our appointment commenced on 1 October 2012 in place of (name of old property management company).

In the circumstances, I feel it important to contact you personally to introduce ourselves.

(CURATE Property Management) is an experienced commercial property management firm with a dedicated support team who are on hand to assist whenever you may need us.

Our service to you underlines our commitment to our clients. This includes a 24 hour service.

If you have any queries, please do not hesitate to contact us at any time.

Yours sincerely

P. Adams

Paul Adams
Property Manager

Jefferson Road, London SW1 HPQ
Tel: + 44 (0) 20 783 496 • Fax: + 44 (0) 20 783 785 • Email: info@curateman.org

6 MANAGING THE PROPERTY

Letter from property manager to tenant regarding prospective new tenant viewing

CURATE
Property Management

6 February 2012

Mr David Newman
6 St Mary's Square
London
SW2 4HT

Dear Mr Newman

6 St Mary's Square, London SW2 4HT

As you are aware, **we are currently seeking** new tenants for the above named property and I am writing **to advise you of** a viewing that I would like to conduct.

I am writing to advise you that a viewing has been scheduled for 5 March 2012 at 2.00 pm.

I hope this is convenient. However, should you wish to discuss this matter, please do not hesitate to contact me.

Thank you for your co-operation in this matter.

Yours sincerely

P. Adams

Paul Adams
Property Manager

Jefferson Road, London SW1 HPQ
Tel: + 44 (0) 20 783 496 • Fax: + 44 (0) 20 783 785 • Email: info@curateman.org

---

we are currently seeking
wir suchen zurzeit

to advise so. of
hier: jemanden von etwas benachrichtigen

6 Managing the Property

Letter from property manager to tenant regarding repair/maintenance contractor visit

CURATE
Property Management

15 November 2012

Mr David Newman
6 St Mary's Square
London
SW2 4HT

Dear Mr Newman

6 St Mary's Square, London SW2 4HT

I am writing to advise you that an appointment has been made for a contractor from (Pure Air Ltd.) to visit your **premises** to carry out repair work on the defective air conditioning **plant**.

An appointment has been scheduled for 7 December 2012 at 11.00 am and if I do not hear from you I will assume that this is convenient.

Thank you for your co-operation in this matter.

Yours sincerely

P. Adams

Paul Adams
Property Manager

Jefferson Road, London SW1 HPQ
Tel: + 44 (0) 20 783 496 • Fax: + 44 (0) 20 783 785 • Email: info@curateman.org

---

premises
Räumlichkeiten

plant
Anlage

6 Managing the Property

Letter from property manager to tenant regarding inspection contractor visit

CURATE
Property Management

10 December 2012

Mr David Newman
6 St Mary's Square
London
SW2 4HT

Dear Mr Newman

6 St Mary's Square, SW2 4HT

As you will be aware, **statutory regulations** require (gas appliances) to be tested annually.

I am therefore writing to advise you that an appointment has been made for a contractor from (EnergiCheck Ltd.) to visit your premises to undertake the required inspection.

An appointment has been made for 17 January 2013 at 9.00 am and if I do not hear from you within 5 working days from the date of this letter, I will assume that this is convenient.

Thank you for your co-operation in this matter.

Yours sincerely

P. Adams

Paul Adams
Property Manager

Jefferson Road, London SW1 HPQ
Tel: + 44 (0) 20 783 496 • Fax: + 44 (0) 20 783 785 • Email: info@curateman.org

---

statutory regulations
gesetzliche Bestimmungen

6 Managing the Property

Requests for payment

The first request for payment should take a polite tone which acknowledges that there may be a good reason why payment has not been made. This can be achieved by using language that is impersonal.

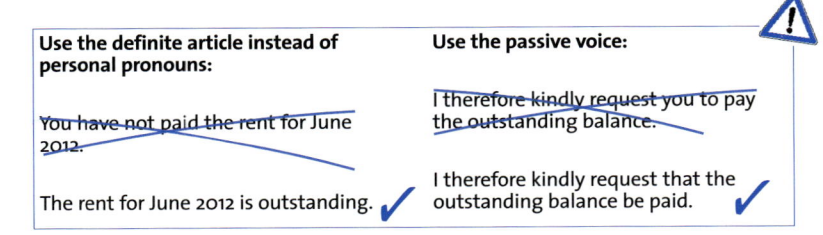

Use the definite article instead of personal pronouns:	Use the passive voice:
~~You have not paid the rent for June 2012.~~	~~I therefore kindly request you to pay the outstanding balance.~~
The rent for June 2012 is outstanding. ✓	I therefore kindly request that the outstanding balance be paid. ✓

Payment phrases

- Thank you for your letter concerning the outstanding rent for June. We are willing to extend the payment period for another four weeks, however we will have to insist on payment by the end of July.
  Vielen Dank für Ihr Schreiben bezüglich der ausstehenden Miete für Juni. Wir sind bereit, die Zahlungsfrist um weitere vier Wochen zu verlängern, müssen jedoch auf Zahlung bis spätestens Ende Juli bestehen.

- Thank you for your letter of 21 September 2012 concerning the outstanding rent for August and September 2012. While we appreciate that (name of tenant company) is currently experiencing financial difficulties, we are unable to extend the payment period.
  Vielen Dank für Ihr Schreiben vom 21. September 2012 bezüglich der ausstehenden Miete für August und September 2012. Uns ist bekannt, dass (Name des mietenden Unternehmens) derzeit finanzielle Schwierigkeiten hat, bedauern jedoch, keinen Zahlungsaufschub gewähren zu können.

- We look forward to receiving your remittance.
  Wir sehen Ihrer baldigen Zahlung entgegen.

- Unfortunately, we are unable to extend the payment period. In view of the financial difficulties (name of tenant company) has been experiencing, we are prepared to compromise and suggest that half the outstanding balance be paid immediately and the remaining amount at the end of the month.
  Wir bedauern, keinen Zahlungsaufschub gewähren zu können. Angesichts der finanziellen Schwierigkeiten von (Name des mietenden Unternehmens) sind wir jedoch zu einem Kompromiss bereit und schlagen vor, dass die Hälfte des ausstehenden Betrags sofort und der Rest Ende des Monats gezahlt wird.

6 Managing the Property

Rent demand 1

CURATE
Property Management

6 April 2012

Mr David Newman
6 St Mary's Square
London
SW2 4HT

Dear Mr Newman

6 St Mary's Square, London SW2 4HT
Formal Demand For Overdue Rent

According to our records **it appears that** the rental payment for March 2012 is currently overdue as follows:

Outstanding rent: € 25,000, due: 3 March 2012

I therefore kindly request that the outstanding balance be paid within 7 working days and that all future rental payments be made in full on the due date.

Thank you for your co-operation in this matter.

Yours sincerely

P. Adams

Paul Adams
Property Manager

Jefferson Road, London SW1 HPQ
Tel: + 44 (0) 20 783 496 • Fax: + 44 (0) 20 783 785 • Email: info@curateman.org

---

it appears that
es scheint/zeigt sich, dass

TIP!
Using less direct and impersonal language helps to maintain goodwill.

6 Managing the Property

Rent demand 2

CURATE
Property Management

4 May 2012

Mr David Newman
6 St Mary's Square
London
SW2 4HT

Dear Mr Newman

6 St Mary's Square, London SW2 4HT
Second Demand For Overdue Rent

I am writing to advise you that despite the previous reminder of 6 April 2012 regarding outstanding rent, payment has not been made.

The current overdue amount is as follows:

Outstanding rent: € 25,000, due: 3 March 2012

I therefore kindly request that the outstanding balance be paid within 7 working days and that all future rental payments be made in full on the due date.

Thank you for your co-operation in this matter.

Yours sincerely

P. Adams

Paul Adams
Property Manager

Jefferson Road, London SW1 HPQ
Tel: + 44 (0) 20 783 496 • Fax: + 44 (0) 20 783 785 • Email: info@curateman.org

6 Managing the Property

Rent demand 3

to note
feststellen

CURATE
Property Management

1 June 2012

Mr David Newman
6 St Mary's Square
London
SW2 4HT

Dear Mr Newman

6 St Mary's Square, London SW2 4HT
Final Demand For Overdue Rent

I regret **to note** that we have received no response to the recent reminders regarding outstanding rent.

I therefore take this opportunity to advise you that should the outstanding rent of € 25,000 not be received within 7 working days we will be forced to take legal action.

Yours sincerely

P. Adams

Paul Adams
Property Manager

Jefferson Road, London SW1 HPQ
Tel: + 44 (0) 20 783 496 • Fax: + 44 (0) 20 783 785 • Email: info@curateman.org

6 Managing the Property

Operating Costs & Service Charges

German and UK operating costs and service charge documents vary in form and content. The items included on service charge reports also depend on the terms of the lease contract and whether costs are recoverable or non-recoverable. The following examples are given in order to serve as a language guide and are not a definitive template for layout.

In German documents, operating costs and service charges are often categorised by Gebäudetechnik and Infrastrukturelle Dienstleistungen. In the UK, costs are often categorised by the terms Soft Services, which include non-technical items such as cleaning, and Hard Services, which include items that can be directly attributed to physical aspects of the property such as structural repairs or maintenance to mechanical and electrical services.

Service charge items

The following list provides a translation of common operating cost and service charge items.

English	German
Soft services	**Infrastruktur**
- external cleaning	- Außenreinigung
- internal cleaning	- Innenreinigung
- landscaping	- Gärtnerdienste, Grünflächengestaltung
- on-site facility manager services	- Hausmeisterdienste
- pest control	- Ungezieferbekämpfung
- security	- Sicherheitsdienste
- snow and ice clearing	- Winterdienst
- street cleaning	- Straßenreinigung
- toiletries	- Hygieneartikel
- waste management	- Müllabfuhr
- window cleaning	- Fensterreinigung
Local tax and rates	**Öffentliche Abgaben**
- rates (UK) / property tax (US)	- Grundsteuer
- drainage	- Oberflächenentwässerung
- street clearance	- Straßenreinigungsgebühren

6 Managing the Property

Life Safety System refers to any elements of a building designed to protect and evacuate the building occupants in emergencies such as heat and smoke detectors, alarms, fire extinguishers and sprinkler systems.

M&E Mechanical & Electrical (engineering)

English	German
Hard services	**Technik**
- access control	- Zugangskontrolle
- **life/safety systems** maintenance	- Instandhaltung der Brandmeldeanlage etc.
- life/safety systems repairs	- Reparaturen der Brandmeldeanlage etc.
- life/safety systems inspections	- Inspektion der Brandmeldeanlage etc.
- lift inspections	- Aufzugsinspektionen
- lift maintenance	- Aufzugswartung
- lift repairs	- Aufzugsreparatur
- **M&E** inspections	- technische Inspektionen (z.B. TÜV)
- M&E maintenance	- technische Wartung
- M&E repairs	- technische Reparaturen
- stand-by service	- Bereitschaftsgebühr
- telephone connection costs	- Telefonanschlussgebühren
- (technical fault)	- Störmeldeüberwachung
Utilities	**Versorgungseinrichtungen**
- electricity	- Elektrizität
- gas	- Gas
- meters	- Zähler
- oil	- Öl
- sewage	- Abwasser
- water	- Frischwasser
Insurance	**Versicherungen**
- building insurance	- Gebäudeversicherung
- liability insurance	- Haftpflichtversicherung
- terrorism insurance	- Terrorversicherung
Management	**Kaufmännisches Management**
- management fees	- Verwaltungskosten
- accounting fees	- Abrechnung und Finanzverwaltung (Buchhaltung)

6 Managing the Property

Letter from property manager to tenant regarding service charge budget

CURATE
Property Management

15 May 2012

Mr David Newman
6 St Mary's Square
London
SW2 4HT

Dear Mr Newman

6 St Mary's Square, London SW2 4HT
Service Charge Budget Year Ending **June 2013**

We enclose the service charge budget for the year ending June 2013, which we hope you will find helpful.

As you are aware, this is an estimate of **anticipated costs** and the **actual expenditure** will be **reconciled** at the year-end and notified to you. We will strive to keep the charge stable at similar levels for future years, subject to normal price rises and **cyclical maintenance** and **unforeseen items**, and to keep the quality of services to the required standard.

The year-end June 2012 account will be reconciled in July and we will inform you as soon as possible of your account adjustment.

Yours sincerely

P. Adams

Paul Adams
Property Manager

Jefferson Road, London SW1 HPQ
Tel: + 44 (0) 20 783 496 • Fax: + 44 (0) 20 783 785 • Email: info@curateman.org

---

Y/E (year ending)
Jahresabschluss (zum Juni)

anticipated costs
Kostenschätzung

actual expenditure
tatsächliche Kosten

to reconcile
abgleichen

cyclical maintenance
zyklische Instandsetzung

unforeseen items
Unvorhergesehenes

6 Managing the Property

Service Charge Budget
(name of property)

Service charge budget for the period 1 January 2012 – 31 December 2012

	Previous year's actual (€)	Current year budget (€)	Current year actual (€)	Variance (%) Actual v budget
Soft services				
Security				
Internal cleaning				
External cleaning				
...				

English	German
Previous year's actual	Kosten Vorjahr
Current year budget	Budget aktuelles Jahr
Current year actual	Ist-Kosten aktuelles Jahr
Variance actual v budget	Abweichung Ist-Kosten v Budget

6 MANAGING THE PROPERTY

Letter from property manager to tenant regarding outstanding service charge payment

CURATE
Property Management

27 July 2012

Mr David Newman
6 St Mary's Square
London
SW2 4HT

Dear Mr Newman

**6 St Mary's Square, London SW2 4HT
Outstanding Service Charge Payment**

We are the **appointed** Managing Agents for 6 St Mary's Square.

Following a review of your account we noticed that the balancing service charge amount for the year 2011 of Euro 5,050.20 that was invoiced on 15 June 2012 has not been paid. I would add that we have written to you in the past supplying full details of the above mentioned service charges.

I therefore **kindly** request that the outstanding balance be paid within the next 7 working days and that you ensure that all future service charge payments be made in full on the due date.

If you have any queries about this please contact me immediately.

Yours faithfully

P. Adams

Paul Adams
Property Manager

Jefferson Road, London SW1 HPQ
Tel: + 44 (0) 20 783 496 • Fax: + 44 (0) 20 783 785 • Email: info@curateman.org

appointed
beauftragt

kindly
höflich, freundlich

6 Managing the Property

Reporting

Many different types of format are used for reporting on property issues to management and clients. Some formats may consist of Excel tables with short statements recording events and action taken while others may be lengthy Word documents with in-depth market analysis. The style chosen depends on the needs of the organisation or the client.

Regardless of the length, it is a good idea to use clear headings in order to organise the report into sections and guide the reader through information quickly and easily.

Below is an example of a short quarterly management report.

QUARTERLY MANAGEMENT REPORT
for (name of owner)

PROPERTY: (name and address of property)
No: (number of property in fund)
DATE:

1.0 Property Condition
The property is in excellent condition.

or

Externally the property is in good condition however internally the finishes look tired and dated.

or

The property would benefit from a substantial refurbishment of the common parts.

2.0 Location Development
The only significant deal to be concluded in (name of town) during the last quarter was the 7,510 sq m letting of (name and address of property) for (name of tenant).

A schedule of the space currently available in (name of town) is shown in Appendix 2.

3.0 Rental Status
A summary of **void** space / existing lease terms is shown in the Tenancy Schedule in Appendix 1.

The property is 83.13% occupied, with currently only the first floor being unoccupied 16.87%. Rents vary from Euro 32 **psm** (name of tenant) to Euro 30 **psm** (name of tenant).

→

---

void
another word for vacancy (Leerstand).

psm = per square metre

6 Managing the Property

4.0 Tenant Meetings

The last tenant meeting was held on 26 April 2012 and representatives from all tenants were present. A separate meeting was held with (name of tenant) on 23 March 2012 to discuss lease renewal.

or

No requirement yet for tenant meetings, however regular contact is kept with office managers.

or

Contact is generally made with the Asset Manager in (name of city) however the tenant has no concerns regarding the building.

or

Monthly inspections are carried out by (name of facility management company) with (name of tenant)'s building manager.

or

(Name of property management company) are in regular contact with the tenant representative.

The key points raised by the tenants are as follows:

- The current service and management of the building are viewed as very satisfactory / not satisfactory
- Improvement of external signage
- Repairs to automatic access doors
- (Name of tenants) have indicated that they may require redecoration of the lobby as a precondition for renewing their lease.

The above matters will be addressed as part of the maintenance programme. The cost of implementation of new signage will need to be met by the landlord.

5.0 Tenant Concerns

Some concerns have been raised over the reliability of the lifts.

The other tenants are not happy about (name of tenant) using the parking spaces for their waste containers.

The tenants are concerned regarding perceived delays in undertaking lift maintenance.

Concerns about the lift reliability: meetings have been held with the lift maintenance company to resolve this matter.

Tenant concerns regarding faults with chillers which we have taken up with suppliers.

Concerns were expressed regarding noise resulting from 2nd floor fit-out.

or

None

TIP!
The word "concern" is often used in business instead of "problem" in order to avoid a negative tone.

6 Managing the Property

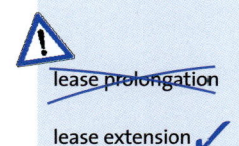

6.0 Operating Costs
We attach a copy of the service charge budget in relation to the year ending 31st December 2011 in Appendix 3.

The service charge currently equates to € 6.52 psm.

At present we do not anticipate a variance of greater than 6% over and above the budgeted annual expenditure.

7.0 Current Matters
The following matters are currently being progressed:
- Vacant ground floor (598.23 sq m) is being marketed by (name of agent). Interest in this space has been expressed by (name of prospective tenant), negotiations continue.
- (Name of tenant)'s lease expires on 15th March 2013. (Name of tenant) has found alternative premises in (name of city) and will be vacating on 1st December 2012.
- Planning consent has been obtained to extend office use to medical.
- (Name of tenant) have **extended** their lease of 4th floor for 5 years to expire September 2017.
- Issues concerning the cleaning of various areas have been improved and the tenants are now generally happy.

⚠ lease ~~prolongation~~

lease extension ✓

No.	Technical issues	Status	Deadline
1.	Capital works instructed. Removal of carpeting from ground floor.	Completed	
2.	To decorate common entrance lift lobbies.	Actioned 23 March	
3.	To upgrade CCTV Security Cameras.	Actioned 23 March	
4.	Staining to façade to be removed.	Outstanding	30 April
5.	Window blinds have been failing on a regular basis due to a design fault. We have contacted the sub-contractor and arranged for repairs to be carried out.	Outstanding	30 April
6.	Gutters have been cleaned.	Actioned 2nd March	
7.	Graffiti cleaned off exterior wall to front.	Actioned 3rd March	

6   Managing the Property

Letter from property manager to owner regarding management meeting minutes

CURATE
Property Management

2 July 2012

Mr David Newman
6 St Mary's Square
London
SW2 4HT

Dear David

Management Meeting Minutes

Following the Management Meeting regarding the Alpha Dynamic Fund, held on 25 June 2012, I enclose a copy of the minutes.

Should you have any queries in relation to these minutes or any other matter then please contact me at any time.

Yours sincerely

P. Adams

Paul Adams
Property Manager

Jefferson Road, London SW1 HPQ
Tel: + 44 (0) 20 783 496 • Fax: + 44 (0) 20 783 785 • Email: info@curateman.org

TIP!
Some business partners use first names in business correspondence if they have regular contact with each other.

6 Managing the Property

Meeting Minutes

Meeting minutes are a written record of everything that happens in a meeting. They are prepared for the company files, as a reference for those in attendance as well as those that are absent. The format may vary between organisations; however the minutes should contain the basic headings and information as provided below.

CURATE
Property Management

MINUTES
of Management Meeting held on 6 July 2012, 11:00 am

PRESENT: Wendy Edwards (Alpha Dynamic)
Mark Stretton (Alpha Dynamic)
Martin Hall (Curate Property Management)
Thomas Wallace (Curate Property Management)

APOLOGIES: Alan Humphries
Susan Smith

1	**MINUTES OF LAST MEETING**	
2	**MATTERS ARISING FROM THE MINUTES**	
3	**Munich**	Position noted re sale. Curate to arrange for outstanding maintenance issues to be resolved. Curate to check for any unauthorised alternations.
4	**Frankfurt Airport Cargo City**	Contractor due to start renovation works to office w/c 19 July. Curate to speak to (name of agents) for update on letting situation for ground floor. Late payment by (name of tenant). No interest payment to be charged in this instance.
5	**Frankfurt**	Inspections to be arranged for 1 September. Damage to fence to be reported to insurers and quote obtained for repair works.
6	**Hamburg**	No matters raised.
7	**AOB**	Send copies of insurance policy to Alpha Dynamic.
8	**DATE OF NEXT MEETING**	It was agreed that the next meeting would be held on Wednesday 3 October 2012 at 11:00 am.

Apologies:
"Absent" is also used

w/c is an abbreviation for "week commencing"

AOB: abbreviation of "any other business" (Sonstiges)

6 Managing the Property

General Property Management Activities

- The monthly/quarterly inspection was carried out by (name of Property Manager) with (name of Facility/Building Manager)
  Die monatliche/vierteljährliche Inspektion wurde von (Name des Immobilienverwalters) zusammen mit (Name des Facility-Managers/Gebäudeverwalters) durchgeführt.

- Notice has been issued to the tenant that works will be carried out by (name of contractor).
  Dem Mieter wurde mitgeteilt, dass die Arbeiten von (Name der Firma) ausgeführt werden.

- (Name of Property Manager) has written to the tenants again concerning unauthorised parking in the underground car park.
  (Name des Immobilienverwalters) hat bezüglich des nicht genehmigten Parkens in der Tiefgarage erneut an die Mieter geschrieben.

- The matter of unauthorised parking in the underground car park has been brought to the tenant's notice.
  Die Angelegenheit des nicht genehmigten Parkens in der Tiefgarage wurde dem Mieter zur Kenntnis gebracht.

- Quarterly tenant meetings have been initiated.
  Vierteljährliche Mieterversammlungen wurden eingeführt.

Tenant concerns

- (Name of tenant) has queried the service charges.
  (Name des Mieters) hat die Nebenkosten in Frage gestellt.

- The other tenants are not happy about any additional (name of tenant)'s signage in the entrance hall.
  Die anderen Mieter haben Einwände gegen zusätzliche Firmenschilder von (Name des Mieters) in der Eingangshalle erhoben.

- (Name of tenant) consider that electricity readings could be inaccurate due to the size of their energy bills.
  (Name des Mieters) vermutet angesichts hoher Stromrechnungen, dass eventuell die abgelesenen Zählerstände nicht stimmen.

- Concerns were expressed by (name of tenant) regarding noise resulting from the 4th floor fit-out.
  (Name des Mieters) hat sich über den Lärm durch die Innenausbauarbeiten im 4. Stock beschwert.

6 Managing the Property

- The tenants are concerned about "excessive" waiting times for lifts. To address this concern (name of manufacturer) have been instructed to install group controllers, which will result in the lifts being on the ground floor during busy times.
Die Mieter haben die „übermäßigen" Wartezeiten auf die Aufzüge beanstandet. Um Abhilfe zu schaffen, wurde der (Name des Aufzugherstellers) mit dem Einbau von Gruppensteuerungen beauftragt, die dafür sorgen sollen, dass die Aufzüge in den Hauptverkehrszeiten im Erdgeschoss sind.

- The tenants raised concern over the entrance flooring as a slip hazard. There have been no further complaints since the cleaners have monitored the area more closely.
Die Mieter beanstandeten, dass der Bodenbelag im Eingang nicht rutschsicher war. Seitdem die Gebäudereiniger diesen Bereich genauer kontrollieren, gab es keine weiteren Beschwerden.

- Issues over the cleaning of various areas have been improved and the tenants are now generally happy.
Mängel bezüglich der Reinigung verschiedener Bereiche wurden behoben und die Mieter sind jetzt im Allgemeinen zufrieden.

- Tenants are complaining about the cost of landscape maintenance and don't feel they are receiving value for money.
Die Mieter beschweren sich über die Kosten für die Pflege der Außenanlagen und sind der Ansicht, dass das Preis-Leistungs-Verhältnis nicht stimmt.

> Negatives words such as „problem" are often avoided in business.
> The alternatives „issue" or „matter" can be used instead.

Issues with tenants

- The tenant has failed to respond to our correspondence and we suspect that given their current financial status they are currently unable to make regular rent payments.
Der Mieter hat nicht geantwortet und wir vermuten, dass er angesichts seiner derzeitigen finanziellen Situation nicht in der Lage ist, regelmäßige Mietzahlungen zu leisten.

- (Name of tenant) have indicated that they are prepared to accept part of the (fit-out) costs.
(Name des Mieters) hat seine Bereitschaft gezeigt, einen Teil der (Innenausbau-) Kosten zu übernehmen.

6 Managing the Property

Tradespersons and contractors

English	German
bricklayer / stonemason	Maurer / Steinmetz
building services engineer	Ingenieur für Gebäudetechnik
carpenter	Zimmermann
dry liner	Trockenbauer
electrician	Elektriker
fire officer	Feuerwehrmann
floorlayer / carpet fitter	Bodenleger / Teppichleger
HVAC engineer (Heating Ventilation & Air Conditioning)	Ingenieur für Klimatechnik
joiner	Tischler
landscape gardener	Landschaftsgärtner
painter	Maler
pest controller	Kammerjäger
plasterer	Gipser / Verputzer
plumber	Klempner / Installateur
roofer	Dachdecker
shopfitter	Ladenausbauer
structural engineer	Statiker

6 Managing the Property

Technical Issues and Works

The following information is a guide to some defects commonly found in commercial buildings.

Common defects in existing buildings

Roof structure and covering

- Some tiles along the verge on the north east have slipped. It is recommended that an inspection is carried out by a specialist roofing contractor to ascertain the cause and replace tiles where necessary.

- Flashing between roof and dormer windows on the top floor has become detached in recent high winds.
- Excessive ponding on built-up felt roof; check drainpipe for blockages.

External walls and cladding

- Weathering and discolouring of façade due to mould growth on north elevation. Specialist cleaning required.
- Rust marks to stone cladding; suggest possible corrosion of fixing cramps.

- Areas of cracked render; in general external decorations need renewing as they have reached end of decoration cycle.
- Vertical/horizontal cracking has appeared on the external masonry to the north elevation. Check for differential movement between brickwork and frame and adequacy of vertical and horizontal expansion joints.

- Outer leaf of concrete cladding panels becoming detached, showing signs of cracking; check for movement between cladding and frame and suitability and condition of fixings.
- There is evidence of failure of sealants between pre-cast concrete panels. This is consistent with the age of the building and it is recommended that all seals are renewed.
- Frost damage to the stone cladding panels on the north elevation. It is recommended that a specialist report is commissioned to ascertain the potential liability and to agree remedial measures.
- Evidence of spalling to pre-cast concrete panels possibly caused by carbonation to concrete and inadequate cover to the reinforcement.
- Patches of efflorescence on external brickwork.
- Cracking to brickwork pointing below parapet caused by differential thermal movement. Repoint brickwork and consider insulating parapet.

Häufige Mängel und Schäden an Bestandsgebäuden

Dachkonstruktion und -belag

- An der Nordostseite sind einige Dachrandziegel verrutscht. Es wird empfohlen, eine Inspektion durch eine Dachdeckerfirma durchführen zu lassen, um die Ursache festzustellen und erforderlichenfalls Ziegel zu ersetzen.
- Das Kehlblech an den Dachfenstern hat sich infolge der starken Winde in jüngster Zeit gelöst.
- Übermäßiges stehendes Wasser auf den Bitumenabdichtungsbahnen; Dacheinläufe auf Verstopfung überprüfen.

Außenmauern und Verkleidung

- Verwitterungen und Verfärbung der Fassade aufgrund von Schimmelbefall an der Nordseite. Reinigung durch Spezialfirma erforderlich.
- Rostflecken auf der Natursteinverkleidung; vermutlich durch Korrosion der Befestigungsklammern.
- Der Putz ist stellenweise rissig; Fassaden allgemein renovierungsbedürftig, das Ende des normalen Renovierungsintervalls ist erreicht.
- Senkrechte/waagrechte Risse außen am Mauerwerk auf der Nordseite. Auf Bewegung zwischen Ziegelmauer und Rahmen kontrollieren und prüfen, ob die senkrechten und waagrechten Dehnungsfugen ausreichend sind.
- Der Sichtbeton weist Risse auf; Bewegung zwischen Sichtbeton und Unterkonstruktion kontrollieren sowie Eignung und Zustand der Befestigungsmittel überprüfen.
- Es gibt Anzeichen eines Mangels im Fugenmaterial zwischen den Fertigbetonplatten. Dies ist angesichts des Alters des Gebäudes zu erwarten. Es wird empfohlen, das Fugenmaterial zu erneuern.
- Frostschäden an der Natursteinverkleidung auf der Nordseite. Es wird empfohlen, ein Gutachten einzuholen, um die potenzielle Haftung festzustellen und Abhilfemaßnahmen zu vereinbaren.
- Anzeichen von Abblättern an Fertigbetonplatten, möglicherweise durch Karbonisierung des Betons und unzureichende Bodendeckung verursacht.
- Stellenweise Ausblühungen am Ziegelmauerwerk.
- Risse in den Mörtelfugen der Ziegelmauer unterhalb der Brüstung, verursacht durch unterschiedliche Wärmeausdehnung. Ziegelmauerwerk neu verfugen und Isolierung der Brüstung in Erwägung ziehen.

6 Managing the Property

Dampness, leaks, condensation & mould

- Water penetration in roof which appears as staining to the ceiling.
- There is rising damp on the ground floor in the north-east corner of the office manifested by flaking of the paintwork at low level.
- There is evidence of water penetration through the retaining wall in the plant room in the basement.
- There is mould formation in the corner at ceiling level on the 3rd floor.
- Damp areas to ceiling finishes on upper floor are potentially evidence of condensation within roof void.

Internal walls and partitions

- Some (horizontal/vertical) cracks have appeared on internal plasterwork which may be a result of settlement. Instruct an engineer to install tell-tails, which will establish whether this is a progressive problem.
- Cracking between wet plaster walls and ceilings due to shrinkage. Filling and repainting required.
- Damage by tenants to plasterboard which needs to be repaired by a specialist contractor.

Windows

- The seal has failed between the two panes of glass in the double glazed units, resulting in condensation forming inside. A general inspection is required to ascertain the extent of this problem.
- Water penetration between spandrel panels and mullions to curtain walling; evidence of potential construction defect.
- Damp to window reveals; evidence of failure of sealant between frame and masonry.

Internal decoration and fit-out

- Scuffing to paintwork in circulation areas.
- Discolouring to walls above radiators.
- Damage to paintwork on doors and doorframes. Rub down and repainting required.
- Damage to metal ceiling panels caused by recent maintenance within the ceiling void.

Building services

- The power circuits have persistently tripped out on the ground floor. The tenant has been requested to test their equipment.
- Complaints of hot water temperature being too high. Temperature may need adjusting.
- Complaints regarding variable temperatures from tenants – check thermostatic control.

6 Managing the Property

Feuchtigkeit, Undichtigkeiten, Kondensation und Schimmel

- Wasser dringt durch das Dach ein und führt zu Wasserflecken an der Decke.
- Im Erdgeschoss an der Nordostecke des Büros wurde aufsteigende Feuchtigkeit festgestellt, die sich durch Abblättern der Farbe im unteren Wandbereich bemerkbar macht.
- Es gibt Anzeichen dafür, dass Wasser durch die Stützmauer im Anlagenraum im Keller eindringt.
- Im 3. Stock ist Schimmelbildung in der Ecke unter der Decke festzustellen.
- Feuchte Stellen an den Decken im oberen Stockwerk deuten auf Kondensation im Dachhohlraum hin.

Innen- und Zwischenwände

- An den Innenwänden wurden einige (waagrechte/senkrechte) Risse im Putz festgestellt, die eventuell auf Setzung zurückzuführen sind. Setzungsmarker vom Vermessungsingenieur anbringen lassen, um festzustellen, ob es sich um ein fortschreitendes Problem handelt.
- Risse zwischen Nassputzwänden und Decken aufgrund von Schrumpfung. Verspachteln und Streichen erforderlich.
- Von Mietern verursachte Beschädigung der Trockenbauwand; Reparatur durch Fachfirma erforderlich.

Fenster

- Die Abdichtung zwischen den beiden Glasscheiben der Doppelverglasung ist defekt, so dass es zu Kondenswasserbildung im Zwischenraum kommt. Eine Grundinspektion ist erforderlich, um das Ausmaß des Problems festzustellen.
- Eindringen von Wasser zwischen Fassadenplatten und Fenstermittelpfosten in die vorgehängte Fassade; Anzeichen für einen möglichen Konstruktionsfehler.
- Feuchtigkeit an Fensterlaibungen; Anzeichen für ein Versagen der Dichtung zwischen Fensterrahmen und Mauerwerk.

Dekorativer Zustand und Einrichtung

- Abgescheuerte Farbe in den Verkehrsflächen.
- Verfärbung der Wände über den Heizkörpern.
- Farbe von Türen und Türrahmen beschädigt. Müssen abgeschliffen und neu gestrichen werden.
- Beschädigte Metalldeckenplatten infolge kürzlich vorgenommener Instandhaltungsarbeiten im Deckenhohlraum.

Gebäudetechnik

- Die Sicherungen im Erdgeschoss springen ständig heraus. Der Mieter wurde gebeten, seine technische Ausstattung zu überprüfen.
- Beschwerden liegen vor, die Temperatur des Warmwassers sei zu hoch. Eventuell muss diese neu eingestellt werden.
- Beschwerden von Mietern liegen bezüglich der Raumtemperatur vor – die Thermostate müssen kontrolliert werden.

6 Managing the Property

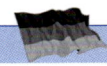

Floors	Böden
• Cracking to floor tiles.	• Risse in den Bodenfliesen.
• Carpet worn in heavily trafficked circulation areas.	• Teppichboden in stark begangenen Verkehrsflächen abgenutzt.
• Uneven finish over raised access floor possible movement of pedestals.	• Doppelböden uneben, eventuell aufgrund einer Bewegung der Ständer.
Elevator/Lift	**Aufzug/Lift**
• ongoing electrical faults	• wiederholte elektrische Störungen
• slow operation and long wait times	• langsamer Betrieb und lange Wartezeiten
• malfunctioning door operators	• Türstörungen
• misalignments between elevator and the intended floor	• nicht bündiger Austritt zwischen Stockwerk und Aufzug
• operation is not smooth, particularly when stopping	• ruckelnder Betrieb, besonders beim Anhalten
Sanitary installations and drainage	**Sanitäre Einrichtungen und Oberflächenentwässerung**
• Report of drain smell from toilet area and drain seals to be checked.	• Abwassergeruch im WC-Bereich gemeldet, Bereich und Abflussrohrdichtungen sind zu überprüfen.
• Water in basement car park is not draining sufficiently due to possible blockage.	• Wasser in der Tiefgarage läuft nicht richtig ab, eventuell ist der Abfluss verstopft.

6 Managing the Property

Repair & Maintenance

English	German
breakdown / fault	Störung
to carry out repairs	Reparaturen durchführen
deferred maintenance	aufgeschobene Instandhaltung
disruption to building users/ tenants (downtime)	Beeinträchtigung für die Nutzer/Mieter (Ausfallzeit)
fault diagnosed and problem rectified	Störung diagnostisiert und Problem behoben
good standard of maintenance	guter Erhaltungszustand
maintenance backlog	Instandhaltungsstau
maintenance planning	Instandhaltungsplanung
maintenance schedule	Instandhaltungsplan
normal wear and tear	normale Abnutzung und Verschleiß
planned maintenance	vorbeugende Instandhaltung / Wartung
preventative maintenance	vorsorgliche/vorbeugende Instandhaltung
to rectify / to remediate	beheben / beseitigen
to repair	reparieren, instand setzen
statutory requirements / compliance with statutory requirements	gesetzliche Vorschriften / Übereinstimmung mit gesetzlichen Vorschriften

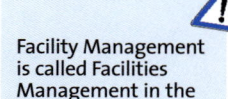

⚠ Facility Management is called Facilities Management in the UK.

Repair works

- An inspection of the drainage will be carried out to check for blockages.
  Eine Inspektion der Oberflächenentwässerung wird durchgeführt, um festzustellen, ob Verstopfungen vorliegen.
- Invitations for tenders for the refurbishment works due to be returned 30.06.2012.
  Ausschreibung von Renovierungsarbeiten mit Frist bis zum 30.06.2012.
- Partial replacement of carpet tiles is required.
  Die Teppichfliesen müssen teilweise ersetzt werden.

6 Managing the Property

- (Name of contractor) have been instructed to carry out repair works.
  (Name des Auftragnehmers) wurde mit der Durchführung von Renovierungsarbeiten beauftragt.
- Some electrical works to the estate lighting were carried out.
  Es wurden Arbeiten an der Außenbeleuchtung durchgeführt.
- Work to the heating plant is in progress.
  Aktuell werden (Wartungs-)Arbeiten an der Heizungsanlage durchgeführt.
- This matter is being taken up directly with the supplier.
  Diese Angelegenheit wird direkt mit dem Dienstleister erörtert.
- Repairs are being carried out by (name of contractor).
  Reparaturarbeiten werden von (Name des Auftragnehmers) ausgeführt.
- Repair works were carried out satisfactorily on 25 May 2012.
  Reparaturarbeiten wurden am 25. Mai 2012 erfolgreich durchgeführt.
- The (heating plant) is now operating satisfactorily.
  Die (Heizungsanlage) funktioniert jetzt wieder einwandfrei.
- Damage was caused to the fire fighting lift by a subcontractor putting it out of action. The subcontractor has accepted liability and informed their insurance company. Work to repair the lift will be undertaken in January 2011 at no cost to (name of owner).
  Der Feuerwehraufzug wurde von einem Subunternehmer beschädigt und ist nicht betriebsfähig. Das Subunternehmen hat die Haftung hierfür übernommen und seine Versicherung benachrichtigt. Die Arbeiten zur Wiederinstandsetzung des Aufzugs werden im Januar 2011 durchgeführt, ohne dass (Name des Besitzers) irgendwelche Kosten hierfür entstehen.
- There have been faults with the chillers which we are taking up with the suppliers.
  Es wurden Defekte an den Kühlaggregaten festgestellt, die wir dem Dienstleister anzeigen werden.
- We have requested three contractors to provide us with quotations for the planned work to the heating plant.
  Wir haben drei Firmen gebeten, uns Kostenvoranschläge für die geplanten Arbeiten an der Heizungsanlage zukommen zu lassen.

6 Managing the Property

Maintenance and inspections

- The tenants were updated on the planned maintenance and are happy with the progress to date.
  Die Mieter wurden über die geplanten Instandhaltungsarbeiten informiert und sind mit dem Fortschritt bis dato zufrieden.
- EPC obtained – C rating.
  Energieausweis eingeholt – Effizienzklasse C.
- Instructions have been received to proceed with a Planned Preventative Maintenance Programme.
  Wir haben Anweisungen zur Durchführung eines planmäßigen präventiven Wartungsprogramms erhalten.
- Meetings are being held with the lift maintenance company to resolve this matter.
  Es finden Besprechungen mit der Aufzugswartungsfirma statt, um eine Lösung in dieser Angelegenheit zu finden.

EPC = Energy Performance Certificate

Facility management issues

- The external window clean has been put on hold.
  Die Außenreinigung der Fenster wurde ausgesetzt.
- Sub-contractors' work is properly/not adequately managed and supervised by principal contractor.
  Die durch den Subunternehmer ausgeführten Arbeiten werden vom Hauptauftragnehmer ordnungsgemäß/nicht ordnungsgemäß verwaltet und überwacht.
- Response to service calls within/not within agreed periods.
  Serviceanfragen werden/werden nicht in den vereinbarten Fristen bearbeitet.
- Inspection of completed work is in accordance with/does not meet good professional practice.
  Abgeschlossene Arbeiten werden/werden nicht gemäß anerkannter Prüfverfahren abgenommen.
- Daily occurrence log is complete/incomplete and issues are (not) closed out.
  Die täglichen Ereignisprotokolle sind vollständig/unvollständig und Probleme werden behoben/nicht behoben.
- Key holding arrangements and storage are (not) maintained as specified.
  Den getroffenen Absprachen bezüglich Verwaltung und Aufbewahrung der Schlüssel wird nachgekommen/nicht nachgekommen.

6 Managing the Property

- Not all/All site entrances are secure and alarmed by staff.
  Alle/Nicht alle Zugänge zur Anlage werden vom Personal verschlossen und alarmgesichert.

- Security vetting procedures for visitors and contractors are (not) adhered to by reception and security staff.
  Rezeptionspersonal und Sicherheitsdienst führen die Sicherheitsüberprüfungen von Besuchern und Lieferanten vorschriftsmäßig/nicht vorschriftsmäßig durch.

- A security patrol log is maintained/not accurately maintained.
  Kontrollgänge des Sicherheitspersonals werden sorgfältig/nicht sorgfältig protokolliert.

- Facility is (not) opened and closed according to specified hours.
  Das Gebäude ist (nicht) zu den angegebenen Zeiten geöffnet und geschlossen.

- Planned maintenance activities are (not) carried out in accordance with the schedule of works.
  Angesetzte Instandhaltungsarbeiten werden (nicht) gemäß Arbeitsplan durchgeführt.

- Waste is stored as specified/not stored to a satisfactory standard.
  Abfälle werden gemäß den einschlägigen Bestimmungen/nicht ordnungsgemäß gelagert.

- Waste holding area is tidy/untidy.
  Der Abfalllagerort ist in aufgeräumtem/unaufgeräumtem Zustand.

- Accurate invoicing for services / Invoicing for services is not accurate.
  (Keine) Mängel bei der Rechnungsstellung erbrachter Serviceleistungen.

- Services are (not) benchmarked for value for money.
  Serviceleistungen orientieren sich (nicht) am Maßstab der Kosteneffektivität.

- A monthly inspection of buildings is (not) carried out by the Contractor and the Facilities Manager.
  Eine monatliche Inspektion der Gebäude durch den Auftragnehmer und den Gebäudemanager erfolgt (nicht).

6 Managing the Property

Installations and alterations

- Planning consent obtained to extend office use to medical.
  Eine Genehmigung zur Ausweitung der Büronutzung für medizinische Zwecke wurde eingeholt.
- Terms have been agreed with (name of contractor/manufacturer) for generator installation.
  Eine Vereinbarung mit (Name des Auftragnehmers/Herstellers) für die Installierung eines Generators wurde getroffen.
- Office fitting out is nearing completion.
  Der Innenausbau der Büros ist nahezu abgeschlossen.
- Entry system cameras and monitors have been installed.
  Überwachungskameras und Monitore für die Zutrittskontrolle wurden installiert.

Landlord consent

- (Name of tenant) have applied for consent to a minor external alteration to the ventilation duct. This is currently under consideration.
  Von (Name des Mieters) wurde die Genehmigung einer geringfügigen externen Änderung am Lüftungskanal beantragt. Der Antrag wird derzeit erwogen.
- (Name of tenant) wishes to carry out alterations to the premises and have requested permission pursuant to clause 2(7) of the lease. The works will involve installing partition walls on the first floor to create cellular offices. (Name of tenant) have sent architect's plans and specifications for the works.
  (Name des Mieters) möchte Änderungen an seinen Räumlichkeiten vornehmen und hat einen entsprechenden Antrag gemäß Artikel 2(7) des Mietvertrags gestellt. Die geplanten Maßnahmen betreffen die Errichtung von Trennwänden im ersten Stock, um Zellenbüros zu schaffen. Architektenzeichnungen und technische Spezifikationen für die Arbeiten wurden von (Name des Mieters) vorgelegt.
- Landlord's approval has been obtained to sublet on 3rd floor 2,500 sq m to (name of sub-tenant). (Name of solicitors/lawyers) were instructed to prepare subletting agreement.
  Die Genehmigung des Vermieters für die Vermietung von 2.500 m² Fläche im 3. Stock an (Name des Untermieters) wurde erteilt. Mit der Erstellung des Untermietvertrags wurde (Name des Rechtsanwalts) beauftragt.

6 Managing the Property

Letting and Leases

English	German
demise	Mietflächen, Mietsache
effective rent	Effektivmiete
escalator clause	Indexklausel, Wertsicherungsklausel
to extend (the lease contract)	(den Mietvertrag) verlängern
Full Repairing and Insuring Lease (FRI Lease)	Der FRI Lease wälzt alle Betriebs- und Bewirtschaftungskosten inkl. der Instandhaltungskosten, Reparatur- und Versicherungskosten auf den Mieter ab.
good covenant (poor covenant)	Mieter mit guter Bonität (schlechter Bonität)
gross rent	Bruttomiete
head lease	Hauptmietvertrag
headline rent	Nominalmiete
heads of terms	Grundsatzvereinbarung
landlord consent	Zustimmung des Vermieters
landlord's improvements	vom Vermieter getragene Verbesserungen der Mietsache
lease (contract)	Mietvertrag
to lease-up (US)	neu vermieten
lessee (tenant)	Mieter
lessor (landlord / owner)	Vermieter
liability	Verbindlichkeit / Haftung / Haftpflicht
net rent	Nettomieteinnahmen
passing rent	aktuelle Miete (Mieteinnahme)
rack rent (UK)	höchstmögliche erzielbare Miete / Marktmiete
rent review	Mietanpassung / Überprüfung und Anpassung bzw. Neufestsetzung der Miethöhe
rent roll	Mieterliste / Mieterbestandsliste

demise
synonymous with the word lease; often used to describe the area of property which forms the lease

good covenant
a good quality tenant who will comply with the lease terms (strong credit standing)

headline rent
the rent payable after all incentives have expired

landlord's improvements
work carried out by the landlord other than repair and maintenance which increases the value of the property

to lease-up (US)
the act of acquiring new tenants

passing rent
the current rent payable under the terms of the lease

rack rent (UK)
rent which is the full letting value of the property (the best rent possible)

rent roll
A document which provides details of rents

6 Managing the Property

English	German
schedule of dilapidations (UK)	Mängelliste
service charges	Nebenkosten
sublease (underlease)	Untermiete, Untermietvertrag
sublessee (underlessee)	Untermieter
sublessor (underlessor)	Untervermieter
subletting	Untervermietung
tenancy agreement	kurzfristiger Mietvertrag
tenant's improvements (TI)	Mietereinbauten / vom Mieter bezahlte Verbesserungen
(to) re-gear a lease	Mietvertrag neu verhandeln
(lease) term	Laufzeit des Mietverhältnisses
(to) terminate the lease contract	Mietvertrag kündigen
turnover rent	Umsatzmiete
vacant / void	leer stehend / Leerstand

schedule of dilapidations (UK)
A list of repair and maintenance items which a tenant is obliged to make good under the terms of a lease contract. Either during but normally at the end of a lease term

charges
The amount payable by a tenant for services provided to the property

tenancy agreement
short term lease – 3 years or less

(to) re-gear a lease
Agreement between landlord and tenant to amend fundamental terms of an existing lease, e.g. the tenant agrees to a lease term extension in exchange for a longer break between rent reviews, break clauses, or a reduction in current rent

For examples of text for letting details, see **Unit 7, Sales and Acquisitions**

125

6 Managing the Property

Tenancy schedule

Property Name	Unit Description (Demise)	Tenant Name	Area in sqm	Current Rent PA in £	Net Effective Rent (per sqm / PA) in £
Birmingham: 5 Lanes House	Offices Ground floor	Reed Software Ltd	448.18	82,000.00	184.28
	Offices Part 1st floor	Walkers Carlton UK Ltd	432.73	84,212.00	194.61
	Offices Part 1st floor	BDF Group International	325.15	63,233.00	194.47
	Offices 2nd floor	Speedway Ltd	942.57	173,000.00	183.54
	Offices 3rd & 4th floor	Total Returns Capital	1,885.04	346,000.00	183.54
				748,445.00	940.44
London: Hanover Square	Ground	Vacant	690.00		-
	1st floor	Techbyte Systems Ltd	1,290.02	261.46	202.68
	2nd floor	Techbyte Systems Ltd	1,293.73	255.30	203.69
	3rd floor	Instant Support Services	1,303.30	266.25	197.34
				783.01	603.71

6 Managing the Property

Lease Start	Break Option (BO)	Lease Expiry Date	Next Review Date	Comments
19.04.2001	-	18.04.2011	-	
11.06.2010	01.06.2017	01.06.2025	01.06.2017	Rent free to 20.11.2010 plus further 2 months if BO not exercised
02.12.2008	-	01.12.2013		
21.08.2009	-	20.08.2014		
11.09.2007	01.05.2012	01.05.2017		
				Marketed by Lorells at £ 260 per sqm
12.09.2007	12.09.2017	11.09.2022	12.09.2012 and 12.09.2017	
01.07.2004	-	30.06.2014		
25.03 2003	12.09.2017	24.03.2018		Sublet to BK Services Ltd

6 Managing the Property

Letting activity

- A summary of void space/existing lease terms are shown on the attached tenancy schedule.
 Ein Überblick über Leerstände/Laufzeiten existierender Mietverträge ist aus der beiliegenden Mieterliste ersichtlich.

- Vacant ground floor. Interest has been expressed by (name of prospective tenant), negotiations continue.
 Leer stehendes Erdgeschoss. Von (Name des potenziellen Mieters) wurde ein Interesse hieran bekundet; die Verhandlungen laufen.

- (Name of tenant) have exercised their break clause as of 10 July 2012.
 (Name des Mieters) hat von seinem Sonderkündigungsrecht Gebrauch gemacht und das Mietverhältnis zum 10. Juli 2012 gekündigt.

- Lease renewal negotiations are ongoing via (name of agent) with (name of tenant) regarding the renewal of their lease as of 30 June 2012.
 Mit (Name des Mieters) laufen derzeit über (Name des Maklers) Verhandlungen bezüglich einer Verlängerung des Mietvertrags ab dem 30. Juni 2012.

- (Name of tenant) is requesting flexible lease terms, including service charge cap to reflect market conditions.
 (Name des Mieters) verlangt flexible Mietvertragsbedingungen, darunter eine Begrenzung der Nebenkosten unter Berücksichtigung der Marktlage.

- (Name of tenant) in re-gear discussions.
 Mit (Name des Mieters) werden derzeit Gespräche über eine Verlängerung des Mietverhältnisses zu neuen Bedingungen geführt.

- The tenant has countered requesting a 6 year term with annual breaks subject to a rent free period/capped service charge.
 Der Mieter verlangt im Gegenzug eine Laufzeit von 6 Jahren mit jährlicher Kündigungsmöglichkeit vorbehaltlich einer mietfreien Zeit/Nebenkostenbegrenzung.

- The tenant has agreed terms for alternative office accommodation and will be vacating the property on 15 June 2012.
 Der Mieter hat einen Mietvertrag für andere Büroräume abgeschlossen und wird am 15. Juni 2012 ausziehen.

6 Managing the Property

- (Name of tenant) have served notice to break the lease of 5th floor in September 2013. Joint letting agents have been instructed (name of agent) and (name of agent).
  (Name des Mieters) hat sein Mietverhältnis für die 5. Etage zum September 2013 gekündigt. (Name des Maklers) und (Name des Maklers) wurden mit der Neuvermietung beauftragt.

- There is just one void in the portfolio being the ground floor unit of Willi-Brandt-Straße 20. This is being marketed by (name of agent).
  Es ist nur ein Leerstand im Portfolio vorhanden, und zwar das Erdgeschoss der Immobilie Willi-Brandt-Straße 20. Diese Räumlichkeiten werden zurzeit von (Name des Maklers) vermarktet.

- We understand from the tenant's agent that their client intends to negotiate a lease renewal and that they will be in contact shortly.
  Laut dem Vertreter des Mieters ist der Mieter an einer Verlängerung des Mietvertrags interessiert und wird sich in Kürze mit uns in Verbindung setzen.

- (Name of tenant) have put their decision to rent additional space on hold.
  (Name des Mieters) hat die Entscheidung bezüglich einer Anmietung von zusätzlicher Fläche vorübergehend aufgeschoben.

- Marketing continuing by (name of agent), however no offers as yet.
  Die Vermarktung durch (Name des Maklers) läuft weiter, bisher gibt es jedoch keine Angebote.

- Ground floor has been newly refurbished and is being marketed by (name of agent).
  Das Erdgeschoss wurde kürzlich renoviert und wird derzeit von (Name des Maklers) vermarktet.

- (Name of tenant) **have exercised their break clause** on 10 December 2012. Joint letting agents have been instructed (names of 2 agencies).
  Der Mieter hat von seinem Sonderkündigungsrecht am 10. Dezember 2012 Gebrauch gemacht. Zwei sich miteinander abstimmende Makler wurden mit der Neuvermietung beauftragt.

Also "served notice to break the lease"

6 Managing the Property

good credit standing / good covenant strength ✓

~~solvent~~

'Solvent' means the tenant can pay their bills. This does not necessarily mean they are in a good financial position, only that they are not bankrupt.

the abbreviation **"k"** is often used for 1000

Tenant's credit standing & payments

- The current rental income is secured against tenants of excellent covenant strength.
  Die derzeitigen Mieteinnahmen sind durch Mieter mit ausgezeichneter Bonität gesichert.

- (Name of tenant) are in arrears with their rent. They have explained this is due to a slow cash flow period.
  (Name des Mieters) ist mit der Miete in Verzug. Laut Erklärung des Mieters sind Verzögerungen im Zahlungseingang hierfür verantwortlich.

- Penalty interest will be applied to the tenant's account.
  Das Konto des Mieters wurde mit Verzugszinsen belastet.

- (Name of tenant) went into administration on 30 June 2012 and (name of administrators) were appointed as administrators to the company.
  (Name des Mieters) hat am 30. Juni 2012 Insolvenz angemeldet und (Name das Insolvenzverwalters) wurde als Insolvenzverwalter für das Unternehmen eingesetzt.

- We were advised last week that (name of tenant) are now in administration. Advice has been sought from (name of solicitor/lawyer) to protect (name of owner)'s interests.
  Wir wurden vergangene Woche davon in Kenntnis gesetzt, dass (Name des Mieters) jetzt in Insolvenz gegangen ist. Wir haben (Name des Rechtsanwalts) konsultiert, um die Interessen von (Name des Besitzers) zu wahren.

- (Name of tenant) is in financial difficulty.
  (Name des Mieters) ist in finanziellen Schwierigkeiten.

- (Name of tenant) are currently in arrears of € 250k. We have been chasing for payment but the situation is now frozen by the administration.
  (Name des Mieters) ist derzeit mit € 250.000 in Verzug. Wir haben uns bemüht, eine Zahlung zu erreichen, die Sache ist derzeit jedoch beim Insolvenzverwalter eingefroren.

- (Name of tenant) explained their financial situation and has requested to sublet some of their space.
  (Name des Mieters) hat seine finanzielle Situation erklärt und um Genehmigung für die Untervermietung eines Teils seiner Fläche ersucht.

6 Managing the Property

Email from letting agent to client confirming instruction

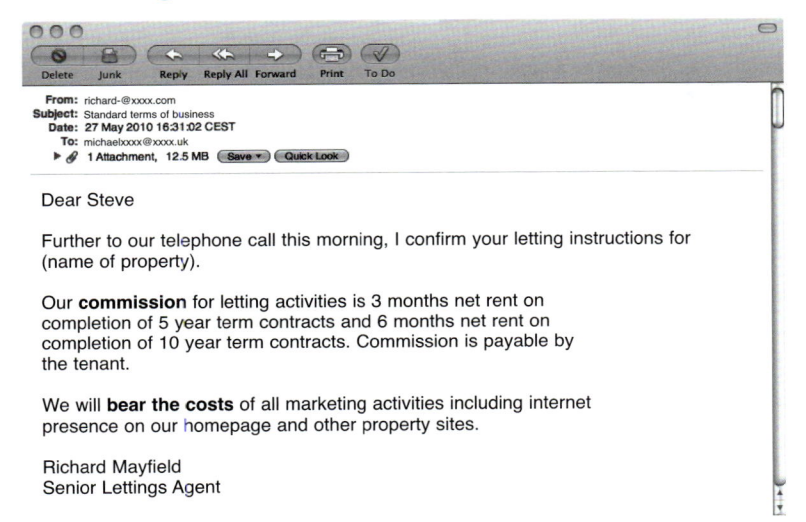

```
From: richard-@xxxx.com
Subject: Standard terms of business
Date: 27 May 2010 16:31:02 CEST
To: michaelxxxx@xxxx.uk
1 Attachment, 12.5 MB
```

Dear Steve

Further to our telephone call this morning, I confirm your letting instructions for (name of property).

Our **commission** for letting activities is 3 months net rent on completion of 5 year term contracts and 6 months net rent on completion of 10 year term contracts. Commission is payable by the tenant.

We will **bear the costs** of all marketing activities including internet presence on our homepage and other property sites.

Richard Mayfield
Senior Lettings Agent

commission/fee
Provision

bear the costs
die Kosten tragen

Negotiating a lease contract

- The rent is adjusted proportionately to the change in the cost-of-living index.
  Die Miete wird proportional zur Veränderung des Lebenshaltungskostenindex angepasst.

- The rent is payable monthly in advance by the fifth working day of each month.
  Die Miete ist monatlich im Voraus zu zahlen, und zwar spätestens am fünften Werktag des Monats.

- Service charges are € 7.50 psm a month and are payable one month in advance.
  Die Nebenkosten betragen monatlich 7,50 €/m² und sind einen Monat im Voraus zu zahlen.

- The lease can be extended for a further period of 5 years.
  Der Mietvertrag kann um weitere 5 Jahre verlängert werden.

- The premises may only be sublet with prior, written consent from the landlord/owner.
  Eine Untervermietung der gemieteten Räumlichkeiten ist nur mit vorheriger schriftlicher Genehmigung des Vermieters/Besitzers gestattet.

6 Managing the Property

- Ground floor tenants are not required to contribute to the service charges for the lift.
  Mieter im Erdgeschoss müssen nicht zu den Nebenkosten für den Aufzug beitragen.

- That is contrary to the provisions in the lease contract, however I will speak to the owners and see if there is a possibility of making an amendment.
  Dies entspricht nicht den im Mietvertrag vereinbarten Bedingungen, ich werde jedoch mit dem Besitzer sprechen, ob eventuell eine Änderung vorgenommen werden kann.

- Please **sign** the lease contract and return.
  Bitte unterschreiben Sie den Mietvertrag und senden Sie ihn zurück.

~~undersign~~

sign ✓

Asset management strategy

- Rebranding and external enhancement study required. There is a need to address the signposting and external branding to improve the lettability of the space.
  Ein Konzept zur Markenbildung und besseren Außendarstellung ist erforderlich. Die Beschilderung und die Außengestaltung müssen überarbeitet werden, um die Vermietbarkeit der Immobilie zu verbessern.

- In order to modernise the office space, the installation of an air-conditioning system and a suspended ceiling with integrated lighting are required.
  Zur Modernisierung der Büroflächen bedarf es des Einbaus einer Klimatisierung sowie einer abgehängten Decke mit integrierter Beleuchtung.

- The warehouse flooring should be upgraded in order to achieve a load-bearing capacity of 2kN/sq m.
  Eine Erneuerung des Hallenbodens ist erforderlich, um eine höhere Traglast von bis zu 2kN/qm zu erreichen.

- Install new windows to the south façade to achieve increased natural daylight in the assembly area.
  Zusätzliche Fenster müssen in die Südfassade eingebaut werden, um mehr Tageslicht im Bereich der Konfektionierung zu erhalten.

Making Recommendations

The property would benefit from ...

It would seem sensible to ....

We propose ....

We suggest ...

We advise you to ...

6 Managing the Property

- Refurbish the entrance hall and install a lounge area with a hospitality area/coffee bar in order to make the property more appealing to prospective and existing tenants.
  Eingangshalle durch die Einrichtung eines bewirtschafteten Lounge-Bereichs umgestalten, um die Attraktivität für potenzielle nteressenten wie auch für Bestandsmieter zu steigern.

- €240,000 has been calculated in the **Capex** schedule for roof insulation and elevator controls. The experience of the last few years has shown that €150,000 should be planned for annual Capex measures.
  Die Kostenaufstellung beinhaltet € 240.000 für Dachdämmung und Aufzugsteuerung. Orientiert man sich an den Erfahrungswerten der letzten Jahre, so ist von einem jährlichen Investitionsaufwand im Umfang von € 150.000 auszugehen.

- Despite the long-term rent guarantee, the vacant space should be let as soon as possible so as not to negatively impact the building's image. Tenants already established in the area are to be targeted and local agents should be instructed to position the property in the market.
  Trotz langfristiger Mietgarantie sollten die leer stehenden Flächen schnellstmöglich vermietet werden, um Schaden am Image der Immobilie zu vermeiden. Dazu sind die am Standort etablierten Mieter gezielt anzusprechen und örtliche Makler mit der Positionierung des Objekts im Markt zu beauftragen.

- The vacant parking spaces should be marketed to neighbouring occupiers via a neighbourhood mailing campaign.
  Unvermietete Parkplätze könnten über eine Rundmail-Marketingaktion den Nutzern benachbarter Stellflächen angeboten werden.

- Every effort needs to be made to retain the existing tenants, even if this means offering incentives.
  Die heutigen Mieter sind unbedingt zu halten, auch wenn dazu eventuell finanzielle Anreize gesetzt werden müssen.

- Due to the long lease term to a tenant with good financial standing, no active measures are being considered at present, apart from ensuring continued good tenant relations and monitoring maintenance requirements.
  Aufgrund des bestehenden langfristigen Mietverhältnisses mit einem bonitätsstarken Mieter stehen aktive Maßnahmen zurzeit nicht an. Selbstverständlich ist das gute Verhältnis zum Mieter weiterhin zu pflegen sowie der Reparaturbedarf zu überwachen.

capital expenditure (capex)
Investitionsaufwand (Kosten für z.B. Nachvermietung, Vermarktung, Renovierung etc.)

6 Managing the Property

- Given the current market situation and the demand for properties with long lease terms and good covenants, consideration should be given to a sale in the near future to a party looking to make a secure investment.
Angesichts der derzeitigen Marktlage und der herrschenden Nachfrage nach Immobilien mit Langzeitmietverträgen mit bonitätsstarken Mietern sollte ein baldiger Weiterverkauf an einen sicherheitsorientierten Anleger in Erwägung gezogen werden.

- The existing leases should be secured and extended wherever possible. Vacant space should be let within the next 1 – 1½ years by means of aggressive letting strategies and proactive tenant acquisition.
Bestehende Mietverträge sind zu sichern und so weit wie möglich zu verlängern. Die freien Flächen sollten in den nächsten 1-1,5 Jahren über eine offensive Vermietungsstrategie und eine aktive Mieterakquise vermietet werden.

- It should be possible to attract further tenants in the near future by targeting local companies in the service sector to take up the vacant units.
Es sollte möglich sein, durch gezielte Anfragen bei lokalen Unternehmen weitere Mieter aus dem Dienstleistungssektor für die leer stehenden Einheiten zu gewinnen.

- The available space meets the standards that prospective tenants demand. Many buildings in this sub-market offer space of poorer quality.
Der Standard der verfügbaren Flächen entspricht dem, was potenzielle Interessenten derzeit nachfragen. Viele Objekte in der Umgebung bieten Flächen von schlechterer Qualität.

- Attention can be drawn to the vacant units and underground parking spaces by erecting a lettings board and banner. This should prove highly effective due to the high level of footfall in the area.
Hinweisschilder und Vermietungsbanner können helfen, die Aufmerksamkeit auf die leer stehenden Büroeinheiten und Tiefgaragenstellplätze zu lenken. Aufgrund des hohen Fußgängeraufkommens in der Gegend dürfte sich diese Strategie als sehr effektiv erweisen.

6 Managing the Property

- The building has a certain competitive advantage compared to other properties in (name of area) due to the attractive façade, prestigious entrance and the high quality landscaping.
  Durch seine attraktive Fassade, den repräsentativen Eingangsbereich und die hochwertigen Außenanlagen hat das Gebäude einen gewissen Wettbewerbsvorteil gegenüber dem übrigen Bestand in (Name des Stadtteils).

- There are three neighbouring properties of similar design and construction putting the building at a slight disadvantage in terms of identity and prominence.
  In der unmittelbaren Nachbarschaft liegen drei in Architektur und Bauweise ähnliche Immobilien, was die Identität und den Wiedererkennungswert des Gebäudes etwas beeinträchtigt.

- The fit-out standard, while adequate, is somewhat basic. This property is therefore not distinguishable from competing properties in the submarket. The absence of air conditioning is a decisive disadvantage in terms of marketing, as this is increasingly being viewed as standard.
  Der Innenausbau der Büroflächen ist angemessen, wenn auch eher einfach. Das Objekt hebt sich dadurch nicht von konkurrierenden Immobilien auf dem örtlichen Markt ab. Das Fehlen einer Klimaanlage muss entschieden als Nachteil gelten, da eine Klimatisierung zunehmend zur Standardausstattung zählt.

- There are a number of problematic issues with the previous marketing strategy employed by (name of former owner), which in our view have impacted the building's marketability. In order to draw a line under the previous marketing campaign and re-launch the property to the market, an aggressive new marketing strategy with attractive incentives is required.
  An der zuvor von (Name des Voreigentümers) verfolgten Marketingstrategie gibt es einige problematische Aspekte, die unserer Ansicht nach die Marktfähigkeit des Objekts beeinträchtigt haben. Um die bisherige Kampagne zu beenden und die Immobilie auf dem Markt ganz neu zu positionieren, ist eine offensive neue Marketingstrategie mit attraktiven Anreizen erforderlich.

6 Managing the Property

- A lack of new developments will lead to a shortage of modern space in the (name of city) office market over the next 2 years. Refurbishment measures should therefore be undertaken as soon as possible in order to benefit from the increase in demand for modern space. Recommended measures include replacing the carpeting on the upper floors and updating the sanitary areas with high quality fittings and by replacing the floor tiles. In order to showcase the entrance point, feature lighting should be installed and new building signage erected. The lack of ambiance in the reception area can be resolved with the installation of a large plasma screen TV and new feature seating. We are working on the assumption that these measures, in combination with an attractive rent of € 15.50/m², will increase interest.
  Da sich keine neuen Bauprojekte abzeichnen, werden moderne Büroflächen in (Name der Stadt) knapp. Eine Sanierung sollte daher rasch in Angriff genommen werden, um von der steigenden Nachfrage nach modernen Büroflächen zu profitieren. Zu den empfohlenen Umgestaltungsmaßnahmen gehören unter anderem der Austausch der Teppichböden in den oberen Stockwerken und eine Aufwertung der Sanitärbereiche durch hochwertige Armaturen und neue Fliesen. Eine auffälligere Beleuchtung sowie eine neue Beschilderung würden den Eingang markanter gestalten. Das atmosphärische Defizit im Foyer lässt sich durch einen großen Plasmabildschirm und neues Sitzmobiliar kompensieren. Wir gehen davon aus, dass das Interesse durch die genannten Maßnahmen in Verbindung mit dem attraktiven Mietpreis von 15,50 €/m² zunehmen wird.

- The sixth and seventh floors are generally in good condition and can be brought up to marketable standard within a short time with usual decorative works.
  Das 6. und 7.OG sind überwiegend in gutem Zustand, so dass die üblichen Schönheitsreparaturen genügen dürften, um die Räumlichkeiten zeitnah auf einen marktfähigen Stand zu bringen.

- Extensive new marketing initiatives are recommended to reposition the property on the market with a new brand/identity. High quality marketing brochures and a dedicated website should be created and a formal launch party should be hosted to showcase the building. Third party fit-out/furniture companies should be approached to create a show suite on the first floor (possibly free of charge).

6 Managing the Property

Zur Repositionierung des Objekts am Markt als neue Marke mit neuer Identität sind umfangreiche Marketinginitiativen erforderlich. Hochwertige Werbebroschüren und ein engagierter Internetauftritt wären zu gestalten. Eine offizielle Launch-Party würde das Gebäude in einem neuen Licht präsentieren. Innenausstatter bzw. Firmen aus der Möbelbranche sollten dafür gewonnen werden, im 1. OG eine (eventuell mietfrei zur Verfügung gestellte) Showsuite einzurichten.

- The building's current high profile and position in the market must be maintained. Vacancy must be avoided.
  Der gegenwärtig hohe Bekanntheitsgrad des Gebäudes und seine Marktposition müssen gehalten werden. Leerstand ist zu vermeiden.

- Due to the ageing construction and outdated entrance, the building does not compare well with properties in the immediate surroundings. The office space has been vacant since March 2010 and even with an aggressive pricing strategy of € 7/m² it has been difficult to achieve lettings. Demand has particularly been a problem in recent years; however we expect this situation to change with the improving economic conditions.
  Wegen seiner in die Jahre gekommenen Bausubstanz und des veralteten Eingangs hat das Gebäude im Vergleich mit Objekten in der unmittelbaren Umgebung einen schweren Stand. Seit März 2010 stehen die Büroflächen leer und trotz aggressiver Mietpreissenkungen auf bis zu 7 €/m² kam es nur schwer zu neuen Vertragsabschlüssen. Die sinkende Nachfrage erwies sich besonders in den letzten Jahren als problematisch, doch dürfte sich die Lage im Zuge der konjunkturellen Erholung bessern.

- Negotiations should be undertaken as soon as possible with the main tenant, (name of tenant), regarding lease renewal, in order to keep this tenant in the building. It is probable that a certain reduction in rent will have to be offered to this tenant – but this will certainly work out cheaper overall than re-letting the space.
  Mit dem Hauptmieter (Name des Mieters) sollten so schnell wie möglich Verhandlungen über eine Vertragsverlängerung aufgenommen werden, um den Mieter im Gebäude zu halten. Wahrscheinlich muss dem Mieter in gewissem Umfang eine Mietreduzierung angeboten werden - doch ist diese Option unter dem Strich sicher günstiger, als eine Neuvermietung der Flächen anzustreben.

Avoid the real estate mistake

Test your knowledge gained in this unit by identifying these common language mistakes. Underline the correct word or phrase.

1. The *service charges / additional costs* currently equate to € 6.25 psm.
2. The tenant has *extended / prolonged* their lease of the 4th floor.
3. The tenant wishes to carry out *changes / alterations* to the premises.
4. The rental income is secured against tenants of excellent *solvency / covenant strength*.
5. The property is 83.13% *occupied / full*.
6. Please *sign / undersign* the lease and return.

Improve your style

Exchange the word/phrase in brackets with a more appropriate expression from this unit.

7. The tenant expressed (anger) _____ regarding noise resulting from the 4th floor fit-out.
8. A summary of the (empty) _____ space is shown in the tenancy schedule.
9. The (problem) _____ with the lifts is being taken up directly with the suppliers.

Test you real estate vocabulary

10. (gesetzliche Bestimmungen) _____ require the gas appliances to be tested annually.
11. The tenant has exercised their (Sonderkündigungsrecht) _____.
12. The tenant is currently in (in Verzug) _____ of € 250,000.

1. service charges | 2. extended | 3. alterations | 4. covenants | 5. occupied | 6. sign | 7. concern | 8. void (or) vacant | 9. matter (or) issue | 10. statutory regulations | 11. break-option | 12. arrears

Acquisitions & Sales   7

Investment Memoranda 140
Example
  Investment Memorandum 140
Agent sending property
details to client 144
Email from client to
agent regarding interest
in property details 146
Letter from client to
agent stating that property
is not of interest 146

Acquisition Decisions 147
Turning down
an investment proposal 147
Arranging a viewing 147
Agent sending standard
terms of business 148

Offer Stage 148
Letters of Intent 149
Agent to client discussing
the Letter of Intent 153
Example
  Heads of Terms 154
Agent confirming agreement to
Heads of Terms 155
Offer stage phrases 156

Negotiating Proposals 157
Proposing amendments 157
Negotiating amendments 158
Signing 162
Transaction costs 163
General contract
terminology 163
Sales and purchase
agreement 164

Sales and Purchase
Agreements Phrases 164
The object of purchase 164
Land register entries 165
Purchase price 166
Warranties and guarantees 166
Leases 167
Costs 167

Avoid the real estate mistake, improve your style and test your real estate vocabulary 168

Investment Memorandum

(Name of property)

Description *(Beschreibung)*
(Name of property) is a prominent, landmark building comprising 11,747 sq m of office accommodation arranged over ground and six upper floors around a full height central atrium.

The building offers a mixture of high quality demountable partitioned offices and meeting rooms, together with open plan offices.

Location *(Makrolage)*
(Name of city) is an internationally recognised commercial centre. *(Name of city)*'s strategic location and excellent transport links have attracted a number of high profile office occupiers. The city further benefits from excellent retail and leisure facilities.

7 Acquisitions & Sales

This unit provides examples of correspondence for each stage of the acquisition and sales process, from the first contact with prospective purchasers through to negotiating the terms of the contract.

Examples are not intended for use in legal documents.

Investment Memoranda

Investment memoranda or sales particulars can vary in content and style in comparison with the German Exposé. In addition to details on the property, its location, situation and the socio-economic profile, information may also be provided on the rent each tenant pays, their credit rating and financial performance. While the style of language in an Exposé tends to be more neutral with the facts outlined in an abbreviated form, the English investment memorandum may include superlatives such as "excellent and unrivalled".

Communications (Verkehrsanbindungen)
(Name of city) benefits from excellent communications as follows:

Road – The (motorway number) motorway is the main arterial route and runs in an east/west direction. It also links with the (motorway number) providing access to (name of other important city) and the north/east/south/west.

Rail – (Name of city) has two mainline railway stations. In addition to the local suburban rail network, regular bus services run from (name of city) Central Station to (names of other important cities). (Name of city) city centre is also served by an underground railway system. The nearest subway station to the subject property is on (name of street).

Air – (Name of airport) International Airport is located approximately 25 km to the west of the city centre. The airport caters for almost (number) million passengers per annum. Approximately (number) airlines use the airport and serve up to (number) destinations.

Bus – (name) Bus Station is situated on (name of street) and in addition to local services offers daily services to other regional cities like (name of other important city) and (name of other important city).

03

7 Acquisitions & Sales

Situation *(Mikrolage)*
The property is prominently situated in the centre of (name of town) at the core of the town's retail and commercial area to the south side of (name of road). The main office entrance is accessed along (name of road) and the property is strategically situated directly opposite the underground station.

Socio-economic Profile
(Soziōokonomisches Profil)
The greater (name of city) conurbation has a resident population of (number) (2008 census). In comparison with the rest of the region, (name of city)'s population has a higher proportion of young adults (age 20-39) and a fewer number of residents in the age group between 40 and retirement. It is anticipated that the city's population will increase slightly over the next decade.

Specification *(Baubeschreibung)*
Internal
- Air conditioning
- 2 passenger lifts (13) person
- Fully accessible raised floors
- Suspended ceilings with recessed light fittings
- Structural grid 9m x 9m
- Shower and locker room facilities
- 24/7 security
- CCTV

External
- Parking for 236 cars
- High quality landscaping
- Bicycle racking
- Standby generator

Tenure *(Art und Bedingungen des Rechtstitels)*
The property is held freehold.

Covenant Information *(Finanzielle und rechtliche Hintergrundinformation zu den Mietern)*
(Name of tenant) is a leading IT consultancy delivering technical, resource and training solutions that contribute to the business transformation and economic performance of private and public sector clients.

	12 months to 31 Dec 2011	12 months to 31 Dec 2010	12 months to 31 Dec 2009
Sales Turnover (Euro)	268,370,000	273,389,000	284,966,000
Profit / (Loss) Before Taxes (Euro)	476,000	9,089,000	21,743,000
Tangible Net Worth (Euro)	67,995,000	72,367,000	73,841,000
Net Current Assets (Euro)	61,431,000	7,351,000	5,761,000

(Name of tenant) is (name of country)'s second largest communications provider. (Name of tenant) deliver a complete portfolio of voice, data and internet solutions nationwide from business broadband to instant messaging over IP multimedia.

	12 months to 31 Dec 2011	12 months to 31 Dec 2010	12 months to 31 Dec 2009
Sales Turnover (Euro)	33,754,000	34,793,000	31,875,000
Profit / (Loss) Before Taxes (Euro)	768,000	1,743,000	409,000
Tangible Net Worth (Euro)	3,126,000	2,348,000	4,175,000
Net Current Assets (Euro)	1,131,000	2,095,000	2,704,000

7 Acquisitions & Sales

Schedule of Areas *(Flächenaufstellung)*

Floor Areas	SQ M	Floor Areas	SQ M
Ground Floor	980.96	Fourth Floor	2,053.81
First Floor	1,814.40	Fifth Floor	1,496.86
Second Floor	2,258.94	Sixth Floor	965.64
Third Floor	2,176.63	**Sub-Total**	**11,747.24**

Tenancy Schedule *(Mieteraufstellung)*

Demise	Tenant	Rating (D&B)	Sq M	Lease Start	Lease Expiry	Remaining Term (Years)	Rent PA (Euro)	Rent PSM
Ground Floor	(name of tenant)	2A1	980.96	29/09/2002	28/09/2017	6.5	242,493	20.60
First Floor	(name of tenant)	2A1	1,814.40	29/09/2002	28/09/2017	6.6	448,520	20.60
Second Floor	(name of tenant)	2A1	2,258.94	29/09/2002	28/09/2017	6.6	558,410	20.60
Third Floor	(name of tenant)	2A3	2,176.63	21/12/2007	20/12/2017	6.8	502,540	19.24
Fourth Floor	(name of tenant)	2A3	2,053.81	21/12/2007	20/12/2017	6.8	474,184	19.24
Fifth Floor	(name of tenant)	2A3	1,496.86	21/12/2007	20/12/2017	6.8	345,595	19.24
Sixth Floor	(name of tenant)	2A3	965.64	21/12/2007	20/12/2017	6.8	222,947	19.24
Sub-Total			**11,747.24**				**2,794,689**	

Proposal *(Angebot)*

An offer in excess of € 30 million is sought, subject to contract and exclusive of VAT. Assuming usual costs of purchase of 5.76%, a purchase at this level would show a net initial yield of 6.22%.

7 ACQUISITIONS & SALES

Agent sending property details to client

Property Details

Further to our conversation this morning, I have compiled the following information on investment opportunities, which I believe may be of interest to you:

(Name of property)

The property is located at (location), prominently situated on (name of road). I have inspected the building internally on a number of occasions and the build quality and flexibility it offers are excellent. The income is secured for a further 10 years to a good covenant subject to **RPI** linked uplifts. At a price of € 28 million, the investment would show a net initial yield of 6%.

(Name of property)

3,852 sq m of office building let to (name of tenant) until September 2017 with a break option in 2012 at a rent of € 28 per sq m. Quoting price of € 21 million, reflecting a NIY of 6.6%. Sold to (name of vendor) for a price reflecting a NIY of 6.4%.

(Name of property)

Two office buildings totalling 20,085 sq m – tenants include (name of tenant), (name of tenant) and (name of tenant) on a weighted unexpired term of 10 years. Rents between € 28 and € 30 per sq m – circa 15% over-rented. Sold to (name of vendor) for € 120 million reflecting a NIY of 6%.

(Name of property)

6,000 sq m recently developed office headquarters building let in its entirety to (name of tenant) for a rent of € 23 per sq m on an 11 year term. It is rumoured in the market that a UK institution has made an offer at a price reflecting NIY of circa 5.85%.

(Name of property)

(Name of property) comprises a headquarters office building constructed in the early 1990s and significantly upgraded in 2005 when (name of occupant) took occupation. The property provides a total net internal area of 6,824.15 sq m with 230 car parking spaces (1:30). The lease expires 25 March 2022 at a current rent of € 32 per sq m. The current rental value is in the region of € 30 lower per sq m.

I hope this provides you with a useful background. If you would like further information on any of the above properties, please do not hesitate to give me a call.

Retail Price Index (RPI)
Einzelhandelspreisindex

Consumer Price Index (CPI)
Verbraucherpreisindex

The RPI and CPI both measure the average changes in the price of consumer goods and services, although there are differences in coverage and methodology. The CPI is based on a European-wide formula allowing international comparison. The RPI is used additionally in the UK and is reflects a more domestic coverage. Lease contracts can specify either index.

⚠️ ~~built-up~~

The property was built / constructed ✓

7 Acquisitions & Sales

- I would be keen to have a brief meeting with you to discuss your investment aspirations for the year ahead as I am confident that we can assist. I am available on (date 1 and date 2). Please let me know if this is convenient. If we could have a discussion on your requirements ahead of this I can come prepared with some investment stock for the meeting.
Ich möchte mich gerne kurz mit Ihnen treffen, um Ihre Investitionsabsichten für das kommende Jahr zu erörtern, denn ich glaube, dass wir Ihnen dabei behilflich sein können. Ich stehe Ihnen dafür am (Datum 1 und Datum 2) gerne zur Verfügung. Bitte teilen Sie mir mit, wann es Ihnen gelegen ist. Wenn wir uns bereits im Vorfeld darüber austauschen könnten, wo Ihre Interessen liegen, könnte ich Ihnen verfügbare Investitionsmöglichkeiten gleich detailliert präsentieren.

- I would be grateful if you could give me a call to discuss the attached at your earliest convenience as we need to move quickly.
Ich wäre Ihnen dankbar, wenn Sie mich baldmöglichst anrufen könnten, um das angehängte Dokument zu besprechen, da wir schnell handeln müssen.

- Please find attached the following documents as requested:
Anbei wie gewünscht die folgenden Unterlagen:
  - The headlease
    Der Hauptmietvertrag
  - The sublease
    Der Untermietvertrag
  - The floor plans
    Die Grundrisse
  - The measured survey
    Das Flächenaufmaß
  - Our most recent market research report
    Unsere aktuelle Marktstudie
  - A schedule of relevant leasing comparables
    Eine Aufstellung relevanter Vergleichsmieten
  - Commentary on recent investment transactions
    Anmerkungen zu Investmenttransaktionen der letzten Zeit

7 Acquisitions & Sales

Email from client to agent regarding interest in property details

To: Andrew.Smith@brownpartners.uk
Cc:
Bcc:
Subject: 6 St Mary's Square
From: David.Thompson@PPD.com

Dear Andrew

Thank you for sending us the investment proposal, relating to the above mentioned property.

Please provide us with further information on the following areas:

a) full postal address for registration purposes
b) detailed tenant schedule in an Excel format
c) statement on net operating income
d) photos
e) **measured floor plans**
f) investment structure (asset or share deal)

I appreciate your assistance.

David

Measured survey / measured floor plans
This is a report which provides detailed measurements and plans of the building.

Letter from client to agent stating that property is not of interest

6 St Mary's Square

Dear Mr Simpkin

Thank you for the above mentioned investment proposal forwarded on 3 June 2012.

Unfortunately, we have already received notification of this opportunity from another party and are therefore unable to pursue discussions with you on this matter.

Furthermore, we regret to inform you that the investment proposal does not meet our investment criteria due to the high investment volume / low investment volume / location / type of use (hotel) / the low initial yield / letting situation.

We would, however, appreciate receiving further proposals from you in the future.

Yours sincerely

Martin Edwards

Vice President

7 Acquisitions & Sales

Acquisition Decisions
Turning down an investment proposal

- On this occasion we have decided not to pursue this investment opportunity as we are not currently investing in share deals.
 Wir haben uns in diesem Fall entschlossen, die Investitionsmöglichkeit nicht weiterzuverfolgen, da wir momentan nicht in Share-Deals investieren.

- We regret to inform you that the investment proposal does not meet our investment criteria as we are not currently investing in (Poland).
 Wir bedauern sehr, Ihnen mitteilen zu müssen, dass das Investmentangebot nicht unseren Anlagekriterien entspricht, da wir momentan nicht in (Polen) investieren.

- We regret we are unable to respond more positively on this occasion but would be pleased to hear from you again.
 Wir bedauern sehr, dass wir gegenwärtig nicht mit einem positiveren Bescheid reagieren können, würden uns aber gleichwohl freuen, wieder von Ihnen zu hören.

- Many thanks for the teaser. Due to (the small investment volume) we have decided not to proceed with this investment opportunity.
 Herzlichen Dank für den Teaser. Aufgrund (des geringen Investitionsvolumens) haben wir uns allerdings entschlossen, diese Investitionsmöglichkeit nicht weiterzuverfolgen.

Arranging a viewing

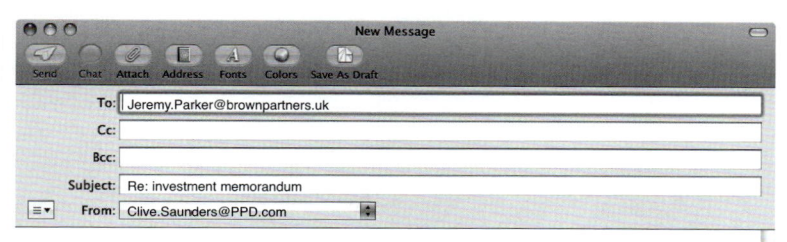

To: Jeremy.Parker@brownpartners.uk
Cc:
Bcc:
Subject: Re: investment memorandum
From: Clive.Saunders@PPD.com

Dear Jeremy

Many thanks for sending us the *requested information / investment memorandum* for the property.

On first review this investment opportunity seems to be very interesting. I am in Warsaw from March 28 to March 30 and would kindly ask you to arrange a viewing. I am flexible with regard to timing so please let me know what time would be most convenient for you.

I look forward to hearing from you.

Best regards

Clive

7 Acquisitions & Sales

Agent sending standard terms of business

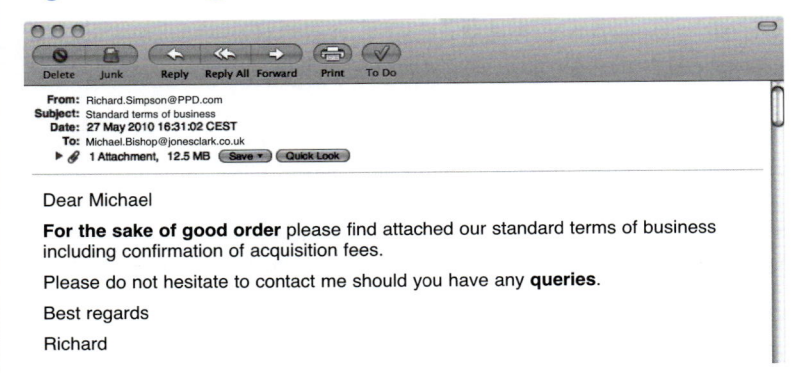

> Discussing **fees** with clients can often require sensitive and indirect language in order not to appear as aggressive.

for the sake of good order
der guten Ordnung halber

queries
Fragen (more formal word for "questions")

From: Richard.Simpson@PPD.com
Subject: Standard terms of business
Date: 27 May 2010 16:31:02 CEST
To: Michael.Bishop@jonesclark.co.uk
1 Attachment, 12.5 MB

Dear Michael

For the sake of good order please find attached our standard terms of business including confirmation of acquisition fees.

Please do not hesitate to contact me should you have any **queries**.

Best regards
Richard

- Please find attached a letter outlining our role in the transaction. For the sake of good order, I also attach a copy of our acquisition fee letter for your approval.
 Anbei erhalten Sie einen Brief, der unsere Rolle in der Transaktion beschreibt. Der guten Ordnung halber fügen wir Ihnen ebenfalls unsere Honorarvereinbarung zu Ihrer Kenntnisnahme bei.

Offer Stage

English	German
Confidentiality agreement	Vertraulichkeitserklärung
Offer to sell	Verkaufsangebot
Offer to purchase	Kaufangebot
Letter of Intent (LOI)	Absichtserklärung
Heads of Terms (HoTs)	Grundsatzvereinbarung

7 Acquisitions & Sales

Letter of Intent

- We wish to thank you for inviting us to consider the sale and purchase of the (type of property) located in (name of town).
  Wir danken Ihnen für die Möglichkeit, ein Angebot zum Kauf der Immobilie (Art der Immobilie) in (Stadt) abgeben zu dürfen.

- We have set out below the terms on which (name of prospective purchaser) would be interested in acquiring the property.
  Nachfolgend finden Sie die Bedingungen, zu denen (Name des interessierten Käufers) an einem Erwerb der Immobilie interessiert wäre.

- We have based our **consideration** on the information provided by your advisor (name of advisor) and by you during our inspection on (date of inspection).
  Unser Kaufpreisangebot basiert auf den uns von Ihrem Berater (Name) und Ihnen während unserer Besichtigung am (Datum) mitgeteilten Informationen.

    consideration
    Vergütung

    "consideration" can also be used as formal expression for "payment" or "price".

- We understand that the site area is (amount) sq m. The (property) provides a lettable area of (amount) sq m retail, (amount) sq m office – in total (amount) sq m. There are (amount) surface parking spaces and (amount) basement parking spaces.
  Wie uns mitgeteilt wurde, ist das Grundstück (Größe) m² groß. Die (Immobilie) umfasst eine vermietbare Fläche von (Größe) m² für den Einzelhandel, (Größe) m² für Büroräume – insgesamt (Größe) m². Es gibt (Anzahl) oberirdische Parkplätze und (Anzahl) Tiefgaragenplätze.

- We understand that the building is to be sold as a **freehold**, free of encumbrances.
  Wie uns mitgeteilt wurde, wird das Eigentum an dem Gebäude (freehold) frei von jeglichen Belastungen verkauft.

    See page 173 for an explanation of the term freehold.

- The vendor is not aware, to the best of his knowledge, of any major problems.
  Dem Verkäufer sind nach bestem Wissen keine wesentlichen Probleme bekannt.

- We will work towards a sale and purchase agreement and will proceed with our due diligence based on a non-binding price for the building of (price) euro which reflects a yield of (yield percentage) % based on projected net operating income.
  Wir werden auf den Abschluss eines Kaufvertrags hinwirken und eine Due-Diligence-Prüfung auf Basis des unverbindlichen Preises von (Betrag) Euro für das Gebäude durchführen, der die Rendite von (Zahl)% auf Grundlage des erwarteten Nettobetriebseinkommens widerspiegelt.

7 Acquisitions & Sales

- Purchase is dependent upon approval of the purchaser's (Supervisory Board) which will be communicated to the vendor in writing.
  Der Erwerb unterliegt der Bedingung der Genehmigung durch den (Aufsichtsrat) des Käufers, deren Vorliegen dem Verkäufer schriftlich mitgeteilt wird.

- We assume that the building meets the technical norms and standards as of the year of construction, taking into account normal wear and tear. In particular the building is free of structural and other major defects and is free of any contamination, deleterious material such as asbestos and substances which are injurious to health.
  Wir gehen davon aus, dass das Gebäude sämtlichen technischen Normen und sonstigen Anforderungen aus dem Jahr seiner Errichtung entspricht, wobei die übliche Abnutzung berücksichtigt wird. Insbesondere bestehen an dem Gebäude keine baulichen oder sonstigen erheblichen Mängel, es ist frei von jeglicher Kontamination, schädlichem Material wie Asbest oder sonstigen gesundheitsschädlichen Substanzen.

- We assume the building is properly maintained (no maintenance backlog), fully functional and has all necessary permits and licenses in place.
  Wir gehen davon aus, dass das Gebäude ordnungsgemäß instand gehalten wird (kein Wartungsrückstand), voll funktionsfähig ist und sämtliche erforderlichen Genehmigungen und Lizenzen vorliegen und wirksam sind.

- We assume the service charge is fully reconcilable and that there are no non-recoverable costs for the owner of the property.
  Wir gehen davon aus, dass die Verwaltungsgebühr vollständig umlagefähig ist und dem Eigentümer der Immobilie keine nicht umlagefähigen Kosten entstehen.

- There are no residual rent free periods or rental concessions which affect income.
  Keine weiteren mietfreien Zeiten noch sonstige Mietkonzessionen beeinträchtigen die Einnahmen.

- Each party shall bear its own advisory and transaction costs.
  Jede Partei trägt die ihr entstehenden Beratungs- und sonstigen Transaktionskosten selbst.

- The vendor shall provide the purchaser with full and comprehensive **representations and warranties**, which shall include amongst others a complete guarantee in respect of tax issues and title to land.

Representations and Warranties
Commonly known as "reps and warranties". These are statements by which one party in a transaction gives certain assurances to the other, and on which the other party may rely. For example, it could be a statement confirming that a specific fact is true or not. For example, a seller may represent and warrant that he has full ownership title in the property being sold.

7 Acquisitions & Sales

Der Verkäufer gibt gegenüber dem Käufer vollständige und umfassende Zusicherungen und Gewährleistungen ab, die u.a. eine vollständige Garantie im Hinblick auf Steuerfragen und das Grundeigentum enthalten.

- We detail below the various activities which need to be performed and criteria which need to be met or about which the purchaser needs to be satisfied:
Nachfolgend sind die verschiedenen Leistungen aufgeführt, die erbracht oder erfüllt werden müssen oder von deren Vorliegen der Käufer sich überzeugt haben muss:

- Satisfactory outcome of a full commercial, legal, financial, environmental, technical, tax and other due diligence over the site and the project as determined by the purchaser in his sole discretion (the „Due Diligence").
Zufriedenstellendes Ergebnis einer umfassenden wirtschaftlichen, rechtlichen, finanziellen, umweltrechtlichen, technischen, steuerlichen und sonstige Fragen untersuchenden Due-Diligence-Prüfung betreffend das Grundstück und das Bauprojekt, vom Käufer nach seinem alleinigen Ermessen festzustellen (die „Due Diligence").

- The (type of property) must comply with all necessary planning, building, fire and environmental regulations, and any conditions, standards or obligations imposed by the governmental or official authorities concerned including the insurance company requirements have been fulfilled.
Die (Art der) Immobilie muss sämtliche erforderlichen planungsrechtlichen, baulichen, feuer- und umweltrechtlichen Verordnungen sowie sämtliche von Regierungs- oder anderen zuständigen Behörden auferlegten Bedingungen, Anforderungen und Verpflichtungen sowie die versicherungsrechtlichen Auflagen erfüllen.

- The purchaser would propose a (number) weeks period for due diligence and negotiation of the sale and purchase agreement, beginning on the day on which the purchaser and their advisors have been provided with access to all necessary and relevant documentation.
Der Käufer schlägt für die Due Diligence und die Verhandlung des Kaufvertrags einen Zeitraum von (Anzahl) Wochen vor, der mit dem Tag beginnt, an dem dem Käufer und seinen Beratern Zugang zu sämtlichen erforderlichen und einschlägigen Dokumenten gewährt wurde.

- The vendor shall not enter into discussions or negotiations concerning the sale of (name of property) with any other prospective purchaser.

7 Acquisitions & Sales

Der Verkäufer führt keine Gespräche und tritt nicht in Verhandlungen über den Verkauf der (Name) Immobilie mit anderen interessierten Käufern ein.

- This letter is valid until (date), after which date it will become null and void.
  Dieses Angebot ist bis zum (Datum) gültig und wird danach nichtig.

- We trust our proposal meets your approval and look forward to rapidly concluding this transaction. To confirm your acceptance of the terms and conditions as set forth in this letter, please sign and return one copy of this letter to our attention.
  Wir hoffen, unser Angebot entspricht Ihren Erwartungen, und sehen einem zügigen Abschluss dieser Transaktion entgegen. Zum Zeichen Ihres Einverständnisses mit den Bedingungen dieses Angebots unterzeichnen Sie bitte ein Exemplar desselben und senden Sie diese Ausfertigung an uns zurück.

- If you wish to discuss, or require clarification of any of the items in the letter please do not hesitate to contact us.
  Für Rückfragen und Anmerkungen zu diesem Angebot stehen wir selbstverständlich gerne zur Verfügung.

- Please find enclosed a revised LOI, taking into account the wishes of both parties, including the points we discussed. Hopefully this is acceptable to you and our client can commence with the due diligence.
  In der Anlage übermitteln wir Ihnen eine überarbeitete Fassung der Absichtserklärung, die die von beiden Parteien geäußerten sowie die weiter erörterten Punkte berücksichtigt. Wir hoffen, dass diese Absichtserklärung für Sie akzeptabel ist und unser Mandant/Klient mit der Due Diligence beginnen kann.

- I have had positive feedback from (name of vendor) that the LOI will be signed today and will be sent over latest this evening.
  I stressed to them that the due diligence starts as from the date of receipt of the documentation.
  Ich habe von (Name des Verkäufers) die Bestätigung erhalten, dass die Absichtserklärung heute unterzeichnet und spätestens heute Abend an uns übersandt wird. Ich habe ihm gegenüber betont, dass die Due Diligence mit dem Datum des Erhalts der Dokumentation beginnt.

- Please find attached the LOI. Please countersign and send back asap.
  Anbei übermitteln wir Ihnen die Absichtserklärung. Wir bitten um Gegenzeichnung und umgehende Rücksendung.

7 ACQUISITIONS & SALES

- Please find attached a first draft LOI for the above opportunity.
  I would appreciate receiving your comments, amendments etc.
  I could be available for a conference call either later this afternoon
  or tomorrow.
  Anbei finden Sie einen Entwurf der Absichtserklärung betreffend
  die vorstehende Erwerbsmöglichkeit. Über Anmerkungen und
  Änderungsvorschläge würde/n wir uns/ich mich freuen. Gerne
  stehe ich später heute Nachmittag oder morgen für eine Telefonkonferenz zur Verfügung.

Agent to client discussing the Letter of Intent

Dear Martin

*Just to update you, I spoke with (vendor's name) this afternoon.
I talked him through the LOI and he **seemed** to accept the remaining
points.*

*I am expecting and hoping that we will get the LOI **countersigned**
tomorrow.*

As soon as I hear further I shall contact you.

Regards

Andrew

*Andrew West
Director
KAM*

TIP!
By adding the verb **to seem** (scheinen) here, the writer is adding protection against the possibility that the client could change their mind.

to countersign
etw. gegenzeichnen

7 ACQUISITIONS & SALES

HEADS OF TERMS
6 St Mary's Square London

1. **Instructions**
   Sale of freehold office and car park investment

2. **Parties**
   Vendor (name and address of vendor)
   Purchaser (name and address of purchaser)

3. **The Property**
   The property known as (name of property), (address) comprising approximately (size) sq m of air conditioned office accommodation over ground and four upper floors, together with 198 car parking spaces.

4. **Tenure**
   The property is held on a freehold interest.

5. **Tenancy**
   The property is let in its entirety to (name of tenant) under a 12 year lease expiring 25 June 2016, at a current rent of € 1.45 million per annum subject to CPI indexing. The parent company (name of parent company) act as guarantors.

6. **Consideration**
   A base purchase price of € 29 million (twenty nine million euros) exclusive of VAT.

7. **Deposit**
   10% of the purchase price will be payable upon exchange of contracts.

8. **Timetable**
   Contracts are to be exchanged by 30 June 2012 or 4 weeks after mutual agreement of Heads of Terms, whichever is sooner. Completion will take place on 25 July 2012.

9. **Conditions**
   Purchaser's Conditions
   a) **Subject to contract**
   b) Satisfactory due diligence
   c) Satisfactory measured surveys
   d) Assignment of all available building warranties and guarantees
   e) Board approval obtained between five working days of agreement of Heads of Terms
   f) Independent valuer's approval

   Vendor's Conditions
   a) Subject to contract
   b) Board approval   →

"Subject to Contract" is used in the UK to indicate that the terms in an LOI or HoT are a basis of discussion and good-will only and are not actually legally binding until the final contract (e.g. the Sales and Purchase Agreement) has been signed. Caution should be used with this term as a recent court decision has concluded that in specific circum-stances the parties of such a document may indeed be bound to it!

7 Acquisitions & Sales

10. **Exclusivity**
    The purchaser will be granted exclusivity until (date) subject to the provisions below.
    Compliance with the timetable outlined above remains a specific condition of this exclusivity.

11. **Confidentiality**
    Both parties are to maintain confidence as to the terms of this transaction and the contents of this letter until after successful completion on (date).

12. **Costs**
    Each party is to bear their own costs.

Agent confirming agreement to Heads of Terms

Dear James

6 St Mary's Square, London

Further to our ongoing discussions in respect of the above and your written offer dated the (date), I am pleased to confirm that my clients are willing to instruct **solicitors** *on the basis of the attached Heads of Terms.*

I would therefore be grateful to receive your written acceptance of the enclosed in order that solicitors may be instructed forthwith.

Yours sincerely

Peter Blake
Enc

TIP!

solicitor
Rechtsanwalt

The word **lawyer** is a general term for a professional who is qualified to practice law. In the US, lawyers are often called **attorneys** or **attorneys-at-law**. In England and Wales the legal profession is divided into **solicitors** and **barristers**. Solicitors deal with clients, for example in business and conveyancing matters, while barristers specialise in presenting cases in court.

7 Acquisitions & Sales

Offer stage phrases

- Just to update you on (name of property). (Name of vendor) has now received all other offers. One at 32 million, which is around 6.4% and another at 6.34%. I will be speaking later in the day to (name of contact at seller) and advise you whether it will be necessary or not to raise the bid in order to clinch it.
  Zu Ihrer Information in Sachen (Name der Immobilie): Bei (Name des Verkäufers) sind inzwischen alle anderen Gebote eingegangen. Eines davon beläuft sich auf € 32 Millionen, entsprechend 6,4%, ein weiteres liegt bei 6,34%. Ich spreche heute im Laufe des Tages noch mit (Name der Kontaktperson beim Anbieter) und werde Ihnen dann sagen können, ob die Gebotssumme erhöht werden muss, um sicher den Zuschlag zu erhalten.

- Further to our telephone conversation, we have been doing some more investigation on the bidding situation and I can now report to you as follows: The feedback is that (name of vendor) has received two other formal offers.
  Im Anschluss an unser Telefongespräch haben wir weitere Erkundigungen über die Gebotslage eingezogen. Wir konnten in Erfahrung bringen, dass (Name des Verkäufers) zwei weitere offizielle Gebote vorliegen.

- (Name of vendor) confirmed with me that in order to secure the deal you would have to offer €18.5 million.
  (Name des Verkäufers) hat mir gegenüber bestätigt, dass Sie € 18,5 Millionen bieten müssten, um den Zuschlag zu erhalten.

- Our recommendation is therefore to wait with the submission of the offer until we hear back from the others. We will then receive the figure necessary to do the deal and submit the offer. I hope you agree with this approach. If you have any questions please do not hesitate to contact me.
  Wir empfehlen daher, mit dem Ausbringen des Gebots zu warten, bis wir von den anderen gehört haben. Wir erfahren dann den für den Abschluss des Geschäfts nötigen Betrag und platzieren das Gebot. Ich hoffe, Sie sind mit dieser Herangehensweise einverstanden. Bei Fragen zögern Sie bitte nicht, sich mit mir in Verbindung zu setzen.

- We do really need to get something to the vendor tomorrow at the latest to maintain our credibility and to demonstrate our ability to move forward quickly.

7 Acquisitions & Sales

Wir müssen dem Verkäufer unbedingt spätestens morgen etwas vorlegen, um glaubwürdig zu bleiben und unsere Fähigkeit zum schnellen Handeln zu demonstrieren.

- I think it would be very useful to have a conference call together to run through these points. Please let me know when it is convenient for you.
  Meiner Meinung nach wäre es sehr hilfreich, diese Punkte gemeinsam in einer Telefonkonferenz durchzugehen. Bitte lassen Sie mich wissen, wann für Sie ein geeigneter Zeitpunkt wäre.

- I have set up a conference call for this evening at 6pm (please see below). (Name of vendor) would like to speak with their agents first, so I suggest that we call in at 6.15. From their side (names of participants) will be joining.
  Ich habe für heute Abend 18:00 Uhr eine Telefonkonferenz angesetzt (siehe unten). (Name des Verkäufers) würde gerne zuerst mit seinen Maklern sprechen, daher schlage ich vor, dass wir uns um 18:15 Uhr zuschalten. Von Verkäuferseite werden (Namen der Teilnehmer) dabei sein.

- Attached is a first draft of the (name of agreement) for your review. Please give us a call should you wish to discuss.
  Im Anhang finden Sie eine erste Fassung des (Name des Vertrags) zu Ihrer Prüfung. Bitte rufen Sie uns an, wenn Diskussionsbedarf besteht.

- We kindly request that you review the (name of agreement) for (name of property) and give your input where needed. Please do not hesitate to call us should you have any questions.
  Wir bitten Sie, den (Name des Vertrags) für (Name des Objekts) zu prüfen und wo nötig mit Anmerkungen zu versehen. Bei Fragen können Sie uns gerne anrufen.

Negotiating Proposals
Proposing amendments

- Please find attached my mark ups to the (Heads of Terms). I am conscious that many of these points are still to be discussed between us but I wanted **to get the ball rolling**, not least to get us all thinking about our position on the points raised.
  Anbei meine Anmerkungen zu den (Vertragsvereinbarungen). Ich weiß, dass wir viele dieser Punkte erst noch besprechen müssen, doch ich wollte die Sache ins Laufen bringen und nicht zuletzt die Beteiligten zur Klärung ihrer Positionen zu den aufgeworfenen Fragen anregen.

to get the ball rolling
den Stein ins rollen bringen

7 Acquisitions & Sales

- Please find attached the amended (name of agreement). Please review and come back with your approval as soon as possible.
 Anbei der geänderte (Name des Vertrags). Bitte prüfen Sie ihn und lassen Sie uns so schnell wie möglich wissen, ob Sie damit einverstanden sind.

- Thank you for the draft (name of agreement) which I have reviewed. I have included some minor amendments.
 Vielen Dank für den Entwurf des (Name des Vertrags). Ich habe ihn geprüft und einige geringfügige Änderungen vorgenommen.

- We have incorporated our modifications directly in the (draft agreement) which is attached.
 Wir haben unsere Änderungen gleich in den angehängten (Vertragsentwurf) eingefügt.

Negotiating amendments

- Please see attached revised (name of agreement) which incorporates all marked-up changes.
 Anbei der überarbeitete (Name des Vertrags), in den alle Änderungen eingearbeitet wurden.

- In general, we agree with your suggestion to …
 Im Prinzip stimmen wir Ihrem Vorschlag zu, …

- We accept your suggestion that …
 Wir sind einverstanden mit Ihrem Vorschlag, …

- We have included some clarifications regarding …
 Wir haben einige Klarstellungen bezüglich … eingefügt.

- We suggest retaining € 500,000 in escrow and that it be paid out to your clients as soon as the issues are resolved.
 Wir schlagen vor, € 500.000 auf dem Notaranderkonto zu belassen und diese Summe unmittelbar nach Klärung der strittigen Fragen an Ihre Klienten auszuzahlen.

- The points on which they have reverted are not as material as I anticipated which suggests that we are well positioned to successfully progress on our discussion.
 Die Punkte, die sie noch einmal aufgegriffen haben, sind nicht so wesentlich, wie ich vermutet hatte, was darauf hindeutet, dass wir uns in einer guten Ausgangsposition für einen erfolgreichen weiteren Gesprächsverlauf befinden.

- Thank you for the (Heads of Terms). I have discussed them with (name of purchaser) and have been instructed to make the following comments:

7 Acquisitions & Sales

Vielen Dank für die (Vertragsvereinbarungen). Ich habe sie mit (Name des Käufers) durchgesprochen und wurde angewiesen, dazu folgende Anmerkungen zu machen:

- Many thanks for your client's proposals which are a big step towards reaching a final agreement.
  Herzlichen Dank für die Vorschläge Ihres Klienten, die uns auf dem Weg zu einer endgültigen Einigung/zum endgültigen Vertragstext ein großes Stück voranbringen.

- I will **chase them up** on this and get back to you as soon as I get confirmation.
  Ich werde sie ein wenig drängen und mich wieder bei Ihnen melden, sobald ich eine Bestätigung habe.

- I will keep pressing them and hopefully we can resolve this quickly.
  Ich werde weiterhin Druck ausüben und hoffe, dass wir die Sache schnell klären können.

- As discussed, let us try to finalise negotiation on the (name of agreement). Obviously, we are available for a conference call or a meeting to resolve the remaining issues.
  Lassen Sie uns versuchen, die Verhandlungen über die Vertragsvereinbarungen wie besprochen zu Ende zu bringen. Selbstverständlich stehen wir für eine Telefonkonferenz oder ein Meeting zur Verfügung, um die verbliebenen offenen Fragen zu klären.

- With regard to your changes in the agreement, our client can accept most of your suggestions. However, some would stretch our client's exposure to an unreasonable and therefore unacceptable extent.
  Mit dem größten Teil Ihrer am Vertrag vorgenommenen Änderungen kann sich unser Klient einverstanden erklären. Einige Ihrer Vorschläge dagegen stellen für unseren Klienten eine unangemessene Belastung dar und sind daher inakzeptabel.

- This is the best and final package we are authorised to offer for your consideration. We are convinced that the package is reasonably balanced now and would be happy if we could meet to finalise the deal.
  Dies ist das beste und endgültige Angebot, das wir Ihnen anzubieten ermächtigt sind. Wir sind überzeugt, dass es nun sehr ausgewogen ist, und würden uns freuen, wenn wir uns bei einem Treffen einig würden.

- I look forward to finalising terms today.
  Ich freue mich, heute zum Abschluss zu kommen/den endgültigen Vertragstext heute aufzusetzen.

UK:
Chase someone up
US:
Chase someone down

jmdm. Dampf machen, damit er/sie etwas tut

7 Acquisitions & Sales

- I have just spoken with (name of vendor/purchaser). They should be ready to come back to us tomorrow and answer our points.
  Ich habe soeben mit (Name des Verkäufers/Käufers) gesprochen. Vermutlich werden sie morgen mit uns Kontakt aufnehmen, um uns unsere Fragen zu beantworten.

- I met with (name of vendor/purchaser) and presented the points we discussed. They still seem to be playing tough on some of the issues but will come back with their summary later today.
  Ich habe mich mit (Name des Verkäufers/Käufers) getroffen und ihnen die Punkte unterbreitet, die wir besprochen haben. Sie scheinen in Bezug auf manche der Fragen noch immer recht unnachgiebig, werden aber im Laufe des Tages eine Übersicht vorlegen.

- At this stage, I believe this is not the final offer they will submit.
  In dieser Phase dürfte das von ihnen vorgelegte Angebot meiner Einschätzung nach nicht das letzte sein.

- Please find enclosed our client's proposal. As you can see (name of vendor) has made great efforts to provide solutions for the critical issues. We hope that the suggestions are appreciated and look forward to your reply.
  Anbei das Angebot unseres Klienten. Wie Sie sehen, hat (Name des Verkäufers) sich sehr bemüht, die strittigen Fragen einer Lösung zuzuführen. Wir hoffen, dass Sie seine Vorschläge würdigen können, und freuen uns auf Ihre Antwort.

- We appreciate that (name of vendor/purchaser) is making efforts to deal with the issues we identified during due diligence.
  Wir wissen es zu schätzen, dass sich (Name des Verkäufers/Käufers) um eine Lösung der bei der Due-Diligence-Prüfung festgestellten Probleme bemüht.

- We require the seller **to make good** the defects stated in the (defect list / due diligence report). The period of time for this is to be agreed and secured by a retainer from the purchase price held in escrow.
  Wir verlangen vom Verkäufer, die im/in der (Due-Diligence-Bericht/Mängelliste) aufgeführten Mängel zu beheben. Der Zeitraum dafür muss ausgehandelt und seine Einhaltung durch einen auf dem Anderkonto einbehaltenen Teil des Verkaufspreises sichergestellt werden.

- We propose a purchase price reduction for this of € 140,000.
  Wir schlagen hierfür einen Preisnachlass von € 140.000 vor.

- We think you will agree that on the basis of the above figures, a compensation figure of € 120,000 is a huge concession and gesture of goodwill from (name of purchaser).

*The term "**make good**" is used in real estate to mean repairing a defect to its previous condition.*

7 Acquisitions & Sales

Wir denken, dass Sie auf Basis der erörterten Zahlen zugestehen werden, dass eine Ausgleichszahlung von € 120.000 ein starkes Entgegenkommen bedeutet und das große Wohlwollen des (Name des Käufers) zeigt.

- We expect a purchase price reduction of € 250,000 for all these items. We believe this is an extremely fair counter-proposal and we therefore expect your agreement to the above terms by Thursday 4 April otherwise we will not be bound to the purchase price as stated in the Letter of Intent.
Für diese Posten erwarten wir einen Preisnachlass von € 250.000. Wir halten dies für einen mehr als fairen Gegenvorschlag und erwarten daher Ihre Zustimmung zu obigen Bedingungen bis Donnerstag, den 4. April. Andernfalls werden wir uns an den in der Absichtserklärung genannten Kaufpreis nicht gebunden fühlen.

- It seems that we are now very close to (name of vendor) taking responsibility for the issues which is a big step in the right direction.
Wie es scheint, ist (Name des Verkäufers) nun fast bereit, die Verantwortung für die Probleme zu übernehmen, was ein wichtiger Schritt in die richtige Richtung ist.

- Thank you for forwarding to us your client's proposal of (date). (Name of vendor) very much appreciates (name of purchaser)'s efforts to come to a final arrangement by making steps towards our client's position. This spirit is taken up by making the following suggestions:
Vielen Dank für die Weiterleitung des Angebots Ihres Klienten vom (Datum). (Name des Verkäufers) weiß die Bemühungen von (Name des Käufers) sehr zu schätzen, eine Einigung zu befördern, indem er der Position unseres Klienten entgegenkommt. Dieselbe Bereitschaft unsererseits spricht aus folgenden Vorschlägen:

- Our client has used the last few days to find a solution to resolve the problems regarding the (fire safety issues).
Unser Klient hat die vergangenen Tage dazu genutzt, in der (Brandschutzproblematik) zu einer Lösung zu kommen.

- Our client proposes to take responsibility for items 12, 18 and 25 raised in the due diligence report and suggests that the other items be taken care of by the purchaser within the general compensation of defects budget.
Unser Klient schlägt vor, die Posten 12, 18 und 25 aus dem Due-Diligence-Bericht selbst zu tragen, und regt an, dass im Rahmen der pauschalen Ausgleichszahlung für Mängel die anderen Posten vom Käufer übernommen werden.

See unit 8 for details on commercial, technical and legal due diligence

7 Acquisitions & Sales

- In order to close the deal, (name of vendor) would be willing to raise the lump sum compensation to € 150,000.
  Um zu einem Abschluss zu kommen, erklärt sich (Name des Verkäufers) bereit, die Ausgleichspauschale auf € 150.000 zu erhöhen.

- I can confirm that (name of client) are in agreement with the revised (name of agreement).
  Ich darf Ihnen bestätigen, dass (Name des Klienten) dem überarbeiteten (Name des Vertrags) zustimmt.

Signing

- The proposed signing date is 10 July 2012. We are in possession of power of attorney to sign for (name of vendor).
  Als Datum der Vertragsunterzeichnung wurde der 10. Juli 2012 vorgeschlagen. Aufgrund der uns vorliegenden Vollmachten sind wir für (Name des Verkäufers) zeichnungsberechtigt.

- Thank you for your update. We require a confirmation that (name of purchaser) intend to transfer the full purchase price into the escrow account within 24 hours.
  Wir danken Ihnen für Ihre Mitteilung. Bitte bestätigen Sie uns, dass (Name des Käufers) innerhalb von 24 Stunden den vollen Kaufpreis auf das Anderkonto transferieren wird.

- We can confirm that we are able to sign on Thursday.
  Von unserer Seite steht einer Unterzeichung am Donnerstag nichts im Wege.

7 ACQUISITIONS & SALES

Transaction costs

English	German
agent's fees	Maklergebühren
due diligence costs	Due-Diligence-Kosten
financing costs	Finanzierungskosten
internal fees	interne Provision
legal advice	Kosten der Rechtsberatung
land register fees	Eintragungsgebühren
real estate transfer tax (UK: stamp duty land tax)	Grunderwerbsteuer
valuation costs	Gutachterkosten

General contract terminology

English	German
addendum	Nachtrag / Zusatz
breach of contract	Vertragsverletzung
clause	Klausel / Ziffer
compensation	Schaden(s)ersatz
completion	Erfüllung
consideration (price)	Kaufpreis / Gegenleistung
defects in quality	Sachmängel
defects in title	Rechtsmängel
(to) draw up a contract	einen Vertrag aufsetzen
execution	Ausführung
force majeure	höhere Gewalt
paragraph	Absatz
performance	Ausführung / Erfüllung
preamble (to a contract)	Präambel
power of attorney / authority to act	Vollmacht
provisions (terms of the contract)	Bestimmungen
right of withdrawal	Rücktrittsrecht
section	Abschnitt
schedule (to a contract)	Verzeichnis / Tabelle
side letter	Nebenabrede
void	nichtig / unwirksam
waiver	Verzicht

execution
to sign a contract or complete the terms of a contract

163

7 Acquisitions & Sales

Sales and purchase agreement

English	German
asset deal	Grundstückskauf
conveyance	Auflassung
escrow account	Notaranderkonto
fittings (chattels)	Zubehör
fixtures	wesentliche Bestandteile
land register	Grundbuch
notarial form / notarisation	notarielle Beurkundung
notary	Notar
possession	Besitz
priority notice	Auflassungsvormerkung
purchaser	Käufer
to reduce the purchase price	den Kaufpreis mindern
right of pre-emption	Vorkaufsrecht
share deal	Anteilskauf
title deed	Eigentumserwerbsurkunde
transfer of possession	Besitzübergang
transfer of title	Eigentumsübergang
vendor (seller)	Verkäufer
warranties	Garantie / Gewährleistung / Zusicherung

A **sales and purchase agreement** is often abbreviated to SPA.

Sales and Purchase Agreement Phrases

The object of purchase

- The property is sold by the vendors to the purchasers together with its fixtures and fittings.
  Die Immobilie wird zusammen mit allen Einbauten und sämtlichem Zubehör von den Verkäufern an die Käufer verkauft.

- The vendor warrants to perform the obligations of the contract under paragraph 11 of schedule 2 to the lease.
  Der Verkäufer sichert zu, sämtlichen vertraglichen Verpflichtungen gemäß § 11 von Anhang 2 zum Mietvertrag nachzukommen.

7 Acquisitions & Sales

- The purchaser hereby acknowledges that he has inspected the property and purchases the same with full knowledge of the actual state and condition thereof and shall take the property as it stands.
  Der Käufer bestätigt hiermit, dass er die Immobilie besichtigt hat und diese in voller Kenntnis ihres aktuellen Zustands erwirbt, sie also unverändert übernimmt.
- The vendor hereby sells the property located in (address), entered in the land register of (city) local court as follows, to the purchaser.
  Der Verkäufer verkauft hiermit die Immobilie (Adresse), eingetragen im Grundbuch des Amtsgerichts von (Ort), an den Käufer.
- The vendor sells the property with all rights, integral parts and fixtures and fittings.
  Der Verkäufer verkauft den Grundbesitz mit allen Rechten, seinen wesentlichen Bestandteilen und mit allem Zubehör.

Land register entries

- The property shall be transferred free of encumbrances.
  Das Eigentum an der Immobilie wird frei von Belastungen übertragen.
- The encumbrances will be deleted from the land register.
  Die Belastungen werden aus dem Grundbuch gelöscht.
- The property is sold subject to and with the benefit of any matters referred to in the entries shown on the property and charges registers.
  Die Immobilie wird vorbehaltlich und unter Berücksichtigung etwaiger Eintragungen oder in Bezug genommenen Angelegenheiten im Grundbuch bzw. Baulastenverzeichnis verkauft.
- The property is encumbered in section (…) of the land register as follows:
  Der Grundbesitz ist in Abteilung (…) des Grundbuchs wie folgt belastet:
- The vendor shall apply for all encumbrances not assumed by the purchaser being deleted from the land register and provide the purchaser with a written confirmation of such cancellation.
  Der Verkäufer wird die Löschung sämtlicher nicht vom Käufer übernommenen Belastungen des Kaufgegenstandes im Grundbuch beantragen und deren Löschung gegenüber dem Käufer schriftlich bestätigen.

7 Acquisitions & Sales

Purchase price

- On completion the purchaser shall pay to the vendor the balance of the purchase price.
  Bei Vollendung zahlt der Käufer dem Verkäufer den noch ausstehenden Teil des Kaufpreises.

- The purchase price shall be transferred to the escrow account indicated for such purpose.
  Der Kaufpreis wird auf das zu diesem Zweck benannte Treuhandkonto überwiesen.

- The benefits and burdens of the property will transfer to the purchaser automatically upon payment of the purchase price.
  Der Nutzen und die Lasten des Grundstücks gehen bei Bezahlung des Kaufpreises automatisch auf den Käufer über.

- The purchase price shall be due and payable when the notary informs the purchaser in writing that the encumbrances of the property have been deleted from the land register as set out in section/clause … above.
  Der Kaufpreis ist fällig und zahlbar, wenn der Notar dem Käufer schriftlich mitteilt, dass die Belastungen des Kaufgegenstandes gemäß vorstehender Ziffer … aus dem Grundbuch gelöscht wurden.

Warranties and guarantees

For the difference between warranty and guarantee see pages 174.

- The vendor warrants to disclose all defects or issues of non-compliance.
  Der Verkäufer sichert zu, dass er sämtliche Mängel oder Fälle von Nichteinhaltung offenlegt.

- The vendor shall transfer the property with full title guarantee.
  Der Verkäufer überträgt die Immobilie unter Zusicherung sämtlicher Eigentumsrechte.

- The vendor warrants that the certificate of use for the retail area on the ground floor has been granted without any restrictions.
  Der Verkäufer sichert zu, dass die Nutzungsbescheinigung für den Einzelhandelsbereich im Erdgeschoss auflagenfrei erteilt wurde.

Leases

- The vendor warrants that the rent amounts to € (amount) per month.
  Der Verkäufer sichert zu, dass die Mieteinnahmen € (Betrag) monatlich betragen.

- The vendor warrants that the non-recoverable operating costs amount to € (amount) per month.
  Der Verkäufer sichert zu, dass die nicht umlagefähigen Betriebskosten monatlich € (Betrag) betragen.

- The provisions of the lease including any addendum thereto are known to the purchasers.
  Die Bestimmungen des Mietvertrags einschließlich etwaiger Anhänge sind den Käufern bekannt.

Costs

- The costs of this agreement shall be borne by the purchaser.
  Die Kosten dieses Vertrags sind vom Käufer zu tragen.

- The purchaser will pay interest on any outstanding amount due at 4% above base rate from the due date for payment until actual payment.
  Der Käufer zahlt Zinsen in Höhe von 4% über dem Basiszinssatz für jede am Fälligkeitstermin ausstehende Zahlung bis zu dem Zeitpunkt, an dem diese tatsächlich erfolgt.

- The costs of the survey pursuant to clause 4 paragraph 2 shall be borne by the vendor.
  Die Kosten der Vermessung trägt gemäß Ziffer 4 Absatz 2 der Verkäufer.

Avoid the real estate mistake

Test your knowledge gained in this unit by identifying the real estate mistakes.

1. The vendor has provided rent guarantees for the vacant *spaces / space*.
2. Each party shall *bear / carry* its own transaction costs.
3. The property was *built / built-up* in the early 1990s.
4. The strategic location and excellent *transport / traffic* links have attracted a number of high-profile tenants.

Improve your style

Exchange the word/phrase in brackets with a more appropriate expression from this unit.

5. The (list of tenants) _____ is provided below.
6. (Just so you know), _____ lease find attached our standard terms of business including confirmation of acquisition fees.
7. We kindly request that you (check) _____ the contact and give your input where needed.
8. The (seller) _____ is not aware, to the best of his knowledge, of any major problems.

Test your real estate vocabulary

9. Please find attached a copy of the (Flächenaufmaß) _____ .
10. We assume that the service charge is fully (umlegbar) _____ .
11. The property shall be transferred free of (Belastungen) _____ .
12. We assume there is no (Instandhaltungsrückstau) _____ .

---

1. space | 2. bear | 3. built | 4. transport | 5. tenancy schedule | 6. For the sake of good order | 7. review | 8. vendor | 9. measured survey / measured floor plans | 10. recoverable / reconcilable | 11. encumbrances | 12. maintenance back-log

Due Diligence

8

Commercial
Due Diligence 170
Location 171
Property 172
Market 173
Tenant(s) 174
Lease Terms 174
Ownership and holding costs 175
Investment appraisal 175
Tax 176

Legal
Due Diligence 176
Vendor 176
Cadastral register / Land register /
Land charge register 177
Restrictive covenants 178
Warranties and guarantees 178
Lease agreements 178

Technical
Due Diligence 180
Construction / Planning law 180
Building design / Flexibility 182
Building construction / Fit-out 184
Building services 188

Avoid the real estate mistake, improve your style and test your real estate vocabulary 194

8 Due Diligence

This unit provides phrases and vocabulary for the commercial, legal and technical due diligence phase. This information does not constitute a complete check list, but rather serves as a guide to the terminology used in practice.

Commercial Due Diligence

The term commercial due diligence is not always used by real estate professionals in the UK, as much of the information is provided in a detailed Investment Memorandum or Purchase Report before the investment decision process is officially started.

8 Due Diligence

Location

English	German
location	Makrolage
- city	- Großstadt
- conurbation	- Ballungsraum
- town	- Kleinstadt
socio-demographic profile	Soziodemografische Struktur
- age	- Alter
- population	- Einwohner
- unemployment levels	- Arbeitslosigkeit
economic climate	Wirtschaftsdaten
- current and forecast economic conditions	- aktuelles und zukünftiges Wirtschaftsklima
situation	Mikrolage
- city centre	- Stadtzentrum
- location image	- Standortimage
- periphery	- Peripherie, Umland
neighbourhood	Nachbarschaft
- amenities	- Nahversorgung, Geschäfte mit Waren des täglichen Bedarfs
- competing properties	- Konkurrenzobjekte, vergleichbare Gebäude, Wettbewerbsobjekte
- image	- Image
- local occupiers	- umliegende Nutzer, nachbarschaftliche Nutzung
- surrounding developments	- ummittelbar angrenzende Liegenschaften, umliegende Bebauung, Nachbarschaftsbebauung
- types of use	- Nutzungsarten
communications (transport infrastructure)	Verkehrsanbindung, Erschließung
- accessibility by car, public transport, foot	- Erreichbarkeit mit dem Auto, mit öffentlichen Verkehrsmitteln, zu Fuß
- local economy	- Wirtschaftsdaten bezogen auf den unmittelbaren Standort
- local parking provision	- Parkplatzsituation, Stellplatzsituation, Parkmöglichkeiten in der näheren Umgebung
- town planning & urban development measures	- Stadtplanung, städtebauliche Maßnahmen

8 Due Diligence

Property

Drittverwendungsfähigkeit

~~third party use~~

potential or demand for alternative uses ✓

"Third party use" would mean another user was occupying the property!

Grade A building: See page 53 for a detailed explanation of property grades and classes.

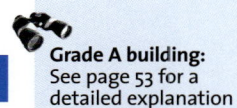

English	German
permitted use	Art und Maß der baulichen Nutzung
- potential or demand for alternative uses	- **Drittverwendungsfähigkeit**, Nachfrage(potenzial) nach alternativen Nutzungen
physical attributes	Gebäudequalität, Gebäudeeigenschaften
- building specification (e.g. **grade A**, B, C)	- Gebäudestandard
- new-build/modern/refurbishment	- Neubau/neuwertig/saniert
- floor areas (net and gross)	- Netto- und Bruttogrundfläche
- ancillary areas	- Nebenflächen
- on-site parking provision	- Stell-/Parkplätze auf dem Grundstück
space efficiency	Flächeneffizienz
- ratio of net to gross internal area	- Verhältnis Netto- zu Bruttogrundfläche
- efficient floorplates	- effiziente Grundrissgestaltung
- structural grid	- Konstruktionsraster
- planning grid	- Ausbauraster
vehicular and pedestrian access	Zugang zur Immobilie (Pkw-Zufahrt und Eingang)
- main entrance	- Haupteingang
- side/rear entrances	- Seiten-/Hintereingänge
- delivery entrance	- Liefereingang
leasing flexibility	flexible Vermietungsgestaltung/Vermietungsmöglichkeiten
- flexibility for multi-tenant and single tenant use	- Immobilie kann flexibel sowohl von einem als auch mehreren Mietern genutzt werden
- flexibility for a variety of work setting configurations	- Flexibilität bei Raumbelegung/Arbeitsplatzgestaltung
service charges	Nebenkosten
- level (total in previous year / estimate for forthcoming year)	- Höhe (tatsächlich angefallene Nebenkosten letztes Jahr / erwartete Nebenkosten kommendes Jahr)
- recoverable costs	- Umlage auf die Mieter / umlegbare Nebenkosten
existing maintenance backlog	Instandhaltungsstau
building's lifecycle	Lebenszyklus des Gebäudes

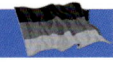

8 Due Diligence

Market

English	German
Rents - market rent - prime rent - current rent in comparison to market rent (overrented / underrented)	Mieten - Marktmiete - Spitzenmiete - aktuelle Miete (Ist-Miete) im Vergleich zur Marktmiete (über/unter der aktuellen Marktmiete)
vacancy rate - marketing/letting concept - agent's contract - fee - letting expenses	Leerstandsquote - Vermarktungs-/Vermietungskonzept - Maklervereinbarung, Maklervertrag - Provision, Maklercourtage - Vermarktungs- und Vermietungskosten
supply / demand - stock - pipeline - demand structure - take-up	Angebot / Nachfrage - Immobilienbestand - Immobilienentwicklungen in der Pipeline - Nachfragestruktur - Flächenumsatz
market outlook	Marktausblick
lettability	Vermietungsmöglichkeiten / Vermietbarkeit
marketability	Vermarktungsmöglichkeiten / Vermarktbarkeit, Marktfähigkeit

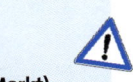

Angebot (Markt)
~~offer~~
supply ✓

8 Due Diligence

Tenant(s)

English	German
rent roll / tenancy schedule	Mieter- und Leerstandsübersicht, Mieterliste
tenant credit standing - excellent/good/poor covenant strength - covenant information	Bonität des Mieters, Mieterbonität - hervorragende/gute/schlechte Bonität - Mieterauskünfte
type of industry - banking & finance - service sector - consulting - accountants & auditors - retail - transport & logistics - IT - telecommunication - (local) government - manufacturing	Branche - Banken & Finanz - Dienstleistung - Beratung - Wirtschaftsprüfung - Einzelhandel - Transport & Logistik - EDV/IT - Telekommunikation - öffentliche Hand - produzierendes Gewerbe
tenant's business sector - current/future market conditions	Geschäftsfeld des Mieters - aktuelle/zukünftige Marktsituation
tenant payment history	Zahlungshistorie
tenant satisfaction and fluctuation	Mieterzufriedenheit und Mieterfluktuation

Lease terms
Mietvertragsbedingungen

English	German
term	Laufzeit des Mietvertrages
lease expiry	Ende des Mietvertrages, Mietvertragsende
break options	Sonderkündigungsrechte
rent review terms (indexed/stepped increase etc.)	Mietanpassungen (indexierte Miete / Staffelmiete etc.)

8 Due Diligence

Ownership & holding costs
Die beim Eigentümer verbleibenden Kosten / Bewirtschaftungskosten

English	German
vacancy/void costs	Leerstandskosten
non-recoverable service costs	Nicht umlegbare Nebenkosten
non-recoverable management costs	Nicht umlegbare Verwaltungskosten
letting costs	Vermietungskosten
capital expenditure (capex)	Investitionsaufwand (Kosten für z.B. Nachvermietung, Vermarktung, Renovierung etc.)
- tenant fit-out, rent-free periods etc.	- Mieterausbau, mietfreie Zeiten etc.
- investment costs	- Investitionskosten
- purchase price	- Kaufpreis
- incidental purchase costs	- Erwerbsnebenkosten
- financing costs	- Finanzierungskosten

Investment appraisal: In the UK, the terms **valuation** and **investment appraisal** differ slightly. Appraisal is distinguishable from market valuation as it is a subjective activity undertaken by or on behalf of investors to assess the likely future performance of an investment, its value and risk. In the US, however, the term appraisal is used for valuation and a UK Valuer is called an Appraiser.

Investment appraisal
Wirtschaftlichkeitsberechnungen / Wirtschaftlichkeitsbetrachtung

English	German
rental income	Mietertrag
security of income	**nachhaltige** Einkünfte
NOI (net operating income)	Nettomietertrag / Nettobetriebseinkommen
valuation	Bewertung
- land value	- Bodenwert
- building value	- Gebäudewert
- market value	- Marktwert / Verkehrswert
- capital value	- Kaufpreis pro Quadratmeter
expected IRR (internal rate of return)	erwartete Rendite auf das eingesetzte Kapital (interner Zinsfuß)
gross income	Bruttomietertrag
net initial yield	Nettoanfangsrendite
land reference values	Grundstücksvergleichswerte
expansion land	Reservefläche
sensitivity analysis	Sensitivitätsanalyse
rental/capital value growth potential	Wertsteigerungspotenzial

The German definition of **Nachhaltigkeit** in the appraisal context refers to rents and the long term cash flow security. The phrase **security of income** is the most appropriate translation here. Caution should be used with the word **sustainable**, as this is primarily used in the context of buildings that meet, for example, LEED or BREEAM standards, where issues such as environmental protection, promotion of social justice and wider socio-economic issues are taken into consideration.

8   Due Diligence

Tax

English	German
capital gains tax	Kapitalertragsteuer
corporate income tax	Körperschaftsteuer
trade income tax	Gewerbesteuer
real estate transfer tax (RETT) (UK: stamp duty land tax)	Grunderwerbsteuer
value added tax (VAT)	Umsatzsteuer
land tax (UK: **rates**)	Grundsteuer
withholding tax	Quellensteuer

Rates (also business rates): An annual tax on commercial property for local authority services.

Legal Due Diligence

Using English to describe legal terms in different jurisdictions is a complex matter. There is no universal legal terminology that is comprehensible in all languages. Each country has unique terminology as its legal system has evolved from its cultural, political and historical background. This complex framework is seldom identical from one country to another and a particular concept in one legal system may have no counterpart in other systems, even for countries that use the same language. This can create a challenge when seeking a suitable translation solution. The list below provides common phrases and vocabulary used in legal due diligence in the real estate acquisition process. Common US terminology is provided in brackets.

Vendor

English	German
excerpt from the commercial register	Handelsregisterauszug
articles of association	Satzung oder Gesellschaftsvertrag
power of attorney	Vollmacht

8 Due Diligence

Cadastral register / Land register / Land charge register
Kataster / Grundbuch / Baulastenverzeichnis

English	German
abstract of **title** / land register extract	Grundbuchauszug
title deeds	Eigentumsurkunde
proof of title / title search	„historischer Eigentumsnachweis"
tenure	„Eigentumsverhältnisse"
- commonhold (US: condominium)	- Teileigentum / Wohnungseigentum
- **freehold**	- Eigentum
- **leasehold**	- (hier ähnlich wie) Erbbaurecht
encumbrances	Grundstücksbelastungen
local land charges	Baulasten
- distance to site boundary*	- Abstandsflächenbaulast
- imposed car parking requirements / restrictions*	- Stellplatzbaulast
land charge	Grundpfandrecht
- land charge / equity charge*	- Grundschuld
- land charge / equity charge*	- Reallast
- mortgage (US: deed of trust)	- Hypothek
easements (US: servitudes)	Grunddienstbarkeiten
- rights of way	- Wegerechte
- rights of access	- Zugangsrechte
- utilities easements	- Leitungsrechte
right of pre-emption	Vorkaufsrecht
usufruct	Nießbrauch
formal legal requirements	Formvorschriften
cadastral plan	Katasterplan
cadastral map	Flurkarte
cadastre of contaminated sites	Altlastenkataster
listed building (US: landmark property / historic site)	denkmalgeschützes Gebäude, Baudenkmal
redevelopment area	Sanierungsgebiet

* no direct translation

Title deeds: An official legal document or a chain of documents which prove the ownership of land. In particular, a Sales and Purchase Agreement, documenting the transfer of the legal right to title to land.

Proof of title / title search: The process of finding a document (or a chain of documents) which confirms the title to the property.

Tenure: The basis on which land (and real property) is held e.g. freehold or leasehold. The verb to hold land is used instead of to own land. This originates from the feudal system where the sovereign was the only person who had the absolute right of ownership. In the US land is held by an individual in his/her own right and is not subject to a superior right.

Freehold: In the US this can be described as the outright ownership of property. In England and Wales this is described as the right to "hold" property for life (see tenure).

Leasehold: The right to hold or use the property for a fixed period of time at a given price on the basis of a lease contract.

Local land charges in one country may not have identical equivalents in another. Common examples in England include local land charges for listed buildings, conservation areas, highway agreements and conditional planning consents.

8 Due Diligence

Restrictive covenants:
An obligation contained in a contract where one party covenants (agrees) to refrain from an act affecting the property or to use the property in a defined way or for a defined purpose.

Warranties & Guarantees:
Warranties and guarantees are often but incorrectly used to express the same meaning. A warranty is a promise or assurance that a certain fact is true or that something is in a specific condition. A warranty may be given by a construction manager to a purchaser. A guarantee (also spelt guaranty) is an agreement by which one party promises to be responsible for debt or default owed by a third party or an assurance that a stated event will occur and the consequences provided if it does not.

Collateral warranty:
Duties of care owed by a contractor and members of the professional team (e.g. architects, contractors, project managers etc.) to the developer or owner. The collateral warranty may be passed onto the buyer, tenant or the lender.

Restrictive covenants

„dingliche Nutzungsbeschränkungen"

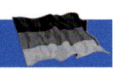

English	German
planning applications - development plan - land use permission - planning permission - preliminary building application - preliminary building notice	Bauanträge - Bebauungsplan - Nutzungsgenehmigung - Baugenehmigung - Bauvoranfrage - Bauvorbescheid
site boundaries	Grundstücksgrenzen

Warranties & guarantees

Gewährleistungen, Garantie & Bürgschaft

English	German
- bank guarantee - construction / **collateral warranty** (e.g. 10 year warranty on roof) - rent guarantee - warranty (e.g. from vendor that property is fit for a specific purpose)	- Bankbürgschaft - Gewährleistung (z.B. 10 Jahre auf das Dach) - Mietgarantie - Garantie (z.B. vom Verkäufer, dass das Gebäude eine spezielle Nutzung erlaubt)
estoppel certificate (US)	Bestätigung vorhandener Rechte und Pflichten

Lease agreements

English	German
alterations and improvements - works permitted with/without consent - works prohibited	Änderungen und Mietereinbauten - mit/ohne Genehmigung - unzulässige Umbauten
options - break options - renewal options	Optionen - Sonderkündigungsrechte - Vertragsverlängerungsoptionen
compliance with statutory provisions (health & safety, fire, and other building regulations) - extent of tenant and landlord compliance obligations	Übereinstimmung mit gesetzlichen Vorschriften (Sicherheit, Feuer und andere Bauvorschriften) - Umfang der gesetzlich geregelten Mieter-/Eigentümerpflichten

8 Due Diligence

English	German
default - default interest	Verzug - Verzugszinsen
demised premises / tenant areas - additional rights (e.g. car parking spaces, reception areas)	Mietfläche - zusätzliche Rechte (z.B. Parkplätze, Empfangsbereiche)
security / deposit - bank guarantee - deposit account - parent company/corporate guarantee - personal guarantee	Mietkaution - Bankbürgschaft - Sperrkonto / Kautionskonto - Konzernbürgschaft - persönliche Garantie / Bürgschaft
insurance obligations - landlord and tenant obligations	Versicherungspflichten - Vermieter-/Mieterpflichten
lease term (length and start date) - fixed term - unlimited period of time	Mietzeitraum - befristet - unbefristet
lease termination rights	Kündigungsrechte
maintenance, repair and redecorating obligations - extent of maintenance obligations - extent of repair obligations - extent and frequency of redecoration obligations	Instandhaltungs-, Instandsetzungs- und Renovierungspflichten/ Schönheitsreparaturen - Umfang der Instandhaltungspflicht - Umfang der Instandsetzungspflicht - Umfang und Häufigkeit der Renovierungen
restrictions on permitted use	Nutzungsbeschränkungen
rent review - fixed increase/stepped rent - index-linked rent - market rent - turnover rent	Mietanpassung - Staffelmiete - indexierte Miete, Indexmiete - Marktmiete - Umsatzmiete
service charges - items recoverable from tenant(s) - cap on service charges	Nebenkosten - umlegbare Kosten - Begrenzung der Nebenkosten
signage	Beschilderung (z.B. Firmenlogo am Gebäude)
subletting & assignment - consent - restrictions	Untervermietung & Vertragsübernahme/Vertragsübergang - Genehmigung / Zustimmung - Beschränkungen
yielding up obligations	Verpflichtungen bei der Rückgabe der Mietsache
competition clause	Wettbewerbsklausel

The terms **maintenance**, **repair** and **redecoration** should be used with caution as their use may have legal implications in both languages.

Assignment: The transfer of a property interest (usually a lease from an existing tenant to a new tenant). The assignment of a lease differs to subletting as the assignor parts with all their rights and obligations.

Yielding up obligations: The obligations a tenant must fulfil before giving up possession at the end of a lease.

8 Due Diligence

Technical Due Diligence

Technical due diligence examines the physical condition of a property. A technical survey might establish defects or deficiencies in the property which could have an impact on its performance. The defects may include repairs which arise from a lack of maintenance, neglect or misuse, insufficient capacity of the building's services, items approaching the end of their useful life, deleterious materials (**schädliche Stoffe**), items that do not comply with statutory requirements or regulations or any other matters that may be of interest to the client such as energy efficiency and environmental standards. An almost indefinite number of items can be identified in the technical due diligence phase, depending on the property's type of construction, location and use. The following – compiled from information kindly provided by Gleeds – provides some of the key items investigated in technical due diligence.

A. Construction / Planning law

A 1
- Is the building situated within an area covered by statutory planning policy or a development plan? Are there any statutory restrictions on changes or similar limitations that apply to the site?

A 2
- Does the building comply with the statutory building lines relative to boundaries and neighbouring buildings and do neighbouring buildings observe these?

A 3
- Is the site subject to encumbrances or easements (on the restriction/usage of the site)? If yes, what are they (e.g. utility easements)?

A 4
- Is there contamination on the site?

A 5
- Are there restrictions or conditions imposed by neighbouring sites?

A 6
- Is the site subject to partial ownership? If yes, what arrangements exist for shared services etc.?

A 7
- Is the building in breach of any official or statutory building regulations which affect its current unrestricted use?

A 8
- Is the building in whole or in part subject to a historic buildings preservation order?

8 Due Diligence

- Befindet sich das Gebäude im Bereich eines Bebauungsplanes oder liegt das Grundstück in einem städtischen Entwicklungsgebiet? Liegen Veränderungssperren oder sonstige Einschränkungen auf dem Grundstück?

- Werden die erforderlichen Grenzabstände, Abstandsflächen gegenüber und von Nachbargrundstücken eingehalten?

- Existieren Baulasten, Grunddienstbarkeiten (zu Lasten/Nutzen des Grundstücks)? Wenn ja welche (z. B. Grunddienstbarkeiten für Versorgungsunternehmen)?

- Gibt es Altlasten auf dem Grundstück?

- Gibt es nachbarschaftliche Einschränkungen oder Abhängigkeiten?

- Besteht Teileigentum? Wenn ja, wie sind die technischen Schnittstellen geregelt?

- Wurde die gegenwärtige unbeschränkte Nutzung des Gebäudes durch den Verstoß gegen geltende behördliche oder baurechtliche Vorschriften ermöglicht?

- Steht das Objekt im Ganzen oder in Teilen unter Denkmal-/Ensembleschutz?

8 Due Diligence

A 9
- Are changes in regulations expected or predicted? If yes, which apply? And will right of continuation under existing regulations be granted?

A 10
- Have all relevant statutory (health and safety) workplace regulations been complied with for the stated use?

A 11
- Have all relevant statutory fire protection and safety regulations been complied with for the stated use?

A 12
- Have public utility company regulations and conditions been complied with for the stated use?

A 13
- Are there any local authority restrictions on usage of the property?

A 14
- Are any potential changes/alterations affected by architects, consultants and artists' copyright (e.g. extensions, additional floors, façade renewal etc.)?

B. Building design / Flexibility

B 1
- Is site access (dimensions of entrances, side entrances) adequate?

B 2
- Do public utilities for the building (electricity, water, gas etc.) depend on agreements with neighbouring properties?

B 3
- Does the arrangement of the internal vertical and horizontal circulation enable an appropriate division into lettable areas? Does the disposition of the elevators support this?

B 4
- What is the maximum viable lettable area which can be achieved within each floor plan?

B 5
- Are the number and location of the wcs, kitchenettes and cleaner's cupboards appropriate to the building's use and possible division into lettable areas?

B 6
- Does the building grid allow for flexible space division?

8 Due Diligence

- Sind Änderungen der Vorschriften abzusehen oder zu erwarten? Wenn ja, welche? Und bleibt der Bestandsschutz erhalten?

- Sind alle arbeitsrechtlichen Vorschriften und Gesetze für die genannte Nutzung eingehalten worden?

- Sind die brandschutzrechtlichen und sicherheitstechnischen Vorschriften und Gesetze für die genannte Nutzung eingehalten worden?

- Sind die Vorschriften und Auflagen der öffentlichen Versorgungsunternehmen für die genannte Nutzung eingehalten worden?

- Bestehen behördliche Nutzungsbeschränkungen für das Objekt?

- Bestehen Urheberrechte von Architekten, Fachplanern, Künstlern, die Veränderungen am Objekt einschränken (z.B. Anbau, Aufstockung, Erneuerung der Fassade etc.)?

- Ist die äußere Erschließung (die Bemessung der Zugänge, Nebeneingänge) ausreichend?

- Ist das Gebäude autark hinsichtlich aller erforderlichen Versorgungen (Strom, Wasser, Gas, etc.) gegenüber Nachbarschaftsgebäuden?

- Ist die innere vertikale und horizontale Erschließung für eine Flächenteilung, die eine kleinteilige Vermietung ermöglicht, ausreichend? Sind die Aufzüge im Grundriss entsprechend angeordnet?

- Welche maximal sinnvolle Mietflächeneinteilung lässt das Grundrisskonzept zu?

- Entspricht die Anzahl und Lage der Toiletten, Teeküchen und Putzräume der Nutzung des Gebäudes hinsichtlich der möglichen Mieteinheiten?

- Lässt das Achsraster des Gebäudes eine flexible Raumaufteilung zu?

8 Due Diligence

B 7
- Do the room heights allow for open-plan usage?

B 8
- Does natural lighting correspond to room depth?

B 9
- Does sound insulation comply with local authority requirements and does this meet tenancy agreement provisions (walls, floors, doors)?

B 10
- Do the lettable units provide sufficient storage space?

B 11
- Are there sufficient parking spaces on the site (tenants/visitors)?

B 12
- Is the delivery area appropriately sized?

B 13
- Is there an internal and external wayfinding system (general signage, direction signs)?

B 14
- Does the refuse removal system meet demand? Are refuse rooms adequately sized?

C. Building construction / Fit-out

C 1
- Are only approved materials used in the building?

C 2
- Does the building incorporate any environmentally harmful materials which could endanger occupants' health, e.g. asbestos, PCB, formaldehyde etc.? Was an asbestos survey carried out and where necessary material removed from the building?

C 3
- Does fire protection comply with the statutory requirements (e.g. escape routes, fire compartmentation, classification of building elements, fire doors etc.)?

C 4
- Do the fire alarm and fire fighting provisions comply with statutory requirements (e.g. fire extinguishers, smoke and heat detection and alarm systems etc.)?

8 Due Diligence

- Lassen die lichten Raumhöhen eine Großraumnutzung zu?

- Ist die natürliche Belichtung für die gegebenen Raumtiefen ausreichend?

- Erfüllt der Schallschutz die herrschenden lokalen Vorschriften und stimmen diese mit den Mietverträgen überein (Wand, Decke, Tür)?

- Sind in den Mieteinheiten ausreichende Lagerflächen vorhanden?

- Gibt es genügend Stellplätze auf dem Grundstück (für Mieter/Besucher)?

- Ist die Anlieferungszone ausreichend dimensioniert?

- Gibt es ein internes und externes Gebäudeleitsystem (Beschilderung/Wegweiser)?

- Entspricht das Abfallentsorgungssystem dem tatsächlichen Bedarf? Haben die Mülllager die nötige Größe?

- Sind nur zugelassene Baustoffe verwandt worden?

- Sind im Gebäude umweltschädliche Materialien verbaut worden, welche die Gesundheit der Nutzer gefährden könnten, wie z.B. Asbest, PCB, Formaldehyd usw.? Wurde im Gebäude eine Asbestsanierung durchgeführt?

- Entspricht der bauliche Brandschutz den behördlichen Anforderungen (Rettungswege, Brandabschnitte, Klassifizierung der Bauteile, Sicherheitsschleusen etc.)?

- Entsprechen die Sicherheitseinrichtungen des Brandschutzes den behördlichen Anforderungen (z. B. Feuerlöscher, Rauch-/ Brandmeldesysteme etc.)?

8 Due Diligence

C 5
- Are there defects to the load-bearing structure which require rectification?

C 6
- Is there any steelwork corrosion which
  a) must be rectified
  b) affects the structural stability?

C 7
- What is the load-bearing capacity of the floors?
- Is the existing load-bearing capacity sufficient for the building's use?

C 8
- Are the upper levels of basements insulated?

C 9
- Does the gradient of the ramp to the underground car park comply with regulations?
- Is the ramp heated, if so how?

C 10
- Are basement levels protected against water penetration?
- Are basement levels connected to a drainage system?
- How will surface water be disposed of?
- Is the underground car park floor covering suitable for its function (e.g. oil and acid resistant / covering / paintwork / sprinklers)?

C 11
- Is access to the underground car park secure? If so how (e.g. barriers, doors etc.)?

C 12
- Will the parking spaces be accessed by external users?

C 13
- Do railings, windows, parapets, stairs etc. meet statutory requirements for protection from falling?

C 14
- Is the structural integrity of curtain walling or cladding façade systems (natural stone, concrete, brickwork, glass or the like) satisfactory?

C 15
- Does the building, in particular windows/façade systems, comply with current sound and thermal protection regulations? If not, is the performance sufficient?

8 Due Diligence

- Gibt es an der tragenden Konstruktion Mängel, welche behoben werden müssen?

- Gibt es an Stahlteilen Korrosionsschäden, die
  a) behoben werden müssen
  b) die Tragfähigkeit beeinflussen?

- Wie hoch ist die Tragkraft der Geschossdecken (Verkehrslast)?
- Ist die vorhandene Tragkraft für die Nutzung des Gebäudes ausreichend?

- Sind die überbauten Untergeschossbereiche im Deckenbereich gedämmt?

- Entspricht das Gefälle der Rampenzufahrt zur Tiefgarage den Vorschriften?
- Ist die Rampe beheizt? Wenn ja, wie?

- Sind die Untergeschosse gegen eindringendes Wasser geschützt?
- Sind die Untergeschosse an ein Entwässerungssystem angeschlossen?
- Wie wird das Oberflächenwasser abgeführt?
- Ist der Bodenbelag der Tiefgarage für die Nutzung geeignet (z. B. öl-/säureresistent / Beschichtung / Anstrich / Sprinkleranlage)

- Sind die Zufahrten zur Tiefgarage gesichert? Wenn ja, wie (z. B. Schrankenanlage, Toranlagen etc.)?

- Werden die Stellplätze auch von Dritten genutzt?

- Entsprechen die Absturzsicherungen an Geländern, Fenstern, Brüstungen, Treppengeländer usw. sowie die Treppen selbst den behördlichen Anforderungen?

- Bestehen bezüglich der Standfestigkeit von vorgehängten bzw. vorgeblendeten Fassaden (Naturstein, Beton, Mauerwerk, Glas oder Ähnlichem) Bedenken?

- Entsprechen das Gebäude und insbesondere die Fenster/Fassade den neuesten Schall- und Wärmeschutzbedingungen? Wenn nein, sind die tatsächlichen Werte ausreichend?

8 Due Diligence

C 16

- Are there any existing or planned external noise sources such as railway, tram, underground lines etc. within the vicinity of the property? If so, have the effects on the building (noise movement, vibrations etc.) been considered in its construction (windows, façades, frame etc.)?

C 17

- Are all metallic fixings manufactured from stainless steel?

D. Building services

D 1

- Have building services been regularly and appropriately maintained and do maintenance contracts comply with common standards and manufacturers' instructions?

D 2

EI&C
electrical, instrumentation and control

- Do electrical, plumbing, HVAC and **EI&C** systems comply with industry standards and can long-term cost-effective use be reasonably anticipated?

D 3

- Identify technical items, plant etc. where the operating life is expected to expire in the next ten years and would normally be replaced.

D 4

- Do power supply installations such as electricity and gas plant etc. as well as sewage and rainwater systems comply with common standards and is their capacity, including reserve capacity, appropriate?

D 5

- Is there capacity to extend services and plant?
- Is this sufficient considering the function of the building?
- Is there structural capacity for increasing plant capacity?

D 6

- Has the mandatory maintenance schedule for plant inspections been adhered to and any possible defects identified and rectified?
- Does the maintenance log comply with the prescribed inspection schedule?
- Are the inspection logs available on site?

- Existieren äußere Schallemissionsquellen wie Eisenbahn-, Straßenbahn-, U-Bahntrassen etc. oder sind welche im Umfeld der Liegenschaft geplant? Wenn ja, sind die Auswirkungen auf das Gebäude wie Schall, Schwingungen, Erschütterungen etc. bei der Gebäudekonstruktion (Fenster, Fassade, Rohbau etc.) berücksichtigt?

- Sind alle metallischen Verankerungen aus rostfreiem Stahl?

- Sind die technischen Einrichtungen regelmäßig sachgemäß gewartet worden und entsprechen die Wartungsverträge dem üblichen Standard und den Herstellervorschriften?

- Entsprechen die Systeme der Elektro-, Heizungs-, Sanitär-, **RLT**- und **MSR**-**Technik** üblichem Standard und ist ein wirtschaftlich sinnvoller Betrieb auch auf Dauer gewährleistet?

RLT
Raumlufttechnische Anlagen

MSR
Mess-, Steuerungs-, Regelungstechnik

- Identifizieren Sie technische Geräte, Anlagen usw., deren zu erwartende Betriebszeit (technisches Lebensalter) in den nächsten 10 Jahren ausläuft und die voraussichtlich ersetzt werden müssen.

- Entsprechen die Energieversorgungsanlagen wie Elektrizität, Gas usw. sowie die Entsorgungsanlagen für Schmutz- und Regenwasser dem üblichen Standard und haben sie ausreichende Kapazität und Kapazitätsreserven?

- Sind Erweiterungsreserven der technischen Einrichtungen vorhanden?
- Sind diese Kapazitätsreserven für die Nutzung des Gebäudes ausreichend?
- Sind die baulichen Voraussetzungen für die Kapazitätserweiterungen vorhanden?

- Sind die Prüffristen überwachungsbedürftiger Anlagen eingehalten und evtl. Mängel beseitigt worden?
- Sind in den Prüflisten fristgerecht ausgeführte Prüfungen ausgewiesen?
- Liegen die Prüfbücher am Betriebsort vor?

8 Due Diligence

D 7
- Does installed or planned pipework prevent legionnaire's disease?
- Are installations provided for the prevention of legionnaire's disease in central hot water heaters etc.?

D 8
- Does the pipework have a corrosion protection system or have corrosion protection measures been carried out?

D 9
- Will the property be served by a transformer within the building?
- Who is the owner and will others be served by this transformer?

D 10
- Are the transformer/battery rooms protected against water ingress? If not, which measures are to be taken?
- Is basement room design appropriate for the ground water level?

D 11
- Are floor coverings to plant rooms (cooling and air conditioning plant rooms etc.) above office and shop areas water-proofed against water penetration? If so how?

D 12
- How is energy consumption metered in the building?
- Can the lettable units be metered separately?
- Can the common areas be metered separately?
- Is there provision for metering small lettable areas?

D 13
- Does the building have lightning protection?
- Is there a potential equalisation system?

D 14
- Which technical installations are covered by an emergency generator and/or uninterrupted power supply?
- Are backup circuits and outlets correspondingly marked?

D 15
- Is the tenant responsible for operating and maintaining any plant? If so which plant items?

- Schützt das ausgeführte oder geplante Rohrleitungssystem vor Legionellenbildung?
- Sind technische Vorrichtungen zur Legionellenbekämpfung bei der zentralen Warmwasserbereitung etc. vorhanden?

- Sind für das Rohrleitungssystem Korrosionsschutzmaßnahmen vorhanden oder durchgeführt worden?

- Wird das Gebäude durch eine im Objekt befindliche Trafostation versorgt?
- Wer ist Eigentümer und werden noch Dritte durch diese Station versorgt?

- Sind die Traforäume/Batterieräume gegen eindringende Feuchtigkeit geschützt? Wenn nein: Welche Maßnahmen sind zu ergreifen?
- Ist bei der Anlage der Kellergeschosse auf den Grundwasserstand Rücksicht genommen worden?

- Sind die Bodenaufbauten der Technikräume (Klimazentralen etc.) über den Büro- und Ladenflächen gegen eindringende Feuchtigkeit abgedichtet? Wenn ja, wie?

- Wie erfolgt die Messung des Energieverbrauchs im Gebäude?
- Gibt es für die einzelnen Mietbereiche getrennte Zähler?
- Gibt es für die Gemeinschaftsbereiche getrennte Zähler?
- Können kleinteilig vermietete Flächen mit Zählern ausgestattet werden?

- Verfügt das Gebäude über Blitzschutz?
- Gibt es einen Potenzialausgleich?

- Welche Systeme (technischen Einrichtungen) werden durch ein Notstromaggregat und/oder unterbrechungsfreie Stromversorgung gesichert?
- Sind die ersatzstromversorgten Stromkreise und Steckdosen entsprechend gekennzeichnet?

- Gibt es technische Einrichtungen, welche vom Mieter eigenverantwortlich betrieben, gewartet und instand gesetzt werden? Wenn ja, welche?

8 Due Diligence

D 16
- Is there an access control system? If so, in which areas?
- Can the system capacity be extended?
- Can the system be separated for different lettable areas?

D 17
- What ventilation and/or air conditioning systems have been installed in the building?
- Which areas are ventilated and cooled?
- Can the system capacity be extended?

D 18
- What medium is used in the cooling equipment?

D 19
- Has the maintenance of the fire protection system been undertaken and documented correctly (fire alarms, fire protection shutters etc.)?

D 20
- Is there a defect reporting mechanism for the fire alarm system?

D 21
- Has the prescribed 25 year sprinkler inspection (including pipe-work and tank) taken place? If so, what were the results?

D 22
- Are there alarm systems? If so what type?

D 23
- Do elevators, escalators etc. comply with industry standards and is there sufficient capacity?
- Are traffic design calculations available?
- Can the elevators and other installations be rated as good?
- What are the maximum/average waiting times for each vertical transportation service?

D 24
- Is there a permanently manned system for reporting malfunctions? If so where?
- Which breakdowns are reported?

D 25
- Is the building management system (if provided) connected to all technical plant and equipment?

D 26
- Are there adequate openings for installing large items of plant such as transformers, chillers or diesel aggregates?

8 Due Diligence

- Gibt es ein Zugangskontrollsystem? Wenn ja, in welchem Umfang?
- Ist dieses System erweiterbar?
- Ist das System in mehrere Mietbereiche aufteilbar?

- Welche Lüftungs- und/oder Kühlungssysteme sind im Gebäude installiert?
- Welche Bereiche werden belüftet oder gekühlt?
- Ist eine Erweiterung der Systeme möglich?

- Welche Kältemittel werden in den Kühlanlagen eingesetzt?

- Wurden die Wartungen der Brandschutzeinrichtungen ordnungsgemäß durchgeführt und dokumentiert (Brandmeldeanlagen, Brandschutzklappen etc.)?

- Verfügt die Brandmeldezentrale über eine eigene Störmeldeüberwachung?

- Sind die vorgeschriebenen 25-Jahres-Prüfungen der Sprinkleranlagen komplett einschließlich Rohrleitungen und Tank durchgeführt worden? Wenn ja, mit welchem Ergebnis?

- Gibt es Alarmmeldesysteme? Wenn ja, welche?

- Entsprechen die Förderanlagen (Aufzug, Rolltreppen etc.) dem üblichen Standard und ist ihre Leistungsfähigkeit ausreichend?
- Liegt eine Förderleistungsberechnung vor?
- Können die Aufzugs- und Förderanlagen als gut kategorisiert werden?
- Welche maximalen/mittleren Wartezeiten ergeben sich bei den jeweiligen Aufzugs- und Förderanlagen?

- Ist eine Störmeldeübertragung an eine ständig besetzte Stelle vorhanden? Wenn ja, wo?
- Welche Störmeldungen laufen auf?

- Sind bei Vorhandensein einer Gebäudeleittechnik alle technischen Anlagen aufgeschaltet?

- Sind ausreichend große Installationsöffnungen für Großgeräte wie Trafo, Kältemaschinen oder Dieselaggregate vorhanden?

Avoid the real estate mistake

Test your knowledge gained in this unit by identifying these real estate mistakes.

1. The office *turnover / take-up* has improved in the last quarter.
2. There are separate electricity *counters / meters* for each tenant space.
3. Does natural *lighting / lightening* correspond to the room depth?
4. The *offer / supply* of office space in the market has increased.

Improve your style

Exchange the word/phrase in brackets with a more appropriate expression from this unit.

5. Is the delivery area (big enough) _____?
6. Does the (rubbish) _____ removal system meet demand?
7. The structural integrity of the curtain walling system is (ok) _____?
8. Does the building (break) _____ any statutory fire regulations?

Test your real estate vocabulary

9. Does the property have potential for (Drittverwendbarkeit)?
   _____

10. The property is subject to (Grundstücksbelastungen)
    _____

11. Does the building comply with (Bauordnungen/Bauvorschriften)?
    _____

12. Is there (Altlasten) on the site?
    _____

1. take-up | 2. meters | 3. lighting | 4. supply | 5. appropriately/adequately sized | 6. waste/refuse | 7. satisfactory | 8. breach | 9. alternative uses | 10. encumbrances | 11. building regulations | 12. contamination

Property Development 9

- Stakeholders and Development Team Members 197
- Development Programme 198
- Drawings and Documents . 203
- Development Appraisal 204
- Property Development Finance 205
- Term Sheets and Loan Agreements 207
  - Term 207
  - Equity contribution 207
  - Conditions precedent 208
  - Development covenants 209
  - Repayment 210
  - Financial covenants 210
  - Drawdown conditions 210
  - Default 211
- Planning and Site Investigation 212
- Types of Contract 213
- Costs and Fees 214
- Payments 215
- Tendering / Procurement 216
- Schedules and Ceremonies 218
- Timing / Delays 218
- Completion, Acceptance and Handover 220
- Snagging Items 222
  - Letter to contractor with schedule of defects 223
  - Letter to contractor regarding latent defects 224
- Avoid the real estate mistake, improve your style and test your real estate vocabulary..................... 226

9 Property Development

> ⚠️ **False friend:**
>
> Projektentwicklung
>
> Property Development / Real Estate Development ✓
>
> ~~Project Development~~

> ⚠️ **abreißen**
>
> ~~to tear down~~
>
> to demolish ✓
>
> "To tear down" is a colloquial term.

Property development is a highly complex area that combines the skills and knowledge of a range of professions from finance, law, planning, architecture, construction and engineering, to name but a few. This unit aims to cover the different stages of the development process from inception and feasibility through to construction and completion.

The different types of development can be generally classified by the type of change the property undergoes during the development process.

- new build (greenfield site)
  Neubau (Neubauland / Rohbauland)
- new build (brownfield site)
  Neubau (Brache / Konversionsgrundstück)
- redevelopment (demolition)
  Sanierung (Abbruch / Abriss)
- redevelopment (partial demolition)
  Sanierung (Teilabriss)
- refurbishment (retention of existing structure/façade)
  Teilsanierung (Gebäude entkernen)
- change of use / conversion
  Nutzungsänderung / Umbau / bauliche Veränderung

9 Property Development

Stakeholders and Development Team Members

There are a number of stakeholders and development team members involved in any project. Some of the key roles are provided below.

English	German
clerk of works	Bauaufseher
client / principal	Bauherr / Auftraggeber
consultants - planning consultant - investment agent - lettings agent - valuation surveyor	Berater - Bauingenieur - Immobilienmakler An- und Verkauf - Vermietungsmakler - Gutachter
contractor - main contractor / general contractor - subcontractor - site agent	Auftragnehmer / Bauunternehmen - Hauptunternehmer / **General-unternehmer** - Subunternehmer - Bauleiter des Auftragnehmers
design team - architect - space planner and interior designer - landscape architect - structural engineer - building services engineer	Fachplaner - Architekt - Innenarchitekt - Landschaftsarchitekt - Statiker - Ingenieur für Gebäudetechnik
planning authorities - local planning authorities (LPA)	Bauämter - regionale und kommunale Planungsbehörden
project manager	Projektleiter
quantity surveyor (UK)	Architekt / Kosten- und Abrechnungsingenieur
supplier	Lieferant

Fachplaner

~~planning specialists~~

design team ✓

The word "planning" in the development context is usually associated with the Baugenehmigungs-prozess

The differences between a **Generalübernehmer** and a **Generalunternehmer** are best described in English as follows:

A Generalübernehmer is a firm that undertakes to supply all the services required for the completion of a building contract but unlike a Generalunternehmer does not carry out any of the work itself but rather employs subcontractors. A Generalunternehmer carries out at least some of the work itself.

9 Property Development

Development Programme
Projektentwicklungsprogramm

The following table provides phrases for general activities in development and project management. The scope of activities can vary between developments and the perspectives and roles of the individuals involved. The activities are grouped under activity headings and are not necessarily in chronological order.

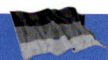

English	German
Opportunity Analysis	**Chancenanalyse**
- identify opportunity	- Chance identifizieren
- undertake market analysis	- Marktanalyse durchführen
- identify needs and prepare business case	- Bedarf ermitteln und Geschäftskonzept erstellen
- identify site	- Standort bestimmen
Feasibility Study	**Machbarkeitsstudie**
- undertake development appraisal	- Projektentwicklungsbewertung/Wirtschaftlichkeitsberechnung durchführen
- estimate revenue and costs	- Einnahmen und Kosten schätzen (Kosten-Nutzen-Schätzung)
- establish profit margin	- Erlösspanne bestimmen
- establish capital investment required	- erforderliches Investitionskapital bestimmen
- establish project budgets	- Projektbudgets bestimmen
- establish funding strategy	- Finanzierungsstrategie ausarbeiten
- prepare feasibility studies and report	- Machbarkeitsstudien und -bericht erstellen
- present briefing and business case and gain approval to proceed	- Briefing und Geschäftskonzept präsentieren und Zustimmung zum Handeln einholen
- prepare strategic brief	- strategischen Ansatz erstellen
Appoint Consultants	**Fachberater beauftragen**
- define consultant's roles, responsibilities, duties and scope of service	- Rollen, Zuständigkeiten, Pflichten und Leistungsumfang von Fachberatern festlegen
- prepare and agree consultant's pre-qualification questionnaire	- Fragenkatalog zur Präqualifikation von Fachberatern erstellen und vereinbaren
- interview consultants	- Gespräche mit Fachberatern führen
- select and appoint consultant	- Fachberater wählen und beauftragen

9 Property Development

English	German
Outline Design	**Allgemeiner Entwurf / Vorplanung**
- prepare outline proposal/ conceptual design	- Vorprojekt/Konzeption erstellen
- determine type of construction, quality of materials, standard of workmanship	- Bauform, Materialqualität, Ausführungsqualität bestimmen
- provide an approximation of construction costs	- grobe Kostenschätzung vornehmen
- prepare, agree and issue initial project brief and objectives and project strategy	- erste Projektbeschreibung mit Zielsetzung und Projektstrategie erstellen, vereinbaren und ausgeben
- consult statutory authorities	- einschlägige Behörden hinzuziehen
Detailed Design	**Ausführungsplanung**
- undertake design development	- Konzeptentwicklung vornehmen
- produce construction drawings	- Bauzeichnungen anfertigen
- produce building specifications	- Baubeschreibungen anfertigen
- revise cost estimate	- Kostenschätzung überarbeiten
Surveys and Investigations	**Messungen und Untersuchungen**
procure and carry out, report and issue:	Beschaffung und Durchführung, Berichterstattung und Ausgabe:
- topographical survey	- topografische Aufnahme
- geotechnical survey	- geotechnische Erkundung / Bodengutachten
- environmental survey	- Umweltgutachten
- traffic survey	- Verkehrserhebung
- ecological survey	- ökologische Untersuchung / Umweltverträglichkeitsprüfung
- existing buildings survey	- Baubestandsaufnahme
- archaeological (desktop) survey	- archäologische Aufnahme (Desktop)
- **asbestos** survey	- Asbestbestandsaufnahme
- noise/acoustic survey	- schalltechnische/akustische Aufnahme
- contamination survey	- Kontaminationsgutachten

Language trap!
English: asbestos
German: Asbest

9 Property Development

English	German
Land Acquisition / Lease Contracts	**Grunderwerb / Mietverträge**
- carry out due diligence and establish site ownership	- Due-Diligence-Prüfungen vornehmen und Eigentumsnachweis ermitteln
- negotiate land acquisition	- Grunderwerb aushandeln
- negotiate leases and agree heads of terms	- Mieten aushandeln und Grundsatzvereinbarungen (Heads of Terms) schließen
- prepare and finalise land purchase	- Grundstückserwerb vorbereiten und abschließen
- prepare and finalise lease contracts	- Mietverträge vorbereiten und abschließen
Statutory Consents and Approvals	**Genehmigungsplanung**
- identify all statutory consents required	- alle gesetzlich erforderlichen Zustimmungen bestimmen
- prepare and agree strategy for obtaining planning and other consents	- Strategie für den Erhalt von Baugenehmigungen und anderen Zustimmungen erstellen und vereinbaren
- engage in pre-application consultation with local authorities and stakeholders	- Konsultationen mit lokalen Behörden und Interessenvertretern aufnehmen
- prepare and conduct public exhibition/public consultation period	- Bürgerbeteiligung/Öffentlichkeitbeteiligung und öffentliche Auslegung der Bebauungsplans vorbereiten und durchführen
- prepare and submit detailed planning application	- detailliertes Baugesuch formulieren und Baugenehmigung beantragen
- obtain detailed planning consent	- detaillierte Baugenehmigung erwirken
Financing	**Finanzierung**
- apply for financing	- Finanzierung beantragen
- obtain offers for financing	- Finanzierungsangebote einholen
- select and sign financing agreement	- Finanzierungsvertrag auswählen und unterzeichnen

9 Property Development

English 🇬🇧	German 🇩🇪
Marketing	**Vermarktung**
- establish sales and marketing strategy	- Verkaufs- und Vermarktungsstrategie festlegen
- send mail shots	- Mailings versenden
- instruct the design of sales particulars and brochures	- Gestaltung des Verkaufsprospekts und von Broschüren beauftragen
- instruct the design and erection of site boards and site hoardings	- Design und Aufstellung von Baustellenschildern und Bauzäunen beauftragen
- arrange launching ceremonies	- Eröffnungsfeiern arrangieren
- send invitations	- Einladungen versenden
- design and install show flats / show suites	- Musterwohnungen/-büros entwerfen und ausstatten
Production Information / Prepare Tender Documentation	**Projektanforderungen / Vorbereitung der Vergabe**
- prepare production information for tender purposes	- Projektanforderungen für Ausschreibungszwecke formulieren
- prepare and agree tender documents	- Ausschreibungsunterlagen erstellen und vereinbaren
- prepare schedules of rates, schedules of quantities, schedules of works	- Stundenlohnverträge, Leistungsverzeichnisse, Bauablaufpläne erstellen
- prepare contracts and appointment documents	- Verträge und Beauftragungsunterlagen erstellen
Tendering / Contracting	**Ausschreibung / Auftragsvergabe**
- selection of appropriate procurement process	- Wahl des geeigneten Auswahlverfahrens
- invite contractors' tenders	- Ausschreibungen zur Angebotsabgabe
- review, evaluate, interview tenders	- Prüfung, Bewertung und Befragung von Anbietern
- select contractor	- Auftragnehmer wählen
- agree construction contract	- Bauvertrag vereinbaren
- appoint contractor	- Auftragnehmer beauftragen

Production Information refers to the detailed completion of all documents (drawings, specifications etc.) ready for the tendering and contract stage.

9 Property Development

English	German
Budget Control / Cost Control	**Budgetkontrolle / Kostenüberwachung**
- prepare and issue pre-tender cost estimate	- Kostenschätzung im Vorfeld der Ausschreibung erstellen und ausgeben
- prepare and issue project budget and total expenditure forecast	- Projektbudget- und Gesamtausgabenprognose erstellen und ausgeben
- prepare and issue interim total expenditure forecast and cost plan	- Kostenprognose und Kostenaufstellung (Zwischenstand) erstellen
- prepare and issue final total expenditure forecast and cost plan	- endgültige Gesamtausgabenprognose erstellen und endgültigen Gesamtkostenplan erstellen und ausgeben (Kostenvoranschlag)
Mobilisation / Preparation	**Bauvorbereitung**
- issue detailed information to the contractor	- eingehende Angaben an den Auftragnehmer ausgeben
- arrange site handover to the contractor	- Übergabe vor Ort mit dem Auftragnehmer vereinbaren
Construction	**Bau**
- monitor planned schedule	- Zeitablaufplan überwachen
- control progress and cost of construction work	- Fortschritt und Kosten der Bauarbeiten kontrollieren
- substructures	- Unterbauten
- superstructures	- Überbauten
- envelope including roof	- Gebäudehülle einschließlich Dach
- building services	- Gebäudetechnik
- fit-out	- Ausstattung
- external works and landscaping	- Außenarbeiten und Gestaltung der Außenanlagen
- services commissioning	- gebäudetechnische Inbetriebnahme
- specialist/tenant fit-out	- Spezialausstattung / Mieterausstattung

The term **"mobilisation"** is used to describe the contractor's preparation activity before the start of construction. The word "mobilise" means to assemble, prepare, coordinate, and put into operation.

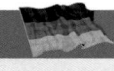

9 Property Development

English	German
Post Practical Completion	**Nach Abnahme**
- identify defects	- nach Mängeln überprüfen
- issue 'as-built' drawings	- Bestandspläne ausgeben
- preparation of final accounts	- Schlussrechnungen erstellen
- reconcile costs	- Kosten abstimmen
- certification of final completion	- endgültiges Übernahmeprotokoll ausstellen
- prepare final accounts	- Schlussrechnungen erstellen
- release retention monies	- Sicherheitssummen/einbehaltene Beträge freigeben

Drawings and Documents

English	German
as-is drawings / as-built drawings	Bestandspläne
details drawings with more specific information about a component or element	Detailzeichnungen
diagrams non-scaled views showing arrangements of systems and connections e.g. lighting or wiring	Strangschema (Wasser- oder Heizungsleitungen) / Schaltschema / Schaltbild (Elektro)
elevation	Ansicht
perspectives, isometric drawings and CAD	Perspektiven, isometrische Darstellungen, CAD
plans	Grundriss-/Aufrissplan
programme	Zeitplan
schedules data about materials, products and equipment	Aufstellungen / Übersichten zu den verwendeten Materialen, Produkten und Ausstattungen
scope of works	Leistungsumfang / Leistungsverzeichnis
sections	Schnitte
specifications	Baubeschreibung

9 Property Development

Development Appraisal

In the UK, the word appraisal refers to the analysis which is undertaken to assess if a development project is feasible as well as to obtain finance. Appraisals are used to determine the price that should be paid for development land, the construction budget required as well as the profit that a project will make.

> See page 171 for differences between valuation and appraisal

English	German
break-even point	Gewinnschwelle / Rentabilitätsgrenze
developers' yield	Projektentwicklerrendite
feasibility / feasibility study	Durchführbarkeits-/Machbarkeitsstudie
internal rate of return (IRR)	interner Zinsfuß
latent value	latenter Wert / potenzieller Wert z.B. von Entwicklungsgrundstücken oder Objekten mit Umbaufähigkeit/Umnutzungsfähigkeit
residual method - assumptions - construction costs - developers' profit/return - gross capital value - gross development value - land price - land value - rental income	Residualverfahren - Annahmen - Baukosten - Projektentwicklungsgewinn - Bruttokapitalwert - Marktwert bei Fertigstellung - Grundstückspreis - Grundstückswert - Mieterträge
sensitivity analysis	Sensitivitätsanalyse

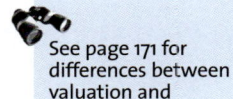

> See page 201 and page 210 for further development costs

9 Property Development

Property Development Finance

Development finance is also known as bridging, building or construction finance. The term is used to describe short-term, interest-bearing loans which cover all or part of the cost of development.

English	German
asset value	Sachwert
base lending rate	Leitzins
borrower	Darlehensnehmer
break-even point	Gewinnschwelle / Rentabilitätsgrenze
capital	Kapital
capitalised income value	Ertragswert
collateral	Kreditsicherheit / zusätzliche Sicherheit
compulsory auction	Zwangsversteigerung
debt	Fremdkapital
default	Verzug
drawdown	Auszahlung / u.a. Inanspruchnahme (bei Krediten)
duty of care letter	Sorgfaltspflichterklärung
equity	Eigenkapital
fees	Gebühren
- administration fee / arrangement fee / servicing fee	- Bearbeitungsgebühr
- commitment fee	- Zusageprovision
- drop dead fee / abortive fee	- vorvertragliche Bearbeitungsgebühr
- market flex clause	- Marktanpassungsklausel
- valuation fee	- Bewertungsgebühr
- prepayment fee	- Vorfälligkeitsgebühr
- non-utilization fee	- Nichtabnahmeprovision
- stand-by fee	- Bereitstellungsprovision
- tail-end fee / exit fee / end fee	- Exit-Gebühr / Erfolgsgebühr

The language used for property financing terms may differ depending on the bank.

9 Property Development

English	German
financial covenants	Finanzkennziffern/-zahlen
- interest cover ratio (ICR)	- Zinsdeckungsgrad
- loan to value ratio (LTV)	- Beleihungsauslauf / Beleihungssatz
- loan to cost (LTC)	- Kostenquote
- debt service cover ratio (DSCR)	- Kapitaldienstdeckungsgrad
foreclosure	Zwangsvollstreckung
guarantee	Bürgschaft / Garantie
hedging	Zinssicherung
indemnity	Ausfallhaftung / Schadloshaltung/ Entschädigung
interest	Zinsen
- floating rate	- variabler Zins / variabel verzinslich
- fixed rate	- Festzinssatz / fest verzinslich
- interest rate	- Zinsrate / Zinssatz
- interest rate hedging instrument	- Zinssicherungsinstrument
- interest on arrears	- Verzugszinsen
lender	Darlehensgeber
leverage (UK: gearing)	Fremdkapitalaufnahme
lien	Grundpfandrecht
- mortgage	- Hypothek
- land charge	- Grundschuld
limited recourse loan	Finanzierung mit eingeschränktem Rückgriffsrecht der Fremdkapitalgeber auf die Projektträger
loan amount	Kreditbetrag / Darlehensbetrag
margin	Marge
maturity	Laufzeitende
mortgage lending value	Beleihungswert
net asset value (NAV)	Nettovermögenswert
outgoings	Ausgaben
overage	Überschuss
pre-letting	Vorvermietung
principal	Kapital / Darlehensbetrag / Hauptsumme
profit	Gewinn / Ertrag

9 Property Development

English	German
repayment	Rückzahlung
- instalment	- Rate / Teilzahlung
- lump sum amount	- Pauschalbetrag
- repayment of principal/capital	- Tilgung / Rückzahlung
security	Sicherheit
term	Laufzeit
underwriting banks	Bankenkonsortium
void (allowance)	Abschlag für Mietausfall
yield	Rendite

Term Sheets and Loan Agreements

The following examples are typical phrases found in term sheets and loan agreements.

> A **term sheet** is a document which outlines the proposed terms between a financing bank and a client and serves as a basis of the final loan agreement.

Term

- The term of the facility shall expire on the interest payment date following (number) months, (number) years after the drawdown date.
  Die Laufzeit des Darlehens endet am Zinszahlungstermin nach Ablauf von (Anzahl) Monaten, (Anzahl) Jahren ab dem Datum der Auszahlung/Inanspruchnahme.

Equity contribution

- The borrower shall provide evidence of contributions in an amount equal to the difference between the total costs and the facility. At the discretion of the borrower, these may take the form of cash equivalent contributions or subordinated shareholder or affiliate loans.
  Der Kreditnehmer hat nachzuweisen, dass die Einlagen in Höhe des Differenzbetrags zwischen den Gesamtkosten und dem Darlehen geleistet wurden (Eigenkapitalbeteiligung). Es steht dem Kreditnehmer frei, diese als Barwerteinlagen oder als nachrangige Gesellschafter- oder Gruppendarlehen zu leisten.

9 Property Development

conditions precedent
The term conditions precedent refers to events which must take place by one party to a contract before the other party must perform their part.

covenant information
Information about the tenant(s), their business and their financial strength

Conditions precedent

- borrower's articles of association and company registration documents
  Satzung oder Gründungsurkunde des Darlehensnehmers sowie Unterlagen über die Eintragung der Gesellschaft im Handelsregister

- audited annual financial statements for borrowers and certified statements from partners (annual report, profit and loss statement and balance sheet)
  geprüfter Jahresabschluss des Kreditnehmers und bestätigte Angaben der Geschäftspartner (Jahresbericht, Gewinn- und Verlustrechnung und Bilanz)

- certified land register extract or priority notice, copy of sales and purchase agreements
  beglaubigter Grundbuchauszug oder Auflassungsvormerkung, Abschrift des Kaufvertrages

- submission of tenancy schedule, lease contracts and **covenant information**
  Vorlage der Mieterliste, der Mietverträge und der Mieterauskünfte

- proof of satisfactory insurance cover and information regarding policy content
  Nachweis über eine ausreichende Versicherung und Angaben zum Inhalt der Versicherungspolice

- submission of planning permission, construction plans and specifications
  Vorlage der Baugenehmigung, der Baupläne und der Baubeschreibung

- a development appraisal including financial analysis, programme, cost plan, drawing and specifications
  eine Projektentwicklungsbewertung einschließlich Finanzanalyse, Bauzeitenplan, Kostenplan, Zeichnungen und Baubeschreibung

- a report from the monitoring surveyor of the development appraisal
  Bericht des leitenden Gutachters/Baucontrollers für die Projektentwicklungsbewertung

- approval of the contractor, terms of all development documents including the building contract and appointments
  Genehmigung des Auftragnehmers, der Bedingungen sämtlicher Projektentwicklungsdokumente einschließlich des Bauvertrags und der in diesem Zusammenhang eingeschalteten Unternehmen/Beteiligten.

9 Property Development

- due diligence reports (commercial, technical, legal)
  kaufmännische, technische und rechtliche Due-Diligence-Berichte
- submission of a current market value and mortgage lending value report
  Vorlage eines aktuellen Marktwert- und Beleihungswertgutachtens
- proof of identity for persons with power of attorney
  Ausweis der vertretungsberechtigten Personen

Development covenants

- practical completion by (date)
  Abnahme / Übergabe (Datum)
- obtaining and complying with all necessary consents, authorisations and approvals for the development
  Einholung und Einhaltung sämtlicher erforderlichen Zustimmungen und Genehmigungen für die Projektentwicklung
- The borrower must not incur costs except as detailed in the approved development plan.
  Dem Kreditnehmer dürfen keine anderen Kosten als die im genehmigten Projektentwicklungsplan dargelegten entstehen.
- Any cost overruns must be funded by the borrower.
  Etwaige Kostenüberschreitungen müssen vom Kreditnehmer finanziert werden.
- The borrower must provide access to the site and allow the bank and monitoring surveyor to participate at site meetings.
  Der Kreditnehmer muss Zugang zur Baustelle gewähren und der Bank sowie dem von der Bank eingesetzten Gutachter/Baucontroller die Teilnahme an Besprechungen auf der Baustelle ermöglichen.
- The lead bank's/agent's consent is required before contractors and professionals are appointed or changes to their appointment are made.
  Die Zustimmung des Konsortialführers muss vorliegen, bevor Auftragnehmer und sonstige Dienstleister benannt/verpflichtet werden oder Änderungen hinsichtlich ihrer Benennung/Verpflichtung erfolgen.
- No changes will be made to the approved development plan except with the lead bank's/agent's consent.
  Änderungen am genehmigten Projektentwicklungsplan bedürfen der Zustimmung des Konsortialführers.

9 Property Development

Repayment

- The facility has to be repaid in quarterly instalments at (amount) % per annum of the total of all allocated loan amounts.
Das Darlehen ist in vierteljährlichen Raten in Höhe von (Betrag)% p.a. des Gesamtbetrags sämtlicher verwendeten Zusatzbeträge zurückzuzahlen.

financial covenants:
Finanzkennzahlen

Financial covenants

- LTV: maximum of (percentage) % at any given time.
LTV to be tested against the value of the completed property in the latest valuation. The lender has the right to call for a new calculation of the property on an annual basis and under an event of default with the costs to be borne by the borrower and at any other time at its own expense.
Beleihungsauslauf: darf zu keinem Zeitpunkt den Höchstsatz von (Betrag)% überschreiten.
Der Beleihungsauslauf ist anhand des bei der neuen Bewertung ermittelten Wertes der fertiggestellten Immobilie zu überprüfen. Der Darlehensgeber hat das Recht, eine neue Bewertung jährlich einmal sowie im Falle eines Verzugs auf Kosten des Darlehennehmers oder jederzeit auf eigene Kosten zu verlangen

- LTC: maximum of (percent) % at any given time. LTC to be tested against the cost of the development.
Kostenquote: darf zu keinem Zeitpunkt den Höchstsatz von (Betrag)% überschreiten. Die Kostenquote ist anhand der Entwicklungskosten zu überprüfen.

Drawdown is a term used in financing to describe how a loan is paid out or "drawn down" in smaller payments over the course of the project.

Drawdown conditions

- The facility will be available for drawing provided: ...
Das Darlehen kann in Anspruch genommen/ausgezahlt werden, wenn: ...

- Subject to the terms of the agreement and upon prior satisfaction of the conditions precedent the facility may be drawn in (number) advances. The minimum drawdown amount per advance shall be (amount) euros.
Vorbehaltlich der vertraglichen Bestimmung und nach Erfüllung der aufschiebenden Bedingung kann das Darlehen in (Anzahl) Auszahlungen in Anspruch genommen werden. Der Mindestauszahlungsbetrag pro Auszahlung beträgt (Betrag) Euro.

9 Property Development

- The build schedule is no more than 30 days behind schedule.
  Der Zeitplan für den Bau ist nicht um mehr als 30 Tage überschritten.
- Each drawdown request is accompanied by evidence of the costs to be financed in accordance with the development plan.
  Jedem Auszahlungsantrag ist ein Nachweis beizufügen, dass die zu finanzierenden Kosten in Einklang mit dem Entwicklungsplan stehen.
- Each drawdown is approved by the monitoring surveyor.
  Jede Inanspruchnahme wird vom leitenden Gutachter/Baucontroller genehmigt.

Default

- non-payment of any sums due
  Nichtzahlung fälliger Beträge
- delayed completion or abandonment of the development
  verspätete Vollendung oder Aufgabe der Entwicklung
- breach of any covenant or undertaking
  Verletzung einer Zusicherung oder Verpflichtung
- misrepresentation
  Falschangabe
- change of ownership or control
  Wechsel des Eigentümers oder Änderung der Kontrollverhältnisse
- a substantial deterioration in the borrower's financial situation
  eine wesentliche Verschlechterung der finanziellen Situation des Darlehensnehmers
- a substantial deterioration in the valuation of the security
  eine wesentliche Verschlechterung der Bewertung der Sicherheit
- termination of any pre-sale or lease agreements
  Kündigung etwaiger Vorkaufs- oder Mietverträge
- If the borrower is in payment default, the bank may charge default interest on the overdue amount calculated on the legal interest rate on arrears, amounting to (amount) percentage points above the base interest rate on an annual basis announced by the Deutsche Bundesbank for the duration of the arrears.
  Ist der Darlehensnehmer in Zahlungsverzug, kann die Bank für die Dauer des Verzugs Verzugszinsen auf den ausstehenden Betrag in Höhe des gesetzlichen Zinssatzes für rückständige Zahlungen (Anzahl) Prozentpunkte über dem von der Deutschen Bundesbank mitgeteilten Basiszinssatz p.a. verlangen.

9 Property Development

Planning and Site Investigation

English	German
plot ratio (US: floor to area ratio)	Geschossflächenzahl (GFZ)
site coverage (ratio)	Grundflächenzahl (GRZ)
area of archaeological interest	Bodendenkmal
brownfield site	Brache / Industriebrache
building regulations	Bauordnung
building control	Bauaufsicht
conservation area	Schutzgebiet
contamination	Altlasten
(detailed local) development plan	Bebauungsplan
flood plain	Aue / Talaue / Überschwemmungsgebiet
greenfield site	Rohbauland / Grundstück auf der grünen Wiese
land use plan (US: zoning ordinance)	Flächennutzungsplan
listed building (US: ancient monument)	denkmalgeschütztes Gebäude
planning application	Bauantrag
- outline planning application/permission	- Bauvoranfrage / Bauvorbescheid
- detailed (full) planning application	- Bauanfrage
- planning permission	- Baugenehmigung
- planning appeal	- Einspruch gegen die Ablehnung eines Bauantrags
preliminary enquiries	Voruntersuchungen
site bearing capacity	Baugrundbeschaffenheit / Tragfähigkeit
site conditions / soil analysis	Bodenbeschaffenheit / Bodenanalyse
remediation (of contamination)	Altlastensanierung
use class	Art der Flächennutzung

Building regulations approval

In the UK, two separate applications are made for planning permission and building regulations approval. The information supplied at the planning stage is therefore considerably less detailed than in Germany where the process is combined.

9 Property Development

- I will be pleased to attend a meeting with your members on (date) in order to speak about the (name of project) and answer any questions.
Selbstverständlich nehme ich gerne an einer Besprechung mit Ihren Mitgliedern am (Datum) teil, um das (Name)-Projekt zu erörtern und etwaige Fragen zu beantworten.

- We are currently in discussions with the planning authority and hope to receive planning permission shortly. We shall let you know as soon as there is any further news.

Gegenwärtig verhandeln wir mit der Planungsbehörde und hoffen, die Baugenehmigung in Kürze zu erhalten. Wir werden Sie unverzüglich in Kenntnis setzen, wenn uns diesbezüglich neue Informationen vorliegen.

Types of Contract

German	English
Vergabe- und Vertragsordnung für Bauleistungen (**VOB**)	General Contractual Conditions for the Performance of Construction Work
Generalunternehmervertrag	the general contractors' agreement
Einheitspreisvertrag	unit price contract
Pauschalpreisvertrag	lump-sum contract
Stundenlohnvertrag	hourly rate contract
Kostenerstattungsvertrag	cost plus/cost price contract

Standard contracts used in the construction industry vary between countries. While in Germany **VOB** is common, in the UK, JCT (Joint Contracts Tribunal) are standard and in the US the AIA (American Institute of Architects) and the AGC (The Associated General Contractors of America) provide standard documents.

9 Property Development

In German, the noun "Kosten" is always used in the plural form. In English, the noun "cost" can be singular or plural depending on how many figures are being referred to.

construction costs refers to a group of costs

estimated final cost refers to one end figure

Where "cost" is used as an adjective to describe a category (e.g. **cost estimate**) it is always used in the singular.

Costs and Fees

English	German
acquisition costs	Grunderwerbskosten
- agent's fee	- Maklerprovision
- land acquisition	- Grundstückskosten
- notary/legal costs	- Notar-/Gerichtskosten
- real estate transfer tax / stamp duty	- Grunderwerbsteuer
actual costs	tatsächliche Kosten
construction costs	Baukosten
contingency sum	Rücklage für Unvorhergesehenes
cost categories	Kostengruppen
cost estimate	Kostenschätzung
cost plan	Kostenaufstellung
(to) deduct	abziehen / einbehalten
demolition costs	Abrisskosten
development charges / connections to all services (water mains, roads etc.)	Erschließungskosten
estimated final cost	geschätzte Endkosten
expense budget	Kostenplan
fee calculation	Honorarberechnung
hourly fees	Stundensätze
incidental building costs / on-costs	Baunebenkosten
letting and agent fees	Vermietungs- und Vermarktungshonorar
lump sum contract	Pauschalvertrag
marketing	Vermarktung
official scale of fees for services by architects and engineers (German)	Honorarordnung für Architekten und Ingenieure (HOAI)
- basic services	- Grundleistungen
- additional services	- besondere Leistungen
professional fees	Honorare für Planungsleistungen
professional indemnity insurance	Berufshaftpflichtversicherung
quote	Kostenvoranschlag
time charge	Vergütung auf Stundenbasis

9 Property Development

Payments

All payment conditions are laid down in the contract. The terms and conditions determine whether payments are to be made at a set date or according to progress.

English	German
advance payment	Vorauszahlung
expenses	Ausgaben
final statement	Schlussrechnung / Endabrechnung
instalment	Abschlagszahlung
interest on default	Verzugszinsen
interim accounts	Zwischenabrechnung
invoice	Rechnung
payment certificate	Zahlungsbescheinigung / Zwischenabnahme
payment conditions	Zahlungsbedingungen
payment schedule	Zahlungsplan
progress payment / interim payment	Abschlagszahlung / Zahlung nach Leistungsabschnitten/Bautenstand
retention	Einbehalt

- We enclose the interim valuation and request payment within the period specified in (clause number) of the contract. Should you have any queries regarding this payment please do not hesitate to contact us.
  Wir übermitteln Ihnen hiermit die Zwischenwertermittlung und erbitten Zahlung innerhalb der in Klausel (Klauselnummer) des Vertrags festgelegten Frist. Sollten Sie zu dieser Zahlung irgendwelche Fragen haben, so setzen Sie sich bitte gleich mit uns in Verbindung.

- I refer to my fee account dated (date) for the sum of € (amount) which is still outstanding. No doubt the matter has escaped your attention. We look forward to receiving your payment of € (amount) by return.
  Ich beziehe mich auf meine Honorarabrechnung vom (Datum) über den noch ausstehenden Betrag von € (Betrag). Sie werden diese Angelegenheit sicherlich übersehen haben. Wir sehen Ihrer umgehenden Zahlung von € (Betrag) entgegen.

9 Property Development

- Payment in the sum of € (amount) for the above project was due to be paid by (date). We note from our records that payment remains outstanding. As you are aware, we are dependent on this payment for funding the project. We would therefore be grateful if you could give this matter your immediate attention.
  Die Zahlung von € (Betrag) für das oben angegebene Projekt war am (Datum) fällig. Aus unseren Aufzeichnungen geht hervor, dass diese Zahlung noch aussteht. Wie Sie wissen, sind wir vom Erhalt dieser Zahlung für die Projektfinanzierung abhängig. Deshalb möchten wir Sie bitten, diese Angelegenheit unverzüglich zu klären.

- I regret that if I do not receive payment for the full amount outstanding within the next seven working days I shall have no alternative but to take whatever steps are necessary to recover the debt including interest and all costs involved.
  Sollte ich die volle überfällige Zahlung nicht innerhalb der nächsten 7 Werktage erhalten, werde ich leider gezwungen sein, die zur Einbringung des ausständigen Betrags nötigen Schritte zu unternehmen, einschließlich der Verrechnung von Verzugszinsen und aller entstehenden Kosten.

Tendering / Procurement

English	German
appointment	Beauftragung
(to) bid for work	sich an einer Ausschreibung beteiligen
competitive tender	Ausschreibung
contract award	Auftragsvergabe/-erteilung
invitation to tender	Angebotsaufforderung
letter of acknowledgement	Empfangsbestätigung
negotiated tender	freihändige Vergabe
open tender	öffentliche Ausschreibung
procurement procedure	Vergabeverfahren
production information	Ausführungsplanung
restricted tender	beschränkte Vergabe
(to) submit a tender	ein Angebot einreichen
tender documentation	Ausschreibungsunterlagen
tender report	Ausschreibungsbericht / Vergabeempfehlung
tender sum	Angebotssumme
tendering	Angebotseinholung

9 Property Development

- We require competitive tenders from three firms for the above sub-contract works.
  Wir benötigen Angebote von drei Unternehmen für die oben angegebenen und im Untervertrag zu vergebenden Arbeiten.

- We learned with interest from (source) that tenders are being invited for the above project. We are specialised in this field of work and should welcome an invitation to tender. Please find attached information on (name of company) and some examples of our recent work.
  Von (Quelle) haben wir erfahren, dass für das oben angegebene Projekt derzeit Angebote eingeholt werden. Wir sind in diesem Arbeitsbereich spezialisiert und würden uns freuen, zur Abgabe eines Angebots aufgefordert zu werden. Anbei finden Sie Informationen über (Firma) sowie aktuelle Referenzbeispiele.

- Thank you for your invitation to tender for the (name of project). We are pleased to be included on the tender list and confirm that we will submit our tender by (date).
  Vielen Dank für Ihre Aufforderung zur Angebotsabgabe für das Projekt (Name des Projekts). Wir freuen uns, dass wir in die Anbieterliste aufgenommen sind, und bestätigen, dass wir unser Angebot bis (Datum) abgeben werden.

- We regret to inform you that we are unable to tender on this occasion due to our current work schedule. We would however be delighted if you would consider us again for any future projects.
  Leider müssen wir Ihnen mitteilen, dass wir aufgrund unserer gegenwärtigen Arbeitspläne kein Angebot abgeben können. Wir würden uns jedoch freuen, wenn Sie uns bei zukünftigen Projekten wieder berücksichtigten.

- Thank you for your letter of (date) accepting our tender for the (name of works) works. We look forward to receiving the contract documents for signing and a successful working relationship.
  Vielen Dank für Ihr Schreiben vom (Datum), in dem Sie unser Angebot für die Arbeiten bezüglich (Name des Projekts) annehmen. Wir sehen dem Erhalt der Vertragsdokumente zur Unterzeichnung entgegen und freuen uns auf eine erfolgreiche Zusammenarbeit.

9 Property Development

- Thank you for your letter of (date) from which we note that our tender was not successful in this instance. We would be delighted if you would consider us again for any future projects should the occasion arise.
  Vielen Dank für Ihr Schreiben vom (Datum), aus dem wir ersehen, dass unser Angebot in diesem Fall nicht erfolgreich war. Wir würden uns jedoch freuen, wenn Sie bei zukünftigen Projekten wieder auf uns zurückkommen würden.

Schedules and Ceremonies

English	German
buffer	Zeitpuffer
completion date	Fertigstellungszeitpunkt
contingency time	Zeitreserve / Zeitpuffer
extension of time	Bauzeitverlängerung
gantt chart	Gantt-Diagramm / Balkendiagramm
master programme	Bauzeitplan
milestone	Meilenstein
overrun	Terminüberschreitung
to resume	wiederaufnehmen
to suspend	unterbrechen
work stages	Leistungsphasen
laying of the foundation stone	Grundsteinlegung
topping out ceremony	Richtfest
opening ceremony	Eröffnungsfeier / Einweihung

Timing / Delays

- The progress of works is being delayed due to (reason).
  Die Ausführung der Arbeiten wird sich verzögern wegen (Grund).

- We are doing our utmost to minimise the delay and its effects and will keep you updated on progress.
  Wir bemühen uns, die Verzögerung und deren Auswirkungen möglichst gering zu halten, und werden Sie über die diesbezüglichen Fortschritte auf dem Laufenden halten.

- A delay is now occurring which could be difficult to make up and may increase the cost of the project.
  Es hat sich eine Verzögerung ergeben, die eventuell nur schwer wettzumachen ist und durch die sich die Projektkosten erhöhen könnten.

9 Property Development

- Thank you for your letter of (date) from which I note that you do not expect to finalise the (name of work) by (date).
  Vielen Dank für Ihr Schreiben vom (Datum), aus dem ich ersehe, dass Sie den Abschluss der Arbeiten (Name der Leistung) bis zum (Datum) erwarten.

- Possession of the site will not be possible on the due date. The commencement and completion dates should be set back by (number of days) days.
  Die Übergabe des Grundstücks wird zum Fälligkeitstermin nicht möglich sein. Die Baustart- und Fertigstellungstermine sollten um (Zahl der Tage) Tage verlegt werden.

- Please be informed that the cause of the delay has been dealt with. We are confident that the measures undertaken during the period of delay and the procedures over the next weeks should enable us to make up for lost time and put the progress of the works back on schedule by (date).
  Bitte nehmen Sie zur Kenntnis, dass die Ursache der Verzögerung nun behoben ist. Wir gehen davon aus, dass die im Verlauf des Verzögerung vorgenommenen Maßnahmen und die Arbeiten der nächsten Wochen es uns ermöglichen werden, die verlorene Zeit wettmachen und für die weiteren Arbeiten bis (Datum) wieder im Zeitplan sein werden.

- We will provide you with an estimate of delay in the completion of the works as soon as the consequences have been evaluated.
  Wir werden Ihnen die geschätzte Verzögerung hinsichtlich der Fertigstellung der Arbeiten mitteilen, sobald die entsprechenden Folgen bewertet sind.

- We estimate that the delay will amount to (delay period).
  Wir erwarten, dass sich die Verzögerung auf (Verzugszeit) belaufen wird.

- We are unable to estimate the total delay at this stage, however we will inform you as soon as any information is available.
  Gegenwärtig können wir die Gesamtverzugszeit noch nicht beurteilen, doch werden wir Sie informieren, sobald wir Näheres dazu erfahren.

- Please be assured that we are doing everything possible to prevent delay to the progress and completion of works.
  Bitte seien Sie versichert, dass wir unser Möglichstes unternehmen, eine Verzögerung im Ablauf und in der Fertigstellung der Arbeiten zu verhindern.

9 Property Development

English	German
delay	Verzögerung
timescale	Zeitraum
to be behind schedule/on schedule	(nicht) im Zeitplan liegen
to be completed on time	fristgerecht fertiggestellt sein
to interrupt work	die Arbeiten unterbrechen
to make up for lost time	verlorene Zeit wieder aufholen
to meet/miss/extend a deadline	eine Frist einhalten/überschreiten/verlängern
to move forward	vorankommen
to bring (the meeting) forward	(eine Besprechung) vorverlegen
to postpone a meeting	eine Besprechung verschieben/aufschieben
to set (a meeting) back	(eine Besprechung) nach hinten verschieben

Completion, Acceptance and Handover

The process of completion, acceptance and handover is similar throughout the world, however there are variations to the exact type of documents used and the extent of the defects rectification period.

English	German
acceptance	Abnahme
Certificate of Making Good Defects	Bauabnahmeprotokoll zur Bestätigung der Mängelbeseitigung bzw. Restmängelfreiheit
Certificate of Partial Completion	Teilabnahmebescheinigung
Certificate of Practical Completion	Abnahmebescheinigung
contractual defects liability period	Gewährleistungsdauer
default	Versäumnis
defect	Mangel
Defect Notification Period	Mängelanzeigefrist
Defect Rectification Period	Mängelbeseitigungsfrist
deferment of possession	Verzögerung der Übergabe an den Auftragnehmer

9 Property Development

English	German
handover	Übergabe
inspection for final completion	Besichtigung zur Endabnahme
latent defects	versteckte Mängel
liquidated and ascertained damages	vertraglich festgesetzte Schadensumme / Verzögerungsschadenersatz
occupation	Besitznahme
performance certificate (UK)	„Erfüllungsbescheinigung"
remedial work / making good defects / defect rectification	Mängelbeseitigung / Nachbesserungsarbeiten
schedule of defects / snagging list	Mängelliste
sectional completion	Fertigstellung in Bauabschnitten
statutory defects liability (Germany)	gesetzliche Gewährleistung / Mängelhaftungsfrist
warranties and insurance - collateral warranty (UK)	Gewährleistung und Versicherung - Ausfallbürgschaft / Gewährleistung
- latent defects insurance (UK)	- Versicherung gegen versteckte Mängel
- warranty bond	- Gewährleistungsbürgschaft

Acceptance

Acceptance is the task of inspecting and approving the work that has been performed before **handover** to the client. During the final inspection, all items that are incomplete or require remedial work are noted on the **schedule of defects**, commonly known as the **snagging list**. In the US the word **punch list** is used which originates from the days when a hole was punched in the margin of the document to show which items were complete.

If the building is in a state ready for **occupation** and no substantial defects are found which restrict the building's use a **Certificate of Practical Completion** is issued. From this point onwards the Defects Rectification Period begins for the period stipulated in the contract. In this time the contractor is responsible for **making good** any defects. This is also referred to as remedial or rectification work. A sum of money known as **retention** may be kept until the works are carried out, after which the money is released and a **Certificate of Making Good Defects** is issued which confirms that all outstanding defects have been rectified.

9 Property Development

snagging list
Mängelliste

Examples of Snagging Items

Snagging items can be divided into different categories. Some items however may fall into more than one category:

English	German
aesthetic issues	ästhetische Mängel
design faults	fehlerhafte Planung
material faults and failures	Materialfehler
omissions / incompletion	fehlende Teile / Unvollständigkeit
poor workmanship	Ausführungsmängel / mangelhafte Ausführungsqualität
variations in working practice	Unterschiede in den Ausführungsarbeiten

- The workmanship is questionable as the brickwork is out of line in areas.
  Die Ausführungsqualität lässt zu wünschen übrig, da die Abmauerung Unebenheiten aufweist.
- Dent to metal cladding panel. Replacement required.
  Eindellung an der Metallverkleidungsplatte. Muss ersetzt werden.
- Throughout the staircases minor scuffs/stains were noted to the wall and floor finishes.
  In allen Treppenhäusern wurden kleinere Verkratzungen/Flecken an Wänden und Böden festgestellt.
- Doors on the second floor are ill-fitting. Further work required.
  Die Passgenauigkeit von Türen im zweiten Stock ist mangelhaft. Nacharbeiten nötig.
- poor finish to paintwork in corridor
  Anstrichmängel im Flur
- staining to stonework
  Flecken am Mauerwerk
- poor workmanship to facing brick section of rear elevation
  mangelhafte Ausführung im Sichtziegelbereich an der Rückfront
- Provide missing seal to fire door at second floor level.
  Die fehlenden Dichtungen an den Brandschutztür im 2. OG sind zu ergänzen.

- suspended ceiling poorly detailed and out of line in places
  abgehängte Decke ungenau ausgeführt und stellenweise nicht maßgenau ausgeführt
- Damaged fire protection within riser. Replace where necessary.
  Beschädigter Feuerschutz in der Steigleitung. Muss möglicherweise ersetzt werden.
- Insulation has come loose to the ductwork above the ceiling on various levels. Re-secure and check all other areas.
  Die Isolierung der Kabelkanäle hat sich in mehreren Geschossen stellenweise gelöst. Losgelöste Isolierung wieder befestigen und alle anderen Stellen überprüfen.
- Provide and fit missing skirting board.
  Fehlende Fußbodenleiste bereitstellen und montieren.
- Grouting to wall tiling in sanitary areas incomplete. Further work required.
  Verfugung von verfliesten Wänden in Sanitärbereichen unvollständig. Muss nachgearbeitet werden.
- (Work / Materials) is/are not in accordance with the contract.
  Die (Leistung / Materialien) ist/sind nicht vertragsgemäß.
- The cost of the outstanding snagging items has been ascertained and deducted from the contract sum.
  Die Kosten für die Behebung der ausstehenden Mängel wurden ermittelt und von der Vertragssumme abgezogen.
- Retention monies will be withheld from contract sum until the developer has remedied.
  Einbehaltene Beträge werden von der Vertragssumme zurückbehalten, bis der Bauträger die Mängel behoben hat.

Letter to contractor with schedule of defects

Dear Mr Reed

24-28 Walton Square

The rectification period ended on (date). *In accordance with clause* (clause number) *of the contract, I enclose a schedule of the defects I found during my inspection carried out on* (date of inspection). *Please ensure that the defects listed are made good.*

Yours sincerely

9 Property Development

Letter to contractor regarding latent defects

Dear Mr Reed

24-28 Walton Square

My client asked me to deal with / I am writing regarding a defect in the above works which became apparent on (date when **latent defect** was discovered). *The problem appears to be* (describe the defect).

Please contact me to arrange a joint site inspection.

Yours sincerely

latent defects
versteckte Mängel

- We anticipate that the works will be complete on (date). Please inform us when it would be convenient to carry out the final inspection so that we can arrange to be on site. We look forward to receiving your practical completion certificate.
Wir erwarten, dass die Arbeiten am (Datum) abgeschlossen sein werden. Bitte nennen Sie uns einen passenden Termin für die Endabnahme, damit wir unsere Anwesenheit vor Ort vorausplanen können. Wir sehen dem Erhalt Ihrer Abnahmebescheinigung mit Interesse entgegen.

- We refer to your letter dated (date), where you state that, in your opinion, practical completion has not been achieved. The items you describe are however insufficient to warrant withholding practical completion. Please be assured that it is our intention to rectify these issues at the earliest possible opportunity.
Wir nehmen Bezug auf Ihr Schreiben vom (Datum), worin Sie uns mitteilen, dass Ihrer Ansicht nach die Abnahmefähigkeit nicht erreicht wurde. Die von Ihnen beschriebenen Mängel sind allerdings nicht ausreichend, um die Erteilung der Abnahmebescheinigung auszusetzen. Seien Sie versichert, dass wir diese Mängel so bald wie möglich bereinigen werden.

9 Property Development

- We enclose a schedule of defects for your attention. Please carry out the necessary remedial work without delay.
  Wir legen eine Mängelliste zu Ihrer Kenntnisnahme bei. Bitte nehmen Sie die erforderlichen Nachbesserungen unverzüglich vor.
- Thank you for your letter dated (date) scheduling the defects you require to be made good. We are making arrangements to make good the items on your schedule.
  Vielen Dank für Ihr Schreiben vom (Datum), in dem Sie die zu behebenden Mängel mit ihren Behebungsfristen aufgeführt haben. Wir werden veranlassen, dass die in Ihrem Verzeichnis aufgeführten Mängel behoben werden.
- We do not consider that the following items are our responsibility as the damage was incurred by the tenants following handover:
  Wir sind nicht der Ansicht, dass wir für die folgenden Punkte haften, da die Schadennahme nach der Übergabe eintrat und von den Mietern verursacht wurde:
- Please be advised, that all defects have been made good according to your schedule. We look forward to receiving a certificate of making good following your inspection.
  Hiermit teilen wir Ihnen mit, dass nun alle Mängel in Übereinstimmung mit Ihrer Mängelaufstellung behoben sind. Wir sehen dem Erhalt Ihres Bauabnahmeprotokolls zur Bestätigung der Mängelbeseitigung bzw. Restmängelfreiheit mit Interesse entgegen.

Avoid the real estate mistake

Test your knowledge gained in this unit by identifying the real estate mistakes.

1. The developer has been granted a *credit / loan* to cover the construction costs.
2. The *project development / property development* is still in the planning phase.
3. The *asbestos / asbest* is being removed from the building.
4. A time *puffer / buffer* is included in the master programme.

Improve your style

Exchange the word/phrase in brackets with a more appropriate expression from this unit.

5. The old section of the building was (torn down) _____.
6. The development will be (finished) _____ in the next two months.
7. Please be (calm), _____ we are doing everything possible to prevent delay to the progress of works.
8. The building is now ready for (using) _____.

Test your real estate vocabulary

9. The development is on a (Neubauland) _____.
10. The (Ausschreibung) _____ documents are being prepared.
11. We have provided the (Bauherr) _____ with an estimate of the delay.
12. Any cost overruns must be funded by the (Kreditnehmer) _____.

1. loan | 2. property development | 3. asbestos | 4. buffer | 5. demolished | 6. completed | 7. assured | 8. occupation | 9. greenfield site | 10. tender | 11. client / principal | 12. borrower

Greetings, Invitations & Personal Correspondence

10

Seasons Greetings 228

Invitations 229

Accepting an Invitation 230

Declining an Invitation 231

Thanking for a
Presentation 231

Congratulations
on a Promotion 232

Congratulations
on the Birth of a Child 232

Retirement 232

Letters of Condolence 233

Thanking for a Gift 234

Declining a Gift 234

Leaving Message 234

Test your prepositions 235

10 Greetings, Invitations & Personal Correspondence

There are many occasions for social business correspondence, these are good opportunities to build goodwill with business partners, colleagues, employees and strengthen personal acquaintances.

The tone of the correspondence varies with the relationship to the recipient and for some occasions it may be more appropriate to send a handwritten message. The language of social business correspondence is sometimes difficult as it must strike a sensitive balance between personal and professional tone.

Seasons Greetings

People in different countries, cultures and religions do not always share the same festivals and holidays. For this reason, the expression **Seasons Greetings** is often substituted for **Christmas** in a greetings message.

Formal

Formal seasons greetings message

> [Name of company] *wishes all its clients and partners Seasons Greetings and* **a prosperous New Year.** *We look forward to seeing you all in 2011.*

a prosperous New Year
ein erfolgreiches Neues Jahr

> *Wishing everyone a Merry Christmas and a Happy 2013 from the* [Name of company] *Team*

more personal

More personal seasons greetings message

> *May the joyous holiday spirit extend throughout the coming year. Wishing you and all at* [name of addressee company] *Season's Greetings from all of us at* [name of company]

10 Greetings, Invitations & Personal Correspondence

Invitations

When inviting guests to attend an opening, reception or other social gathering it is often necessary to request a response in order to plan the event. Formal invitations use the French expression **réspondez s'il vous plait** which is abbreviated to R.S.V.P. For informal invitations a short phrase may be added for example: **Please let us know if you plan to attend**.

> *JQP Associates have moved their offices to* [location]
> *We would be delighted if you could join us between 6.00 and 9.00 pm on Wednesday 3 November 2012*
> *to celebrate our new space*
>
> *JQP Associates*
> *210a Whitcross Street*
> *London W1D 4QZ*
>
> *Please confirm your attendance by*
> *Telephone: 020 5678 9101*
> *E-mail: rsvp@jqpassociates.com*

Formal invitations

> *I have pleasure in enclosing an invitation for our annual conference, which will take place on 15 May. As a **distinguished** and respected professional in the* [logistics sector]*, we would like to ask if you were willing to give a presentation on a subject of your choice.*
>
> *We would be delighted if you are able to accept our invitation. I look forward to hearing from you.*

> [Name of company]
> **cordially invites** you to join us
> for a festive holiday celebration.
> Cocktails, Dinner and Dancing
> Friday, the ninth of December
> Two Thousand and Eleven
> Six o'clock p.m.
> Hotel Bayerischer Hof
> Promenadeplatz 2-6
> 80333 Munich
> R.S.V.P.

Formal

distinguished
angesehen

to cordially invite
herzlich einladen

10 Greetings, Invitations & Personal Correspondence

> Please join us for
> Cocktails / Dinner
> On Saturday, the fourth of November
> At seven o'clock
> Cecconi's
> 12 St. Martins Lane
> London W2T 3NP
> [Name of company]

> [Name of company]
> Invite you to the opening of their new office at
> Eschersheimer Landstrasse 12
> 65812 Frankfurt am Main
> On Friday, November 2, 2012
> At 6 in the Evening
> Drinks & Hors d'Oeuvres

Informal invitations

> I will be in Paris in November and would very much like to take the opportunity to catch up with you. Perhaps you have time to meet for dinner on Wednesday 14 or Thursday 15 November?
> I look forward to hearing from you.

Accepting an Invitation

> Thank you for the kind invitation to dinner on Thursday 12 March. I very much look forward to coming.

> It is a great pleasure to accept your invitation to be a speaker at your conference on 15 May. The topic of my speech will be [Sustainability in Practice].
> I will have the relevant information with me on the day; however I will need a microphone, a **projector**, a pointer and connectivity to my laptop. I would be grateful if you could give me further details on how many people will be attending. I would like to thank you again for the invitation.

⚠ ~~beamer~~
projector ✓

230

10 Greetings, Invitations & Personal Correspondence

Declining an Invitation

Giving a short explanation of why you cannot accept the invitation helps preserve goodwill, but you are not obliged to give a detailed response.

More formal

> *I would like to thank you for your kind invitation to attend the reception being held at your offices / The Langdon Hotel.*
> *Unfortunately, I will be in Brussels at that time. I send my sincere apologies and hope to be able to attend on another occasion.*

> *Thank you for the invitation to* [dinner/your opening event] *on Tuesday May 6. Unfortunately, I have a prior arrangement on that date and will be unable to attend.*
> *I wish you an enjoyable evening / I wish you a successful evening.*

Less formal

> *Thanks for the invitation to dinner next month. Unfortunately, I am travelling and will not be able to attend. However, I look forward* **to catching up** *with you sometime soon.*

Thanking for a Presentation

> *Thank you for presenting at the conference in Munich. We appreciate the work and time that you put into making your presentation so informative and inspiring.*
> *Once again many thanks for making time in your busy schedule to attend.*

More Formal

Less Formal

to catch up
sich treffen

10 GREETINGS, INVITATIONS & PERSONAL CORRESPONDENCE

Congratulations on a Promotion

> *I would like to offer my congratulations on your **appointment** as Managing Director.*
> *I know how you have worked hard to achieve this and I wish you every success in your new position.*
> *With best wishes*

⚠️ Senior managers are often **appointed** or elected rather than promoted.

Congratulations on the Birth of a Child

> *Dear Anna,*
> *My warmest congratulations on the birth of your [daughter / son].*
> *This small gift is a **token** of the joy [I / we] share with you on this wonderful occasion.*
> *Best regards*

token
ein Zeichen

Retirement

> *Dear Adam*
> *I would like to take this opportunity to thank you for all your **dedication** and **commitment** to [name of company/name of department]. It has been a great pleasure working with you and we will miss your humour and expertise.*
> *May I offer my best wishes for a long and happy retirement.*
> *John*

dedication
Einsatz

commitment
Engagement

10 Greetings, Invitations & Personal Correspondence

Letters of Condolence

Letters and notes of condolence are often handwritten to show personal consideration. If you are writing to the family or business partner of someone you knew well you may want to include some personal comments.

Dear Mrs Saunderson,

We were very sorry to hear the sad news. Jonathan will be greatly missed by all of us at Carter & Jones.

*Jonathan was a wonderful person and highly respected colleague. We were very **fortunate** to have known him.*

*We all join in expressing **our sympathy** to you and your family at this very sad time.*

If there is any way in which we can be of help through this difficult time, please let us know.

Yours sincerely

Paul Edwards

Dear Mr Andrews

***We learned today with regret that** your Chief Executive Officer Jonathan Peterson has died and I am writing to express our deep sympathy.*

Mr Peterson was a highly respected member of our industry who contributed so much. He will be greatly missed by all those who knew him.

*Please **convey** our sympathy to Mrs Peterson and her family.*

Yours sincerely

Simon Waterstone

---

fortunate
glücklich

our sympathy
unsere Anteilnahme

We learned today with regret that ...
Mit bedauern haben wir heute erfahren, dass ...

to convey
übermitteln

10 Greetings, Invitations & Personal Correspondence

Thanking for a Gift

Thank you very much for the [bottle of whisky]. *I appreciate your thoughtfulness and look forward to enjoying it.*

Declining a Gift

Thank you for your gift of [the case of Château de Rothschild], *it was a kind gesture.*

With regret, I shall have to return the gift as our company policy restricts us from accepting gifts from business partners/suppliers. However, I would like to assure you that the thought was very much appreciated.

Leaving Message

Working with you for the last five years has been a privilege. Your knowledge has been a benefit to everyone and will be greatly missed. We recognise that there are many exciting opportunities for you in your new position and wish you all the best for your future career.

Test your prepositions

Fill the gaps in the text with the prepositions from the box.

for	to (x2)	on (x2)	in (x2)	at (x2)

I will be in Paris _____1 November and would very much like to take the opportunity _____2 catch up with you.

Perhaps you have time to meet for dinner _____3 Wednesday 14 or Thursday 15 November?

Thank you _____4 the invitation _____5 your opening event on Tuesday May 6. Unfortunately, I have a prior arrangement _____6 that date and will be unable to attend.

I would like to thank you for your kind invitation to attend the reception being held _____7 The Landon Hotel. Unfortunately, I will be _____8 Brussels _____9 that time. I send my sincere apologies and hope to be able to attend on another occasion.

1. in | 2. to | 3. on | 4. for | 5. to | 6. on | 7. at | 8. in | 9. at

Job Applications

11

Curriculum Vitae 238
Length and format 238
Information not to be included 239
Optional information 239
Educational qualifications 240
Academic grades 240
Job titles 241
Personal profiles and career objectives 243
Employment history 243
Using action verbs 244
Additional information 246
Hobbies and interests 246
References 246
Examples
    Student / Graduate CV
    (chronological) 247
    Experienced CV (functional) 248
    Experienced Résumé (US) 248

The Covering Letter 250
Examples
    Graduate applicant 245
    Experienced applicant 246
    Speculative covering letter 246
    Internship / Work placement 247
Online applications 247

**Duties and Responsibilities
of Real Estate Professionals** .. 254
Acquisitions Manager 254
Architect 255
Asset Manager 256
Property Manager 257
Building Services Engineer 258
Construction Manager 258
Developer / Development Manager 259
Facilites Manager 260
Fund Manager/ Portfolio Manager 260
Investment Agent 261
Land Surveyor 261
Lettings Agent 262
Planning Consultant / Planning Officer ... 262
Project Manager 263
Residential Agent 263
Shopping Centre Manager 264
Valuer / Valuations Surveyor 265

Example Correspondence
    Thank you for the interview! 266
    Accepting a job offer 267
    Declining a job offer 267
    Letter of resignation 267

**Avoid the real estate
mistake, improve your
style and test your real
estate vocabulary** 268

11 Job Applications

Curriculum Vitae

A **curriculum vitae (CV)** – which is known as **résumé** in the US – differs in content and style to German job applications. In order to create a good impression with recruiters and employers it is important not to translate a German CV into English but to adapt the contents to create an application that meets the prospective employer's expectations.

The application usually consists of a two-page CV and a one-page covering letter. Certificates, diplomas and references are not included unless explicitly asked for. As this additional information is not provided, it is important that the language used in the application emphasises and "sells" your competencies. Rather than giving a short list of tasks undertaken while working for a company, many applicants choose to describe their work in terms of what they have achieved.

The CV and covering letter should be tailored to suit the company and the position that is being applied for as an application that appears to have been sent to many companies is unlikely to impress employers.

> ⚠ No folder (Bewerbungsmappe) is used when sending an application. Only a CV and a covering letter is required.

English	German
curriculum vitae (CV) / résumé	Lebenslauf
length and format	Länge und Aufbau
educational qualifications	Schul- und Hochschulabschlüsse, berufliche Qualifikationen
academic grades	Noten
job titles	Berufsbezeichnungen
personal profile	Angaben zur Person
career objectives	Berufsziel
employment history	Stationen des Berufslebens
references	Referenzen
covering letter	Anschreiben
online applications	Bewerbungen im Internet
letter of resignation	Kündigungsschreiben

Length and format

There is no absolute rule regarding the length of a CV, but in general it should be no more than two pages. There are different formats for presenting the information in a CV. The exact structure is not as important as a clear and attractive format. The three most common formats are given below and illustrated in the examples at the end of this chapter.

11 Job Applications

Chronological Curriculum Vitae	In the traditional format, personal details are followed by education and work experience, then achievements, interests and referees. Usually the most recent training or jobs are listed first, with earlier career experience at the end. This is known as the 'reverse chronological CV'.
Functional Curriculum Vitae	This format focuses on the key skills and achievements required for the job and evidence of how these skills have been demonstrated. A functional CV is ideal for applicants that have held many different jobs where there is a less clear career progression or gaps in their employment history.
Hybrid Curriculum Vitae	A hybrid CV is becoming increasingly popular. It combines the best of both the chronological and functional CV. The format is generally chronological with an emphasis on skills and achievements.

Information not to be included

Certain information should not be included in a CV as it is considered to be discriminating. Do not include the following information:

- photograph
- information about parents' profession
- date and signature
- certificates, diplomas or references
- school or higher education transcripts
- salary expectations

Optional information

The following information is now not required by employers but is optional. An employer can usually calculate your age from your educational background and career history. Although it is not necessary to state nationality, an employer may be concerned that an international applicant may require a work permit and visa. For this reason you may decide to include this information so that the employer is clear of the situation.

- date of birth
- marital status
- nationality

11 Job Applications

Educational qualifications

Many qualifications cannot be translated directly due to the differences in national academic systems. It is recommended to use German titles and to add the English equivalent (relevant for the country in which the application is being made) in brackets behind in order to assist the recruiter and employer in understanding the qualification.

The Bologna Process seeks to create a system of easily comprehensible and comparable higher educational qualifications. With the introduction of Bachelor and Master programmes at German **Hochschulen** and **Fachhochschulen**, academic degrees have become internationally recognisable.

German Qualification	UK / US Qualification / "Translation"
Realschulabschluss / Mittlere Reife	GCSE's High School Diploma (US)
Abitur / Fachhochschulreife	A levels (UK) / High School Diploma (US)
Lehre / Ausbildung	Traineeship (office) / Apprenticeship (manual professions)
Fachhochschulabschluss	Bachelors Degree (Honours)
Diplom / Magister	Masters Degree
Immobilienkaufmann/-frau	"Management Assistant in Real Estate"
Immobilienfachwirt/in	"Certificate in Real Estate Management"
Immobilienökonom	"Postgraduate **Diploma** in Real Estate"

⚠ A **diploma** in English is a qualification often lower than a Bachelor degree.

Academic grades

The inclusion of grades on a CV is optional. While a student or graduate is usually expected to include the most relevant grades on their CV, a mid-career applicant may choose to exclude grades as their experience and skills have become more important.

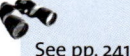

See pp. 241-243 for Example CVs

11 Job Applications

Job titles

Job titles do not always translate well into other languages due to differences in national educational and market structures. While English job titles are becoming more popular in Germany, there are still some significant differences between the scope of work professionals in the property industry undertake and the title their job is given.

What is a Surveyor?
The word surveyor originated from the practice of cartography. Particularly in the UK, the title surveyor is used today as a collective name for professionals who work in the real estate industry. The title can be used to describe the area of work: Valuation Surveyors, Land Surveyors or Commercial Surveyors; within each discipline there are different levels of seniority, e.g. Graduate Surveyor, Junior Surveyor, Trainee Surveyor, Senior Surveyor.

A Chartered Surveyor is a protected title given to individuals who have the required qualifications and experience and who have satisfied the professional standards of the Royal Institution of Chartered Surveyors.

What is a Quantity Surveyor?
A quantity surveyor is a professional qualification and title in the UK and many other countries. A quantity surveyor is specialised in managing building project costs. The work can range from calculating initial construction costs, undertaking feasibility studies, preparing and analysing tender costs, to ensuring quality standards are complied with, writing progress reports and arranging payments. In Germany this work is usually undertaken by an architect, construction manager or structural engineer.

11 Job Applications

The following list provides common real estate job titles and where possible a translation.

> Job titles can sometimes be misleading. With some titles it is not always clear what type of work the position involves. Indeed, a position with the same title may differ between companies.

> See pp. 248-259 for the Duties and Responsibilities of Real Estate Professionals

UK Job Title	German Title
Acquisitions Manager	Immobilieneinkäufer
Architect	Architekt
Asset Manager	Asset-Manager
Construction Manager	Bauleiter
Building Services Engineer	Gebäudetechnik-Ingenieur
Building Surveyor	Bausachverständiger
Civil/Construction Engineer	Hochbau-/Bauingenieur
Developer	Projektentwickler
Facilities Manager	Facility-Manager
Fund Manager	Fondsmanager
Portfolio Manager	Portfoliomanager
Investment Agent	Investmentmakler
Land Surveyor	Landvermesser
Landscape Architect	Landschaftsarchitekt, -planer
Lettings Agent	Makler (Vermietung)
Lettings Manager	Vermietungsmanager
Planner / Planning Officer	Stadtplaner
Project Manager	Projektsteuerer, Projektmanager
Property Manager	Hausverwalter / Objektmanager
Quantity Surveyor	see page 235
Residential Agent	Wohnimmobilienmakler
Shopping Centre Manager	Centermanager
Structural Engineer	Statiker
Valuer / Valuation Surveyor	Sachverständiger / Gutachter

11 Job Applications

Personal profiles and career objectives (optional)

A Personal Profile is a short statement which can be included at the beginning of a CV to summarise your knowledge, experience, skills, attitudes and career objectives. The attributes chosen should demonstrate how you 'match' the specific criteria that are set out in the job description or advertisement. It is important that the statement is evidenced in the CV.

Alternatively, you may call it a Career Objective and can state the type of position you are looking for. This is useful when writing speculative letters.

Examples of personal profiles

> *A highly motivated and ambitious Acquisitions Manager with 10 years' experience in the European property investment market and a proven track record in a range of different property sectors. Now seeking to respond to new challenges and contribute to the successful performance of a multinational company.*
>
> *Enthusiastic Industrial and Logistics agent with a solid market knowledge and understanding of occupiers' operations and needs. Now seeking to develop career with a multinational agency where I will be continually challenged and stretched.*
>
> *Real Estate Graduate with highly developed interpersonal and communication skills. Nine months of work experience in the Property and Asset Management field and solid theoretical knowledge of real estate business. Seeking entry-level position.*

Employment history

In addition to details of previous employers, the work undertaken should be presented in terms of achievements and accomplishments rather than a simple list of tasks. Descriptions are generally listed with bullet points (•) or hyphens (–). Use action verbs and avoid words like 'I' or 'a' to keep the statements short and to the point:

- Turned the occupancy rate of a multi-tenant office building from 40% to 100% in 4 months.
- Managed 5 external companies and ensured that contracts were carried out effectively and efficiently, to the agreed service levels and within budget.
- Developed service levels across the portfolio to exceed client expectations.

TIP!
Concentrate on the tasks in your employment history that are most relevant for the job you are applying for.

Branche:
A branch translates as a „Filiale" in English.

The bank has a branch on the high street

branch ✗

industry / sector / field ✓

11 Job Applications

Using action verbs

Using active words in a CV can make it more dynamic and help create a positive impression on employers. Use action words to describe what you have achieved and the tasks you have carried out.

For current employment use the present tense: **advise**

For previous employment use the past tense: **advised**

These verbs will give you some ideas:

achieve	achieved 15 % reduction in operating costs by renegotiating utilities contracts and updating heating plant
advise	**advised** clients on portfolio and asset management strategies
analyse	analysed the office and retail markets in the EMEA region
arrange	arranged meetings with staff and clients throughout the construction phase
assess	assessed client credit applications for development financing to the value of €10m
assist	assisted the Head of Acquisitions with the compilation of commercial due diligence reports and appraisal calculations
calculate	calculated construction costs for development projects in the region of €8 – 10m
compile	compiled valuation reports for real estate lending purposes
conduct	conducted client presentations on company's services
contract	contracted facility management services for the portfolio to a value of €50,000
control	controlled maintenance contractors' work to ensure compliance with regulations
coordinate	coordinated due diligence work on acquisition projects
consult	consulted clients on investment matters
create	created strong business relationships with institutional pension funds
design	designed new office layouts to increase efficiency
determine	determined the loan values of development projects
develop	developed company policy for procurement of external services
devise	devised new fund management strategy
establish	established marketing initiative to maintain occupancy rates and protect future cash flow
evaluate	evaluated tender submissions for € 120,000 cleaning contract
generate	generated over € 800,000 per annum in fee income with transactions in the North-West region
head	headed a department of 20 letting agents in the office and retail sectors
hire	hired and managed subcontractors to undertake property maintenance

11 Job Applications

identify	identified new sites for logistic development opportunities in central and eastern Europe	
implement	implemented a benchmarking process to evaluate facility management performance	
increase	increased brand awareness	
initiate	initiated tenant retention programme to secure lease extensions	
integrate	integrated property management software into existing systems	
liaise	liaised between tenants and owner, managing conflict and ensuring understanding	*to liaise* vermitteln
maintain	maintained database with client investment profiles and contact details	
manage	managed multiple development projects in Poland, the Czech Republic and Hungary	
monitor	monitored construction progress and compliance with client's instructions	
negotiate	negotiated lease contracts on behalf of owners	
organise	organised the construction process on behalf of the client	
oversee	oversaw fit-out works for 23 retail units for national multiple	
plan	planned a new shopping centre development in Southern Germany	
prepare	prepared monthly and quarterly reports for management and investors	
produce	produced statistics on Frankfurt office letting market	
promote	promoted the company's services at trade fairs and events	
provide	provided employee training on health and safety matters	
recruit	recruited 5 new members to the lettings team to increase market coverage in the Frankfurt region	
redesign	redesigned organisational structures following merger	
reduce	reduced administration costs by renegotiating property management contracts	
renegotiate	renegotiated lease contracts with tenants on behalf of the owner	
represent	represented the client at lease negotiations	
(to be) responsible	was responsible for high profile investment clients	
secure	secured lease extensions with 3 major, international tenants	
select	selected local property management partners for France and Poland	
supervise	supervise all fire safety maintenance works and ensure compliance with regulations	
train	train new members of staff to use Asset Management software	
undertake	undertake regular inspections of tenants' premises	
value	value retail and office properties for lending purposes	
work	worked closely with CEO on portfolio strategy	

11 Job Applications

Additional information

Items such as language and computer skills and information regarding a driving licence can be included in this section of the CV. Below are some common phrases used to describe skills and competencies:

Languages

German: Mother tongue
English: Fluent
French: Good working knowledge
Spanish: Basic knowledge

IT skills

Good knowledge of standard MS Office applications, including email and the internet

Driving licence

Full, clean

Hobbies and interests (optional)

The inclusion of hobbies and interests is optional. Some employers want to know about an applicant's personal interests to get a better picture of what type of person they are, what motivates them and their personal skills. If possible give examples of how your interests relate to the qualities that are required for the job. Giving information about personal interests is particularly important for students or applicants with little work experience as it will give employers evidence of maturity (Reife) and team ability.

References

When applying for a job in English speaking countries certificates and references are **not submitted** with the cover letter and CV. Indeed it is not common to receive a '**Zeugnis**' when leaving employment with a company. Instead, the details of two 'referees' are often provided (BE) or the name of two people who will provide 'references' (AE). The best referees are previous employers, although this is not always possible, in which case other suitable referees include professionals such as teachers and university lecturers and senior business contacts. It is important to ask the referee before using their name. An alternative is to add the sentence '**References available on request**'.

TIP!

In the UK a "**full, clean driving licence**" is a standard phrase. This refers to a standard driving licence for cars:
"**full**", i.e. not provisional or for learners
"**clean**", no penalty points

11 Job Applications

Student / Graduate CV (Chronological)

Markus Schmidt
Street Name, Town Name
County, Postcode, Country
Tel: (+49 069 824 58672)
Mob: (+49 173 310779)
Email: m.schmidt@emailaddress.de

Profile:
Real Estate graduate with agency experience at the London subsidiary of Müller & Partner. A good understanding of institutional clients' needs and the commercial property market. Enjoys meeting new challenges and seeing them through to completion while remaining confident and good-humoured under pressure.

Education & Qualifications:

2007 – 2010	BSc (Hons) in Business and Real Estate Grade: 1.8 (upper second class) University of Applied Sciences. Name of Town, Germany Subjects included: - Valuation - Construction Technology - Planning & Contract Law - Development Appraisal - Investment & Finance - International Real Estate Markets Dissertation topic: The Development of Institutional Demand for Logistic Assets
1995 – 2007	Abitur (A Levels) Name of School, Name of Town Subjects: Mathematics, English, German, Geography

Work Experience:

March – Aug 2009	James Wooton, Frankfurt Student Work Placement - Provided assistance to six senior consultants in the Office Investment Team - Prepared slides for a number of prestigious client presentations - Prepared Investment Memoranda for a variety of office properties including several landmark buildings - Accompanied consultants on client viewings - Solely responsible for maintaining the enquiries database

Additional information:

Languages:	German:	native speaker
	English:	fluent in written English with competent technical English
	French:	proficient user
Driving licence:	Full, clean	
Interests:	**Keen interest** in sport	
	Played in college football team	
References:	Available on request	

There are no mother or daughter companies in English!

~~mother company~~
parent company / holding company ✓
~~daughter company~~
subsidiary ✓

TIP!

UK: In the UK the term **"dissertation"** is usually associated with a substantial piece of work as part of a bachelor or master programme, while a **"thesis"** is part of a PhD or Doctor programme.

USA: In the US a **"thesis"** is usually associated with a substantial piece of work as part of a bachelor or master programme, while a **"dissertation"** is the required submission of a doctoral degree.

keen interest
großes Interesse

11 Job Applications

Experienced CV (Functional)

Elizabeth Parker
Street Name, Town Name
County, Postcode, Country
Tel: (+44 20 41728316)
Mob: (+44 172 814620)
Email: m.smith@emailaddress.com

Profile:
A committed Senior Quantity Surveyor with extensive experience in industrial, office, retail, residential and education projects ranging from home extensions to high profile retail and industrial schemes. An excellent communicator with strong project management, analytical and organisational skills as well as strengths in feasibility, cost planning, control and post contract administration.

Major Achievements:
- Managed a number of major projects up to £35m in value
- Led teams of 4 Quantity Surveyors and 8 Site Agents
- Experienced in procurement process from tendering stage to final account settlement
- Confident in the preparation of complex and detailed final accounts of up to £20m in value
- Extensive experience in the preparation of monthly management figures, and also monthly reports for managing director on project status

Career History:
Senior Quantity Surveyor, Hardcastle Associates, 2002 – Date
- Responsible for the commercial management of all projects run from the northern area office
- Responsible for the management and development of all regional staff
- Provide post-occupancy, facilities management and lifecycle costing advice

Quantity Surveyor, Broadmead & Partners Ltd, 1995 – 2002
- Undertook full range of quantity surveyor duties in mid to large scale office and retail schemes
- Prepared tender and contractual documentation and procedures for office fit-out projects
- Involved with cost control, financial reporting and final accounts for major building works
- Assisted in valuation of completed work

Graduate Surveyor, Street, Brown & McGougan, 1992 – 1995
- Provided assistance with traditional private practice quantity surveying services including new-build housing and small and mid-sized industrial units

Education / Qualifications:
- Qualified as a professional Member of The Royal Institution of Chartered Surveyors 1996
- Diploma in Project Management, Salford University 1999 – 2000
- BSc (Hons) Quantity Surveying, Reading University 1989 – 1992
- A-Levels in Maths, English and History, St Martins College, Bristol 1987 – 1989

Additional information:
- IT Skills: Considerable experience using Siteman, MS Project, Primavera and Microsoft Office
- Driving Licence: Full, clean

11 Job Applications

Experienced Résumé (US)

GREG. F. MARSHALL
273 Street Name – City Name CA 87349 – (821) 555-3198 – greg-marsh@info.com

PROPERTY MANAGEMENT PROFESSIONAL
Over 10 years of commercial and residential property management experience in both strategic planning and day-to-day operations.

Career Contributions
- Consistently achieved owners' target return on investment
- Developed service levels across the portfolio to meet and exceed client expectations
- Introduced tenant feedback mechanism to improve customer service
- Reduced operating costs by renegotiating utilities contracts
- Ensured smooth transition of properties during handover

Career History
Property Manager • B&H Property Management INC,   2005 – **present**
Brea, CA, 36 buildings comprising 26 office and 10 retail units

Property Manager • Corporate Property Services INC, Los Angeles,   2003 – 2005
CA, 8 office complex buildings in Los Angeles CBD

Real Estate Manager • JJ Homes, Fullerton, CA   1999 – 2003
12 residential buildings with 350 units for privately owned housing company

Education
Bachelor of Science in Real Estate, Name of College, Town   1996 – 1999

Affiliations
Certified Property Manager (CPM ®)
Institute of Real Estate Management (IREM ®) California Chapter

TIP! The word **"present"** shows this is your current position

11 Job Applications

The Covering Letter

A CV should always be sent with a covering letter, whether it is sent by email or by post. While the CV is more factual, the letter is an opportunity to expand and demonstrate your skills and enthusiasm. It should be prepared with the same care as your CV.

Start by stating the purpose of your letter, mentioning the specific job you are applying for and if the job was advertised, where you heard about it. Continue by highlighting your qualifications and achievements and specify how they suit the job you are applying for. The letter should always be tailored to the company and position that is being applied for, providing specific examples of how you are suitable. Conclude by requesting an interview or for the employer to make contact with you and mention the best hours they can reach you.

Both the letter and the CV should be posted in a large envelope and not folded.

Job applications by email are now very common. The information provided in the covering letter can be sent in the text of an email with the CV as an attachment. Although email is more informal, the spelling, grammar and content still need to be accurate.

11 Job Applications

Covering letter: Graduate applicant

Phillip Curtis
4 Highgrove Street
Teddington
TW11 9JB
phillip.curtis@mail.com

Name of Company
20 Grosvenor Hill
Berkeley Square
W1K 3HQ London

01 October 2012

GRADUATE RECRUITMENT PROGRAMME 2013

Dear Ms Wakefield

I will be completing a BSc Degree in Real Estate this year and I am writing to apply for a position on the graduate recruitment programme in 2013. My undergraduate courses included international valuation methods, investment appraisal and planning law and have given me a sound theoretical knowledge of the real estate sector and a thorough grounding in management principles.

My work experience includes a placement with James Wotton in Frankfurt assisting in the preparation of sales details for the office investment department. I very much enjoyed working for an agency and found the experience both interesting and rewarding. During my placement there, I discovered I had an **aptitude** for detailed and accurate work. I also learned how to meet tight deadlines and to communicate effectively at all levels.

I have enclosed my CV with further details about my responsibilities and duties at (name of company) and the topics covered on my degree course.

Should you not be recruiting currently, I would appreciate your keeping my name on file for future reference. I would, in any case, be very interested in a brief meeting with you to discuss possible career prospects at (name of company).

Yours sincerely

Phillip Curtis

---

aptitude
Befähigung, Neigung, Tauglichkeit

11 Job Applications

Covering letter: Experienced applicant

Dear Mr Warner

Further to our telephone conversation, I would like to apply for the position of Asset Manager.

Having worked within the property and asset management sector for over ten years, I have extensive experience in managing a range of property types across different geographic regions. In my current position, I am jointly responsible for a pan-European portfolio valued at over £ 800 million.

I have a proven ability to **embrace** challenges, work on demanding **high pressure** projects, while remaining flexible and meeting and exceeding expectations. I am a strong team player with excellent communication skills and look forward to the opportunity of working with like-minded high calibre individuals.

I am confident that I can bring success to the business and look forward to taking my application a step further at interview. Please feel free to contact me if you require any further information.

Yours sincerely

Elizabeth Simpson

to embrace
begeistert annehmen

high pressure
hoher Druck

Speculative covering letter

Dear Ms Johnson

I am writing to enquire whether you have a vacancy in your company for a Senior Surveyor.

I enclose a copy of my CV for your consideration.

In my present position I have been involved in a number of projects including retail, office and industrial schemes. I have experience in all aspects of Quantity Surveying with strengths in cost planning, cost control and post contract administration.

With my proven organisational ability and clear sense of motivation, I feel that I would be able to make a significant contribution to your company's quantity surveying team.

I would be grateful if you would contact me if you have any vacancies in your company; otherwise please keep my information on file in case any future openings arise. I look forward to hearing from you.

Yours sincerely

Ruth Parker

11 Job Applications

Covering letter: Internship / Work placement

Dear Ms Ryder

Application for a six-month work placement in Asset Management.

I am writing to apply for a work placement at Barstow and Partners. I am currently in the second year of a BSc in Real Estate at the University of Applied Sciences in (name of city) and expect to graduate in 2012.

As an integral part of the degree, I am required to undertake a 6 month / one year work placement commencing in March 2011.

I am very keen to work for Barstow and Partners as I understand that you are leaders in the field of asset management.

As you can see from my CV, I have gained valuable skills through my university course and my previous work experience placement and feel confident that I will be able to make a significant contribution to your company.

I would be most grateful if you would consider me for a work placement position. I am available for an interview at your convenience.

Yours sincerely

Susan Edwards

Enc.

Online applications

Many companies and organisations prefer job applicants to complete an online form rather than sending an application by email or post. By using a form the company can ask specific questions and ensure they receive the information they require rather than just the information the applicant chooses to give. This also enables the company to compare applications with more ease.

It is important to take as much care over an online application as a paper one. Make sure you allow yourself plenty of time to look through the form and read the instructions so you know exactly what is involved. It is advisable to copy and paste the questions into a word processing document so you can prepare your answers, particularly for those you find difficult. Consider what the question is asking and give a suitable example that demonstrates the skill or competence the company is looking for.

Use formal language and provide clear, concise answers to all questions. Finally check your text for errors, edit any unnecessary words and make sure your contact details are accurate before submitting.

TIP!

Print off the form first and prepare your answers

Print out the completed copy and proofread it before sending

Keep a copy for reference

11 Job Applications

Duties and Responsibilities of Real Estate Professions

Acquisitions Manager	
Identify and evaluate investment opportunities predominantly through own existing network of property contacts and market knowledge	Identifizierung und Bewertung von Investitionsmöglichkeiten, hauptsächlich durch eigenes Netzwerk im Immobilienbereich und Kenntnis des Marktes
Prepare and present proposed transactions to the investment committee	Vorbereitung und Präsentation der beabsichtigten Transaktionen vor dem Ausschuss
Enact and complete transactions including due diligence, structuring, financial analysis and closure	Abwicklung von Geschäften einschließlich Ankaufprüfung, Strukturierung, Finanzanalyse und Abschluss
Work with and manage external property managers and advisors	Zusammenarbeit mit und Führung von externen Immobilienverwaltern und Beratern
Liaise with external legal, finance and tax advisors, with direct responsibility for the detailed preparation and oversight of all requisite documentation related to acquisitions and disposals	Zusammenarbeit mit externen Anwälten, Finanz- und Steuerberatern mit direkter Verantwortung für die detaillierte Vorbereitung und Aufsicht aller erforderlichen Unterlagen in Verbindung mit Akquisitionen und Veräußerungen
Assist with acquisitions, undertaking due diligence and deal execution	Unterstützung bei Akquisitionen einschließlich Ankaufprüfung und Abwicklung
Assist with the preparation of annual business plans and asset strategies	Unterstützung bei der Vorbereitung von jährlichen Geschäftsplänen und Anlagestrategien
Attract new business with extensive contacts within the investment market	Erschließung neuer Investitionsgelegenheiten mit Hilfe eines umfangreichen Netzwerks im Investmentmarkt
Responsible for sourcing and purchasing land throughout the Northwest	Zuständigkeit für die Beschaffung und den Ankauf von Grundstücken im Nordwesten

11 Job Applications

Architect	
Lead feasibility study, concept design, design development, detailing, client presentations, planning applications	Leitung einer Machbarkeitsstudie, Konzeption und Ausarbeitung von Projekten, Klientenpräsentationen, Bauanträgen
Responsible for design, client liaison and project management	Zuständigkeit für Design, Zusammenarbeit mit Klienten und Projektmanagement
Responsible for the overall management of the office and the work that is produced	Zuständigkeit für die Gesamtleitung des Büros und der auszuführenden Arbeiten
Responsible for tender documentation and detail design	Zuständigkeit für Ausschreibungsunterlagen und die Ausführungsplanung
Assist with the preparation of submissions, projects submittals, tender and construction drawings and documentation including specifications	Unterstützung bei der Vorbereitung von Ausschreibungsangeboten, Projektvorlagen, Angebots- und Bauzeichnungen und Unterlagen einschließlich Baubeschreibungen
Negotiate with clients and contractors	Verhandlungen mit Klienten und Bauunternehmern
Liaise with external consultants and clients	Zusammenarbeit mit externen Beratern und Klienten

11 Job Applications

Asset Manager	
Identification of opportunities for asset enhancement	Identifizierung von Möglichkeiten zur Vermögenssteigerung
Responsible for all aspects of the day-to-day management of a commercial property portfolio	Zuständigkeit für alle Bereiche des täglichen Managements eines gewerblichen Immobilienportfolios
Responsible for rent reviews and lease renewals	Zuständigkeit für Mieterhöhungen und Mietvertragsverlängerungen
Responsible for EMEA property portfolio, managing all aspects of the commercial real estate business	Zuständigkeit für das EMEA-Immobilienportfolio, Leitung aller Bereiche des gewerblichen Immobiliengeschäfts
Management and coordination of agents on lease renewal and void re-letting matters	Management and Koordination von Maklern bei Mietvertragsverlängerungen und Neuvermietungen leer stehender Immobilien
Assistance in the periodic valuation of the portfolio	Unterstützung bei der regelmäßigen Bewertung des Portfolios
Assistance in the preparation of Asset Management plans	Unterstützung bei der Erstellung von Asset-Management-Plänen
Responsible for managing the occupier-profile-mix by facilitating the relocation of existing occupiers and undertaking lettings and renewals	Zuständigkeit für Mietermix durch Aufhebungen bestehender Mietverträge und Neuvermietungen sowie Mietvertragsverlängerungen
Responsible for managing the property risk and maximising opportunities within the portfolio	Management des Immobilienrisikos und Ertragsmaximierung des Portfolios
Negotiate and supervise lease renewals, rent reviews, lettings, disposals and acquisitions	Verhandlung und Beaufsichtigung von Mietvertragsverlängerungen, Mieterhöhungen, Vermietungen, Veräußerungen und Akquisitionen

11 Job Applications

Property Manager	
Responsible for 500 residential units of new-build properties in the South Eastern region	Verantwortung für 500 Wohneinheiten in neu erbauten Immobilien in der südöstlichen Region
Ensure maximum occupancy of properties including securing tenants via marketing and maintenance of website	Sicherstellung maximaler Vermietungsauslastung der Immobilien einschließlich Gewinn neuer Mieter durch Marketing und Pflege der Website.
Deal with day-to-day estate management issues including subletting, alterations, letting, renewals and rent reviews	Bearbeitung von alltäglichen Themen im Immobilienmanagement wie z.B. Untervermietung, Umbaumaßnahmen, Vermietung, Mietvertragsverlängerungen und Mieterhöhungen
Responsible for property management of two client portfolios, including landlord and tenant liaison, supervision of facilities management and liaison with on-site staff, service charge budgeting, property inspection, insurance monitoring	Verantwortung für das Immobilienmanagement von zwei Klientenportfolios einschließlich der Zusammenarbeit mit Vermieter und Mieter, Beaufsichtigung des Facility-Managements und Zusammenarbeit mit den Mitarbeitern vor Ort, Budgetierung der Nebenkosten, Immobilienbesichtigung, Kontrolle der Versicherungen

11 Job Applications

Building Services Engineer	
Advise clients and architects on energy use and conservation for a range of buildings and sites	Beratung von Klienten und Architekten im Bezug auf Energieverbrauch und Energieeinsparung für ein größeres Portfolio von Gebäuden und Grundstücken
Manage and forecast spend, using whole life cycle costing techniques, ensuring that work is kept to budget	Management und Vorausplanung der Ausgaben unter Zuhilfenahme von Lebenszykluskosten-Methoden, um die Einhaltung von Budgets sicherzustellen
Develop and negotiate project contracts	Erstellung und Verhandlung von Projektverträgen
Close liaison with structural engineers, builders, architects and surveyors, and in-house project teams	Enge Zusammenarbeit mit Bauingenieuren, Handwerkern, Architekten und betriebsinternen Projektteams
Responsible for the commissioning, organisation and assessment of contractors' work	Zuständigkeit für die Auftragsvergabe, die Organisation und Kontrolle der Arbeit des Bauunternehmers
Oversee and supervise the installation of building systems	Beaufsichtigung und Kontrolle der Installation der Gebäudetechnik

Construction Manager	
Responsible for appointing consultants and contractors, managing all elements of the "build process" including contract administration	Zuständigkeit für die Benennung von Fachberatern und Bauunternehmern, Leitung aller Bereiche des Bauprozesses einschließlich Vertragsverwaltung
Close liaison with the development and sales and marketing teams	Enge Zusammenarbeit mit der Projektentwicklung und der Vertriebs- und Marketingabteilung

11 Job Applications

Developer / Development Manager	
Responsible for mixed-use development projects from acquisition through to completion	Zuständigkeit für Entwicklungsprojekte für gemischt genutzte Immobilien, von der Akquisition bis zur Fertigstellung
Deal with planning consents	Bearbeitung von Baugenehmigungen
Responsible for preparing schemes and appraisals for board consideration, negotiation of planning permissions and securing pre-lets and pre-sales	Vorbereitung von Projekten und Kalkulationen zur Vorlage im Vorstand, Verhandlung von Baugenehmigungen und Sicherstellung von Vorvermietungen und Vorverkäufen
Undertake market research analysis	Durchführung von Marktforschungsanalysen
Preparation of board reports showing progress against targets	Erstellung von Soll-Ist-Berichten für den Vorstand
Manage and coordinate both internal and external teams	Führung und Koordinierung von internen sowie externen Teams
Manage project teams, including the appointment and management of professional consultants and contractors.	Leitung von Projektteams einschließlich Benennung und Führung von Fachberatern und Bauunternehmern
Identification of new development opportunities	Identifizierung neuer Projektentwicklungsmöglichkeiten
Carry out feasibility, appraisal and due diligence studies	Durchführung von Machbarkeitsstudien, Wirtschaftlichkeitsrechnungen und Ankaufprüfungen
Liaison and negotiation with planners, local authorities, statutory bodies and others involved at the pre and post-planning stage	Zusammenarbeit und Verhandlungen mit Stadtplanern, örtlichen Behörden und anderen Beteiligten vor und nach Erteilung der Baugenehmigung
Handle mid-sized commercial schemes from inception to completion	Bearbeitung von mittelgroßen gewerblichen Projekten von der Planung bis zur Fertigstellung
Appoint and monitor specialist design teams and contractors	Benennung und Beaufsichtigung von Fachdesignteams und Bauunternehmern
Responsible for handover and co-ordination with Project and Asset Management teams	Zuständigkeit für die Übergabe und Abstimmung mit den Projektmanagement- und Asset-Management-Teams
Lead role in producing marketing and promotional material	Leitende Funktion bei der Produktion von Marketing- und Werbematerial

11 Job Applications

Facilities Manager (US: Facility Manager)

Responsible for ensuring the satisfactory operation and maintenance of equipment and building services, project management and minor works (up to €30K)	Verantwortlich für den zufriedenstellenden operativen Ablauf und die Instandhaltung der Anlagen- und Gebäudetechnik, Projektmanagement sowie Reparaturmaßnahmen (bis zu 30.000 EUR)
Lead, supervise, monitor and control the in-house maintenance and caretaking staff	Leitung, Beaufsichtigung und Kontrolle der betriebsinternen Mitarbeiter, die für die Instandhaltung und Hausmeister- arbeiten zuständig sind
Administer and consult on all aspects of facility management	Verwaltung und Beratung im Hinblick auf alle Bereiche des Gebäudemanagements
Control maintenance contractors and liaise with suppliers	Kontrolle der Instandhaltungsfirmen und Zusammenarbeit mit Anbietern
Analyse procedures and processes and recommend strategy	Analyse von Arbeitsabläufen und Empfehlung von Strategien
Advise on repair issues and likely costs	Beratung im Hinblick auf Reparaturarbeiten und voraussichtliche Kosten
Responsible for project management from tendering to negotiation and implementation	Zuständigkeit für das Projektmanagement, von der Ausschreibung bis zur Verhandlung und Durchführung
Liaise with the tenants and the property department	Zusammenarbeit mit den Mietern und der Hausverwaltung

Fund Manager / Portfolio Manager

Devise and implement the fund strategy, including the co-ordination and oversight of all asset and property management functions	Ausarbeitung und Durchsetzung der Fondsstrategie einschließlich der Abstimmung und Aufsicht aller Asset- und Property-Management-Funktionen
Acquisition and disposal of assets across the portfolio	Akquisition und Veräußerung von Assets innerhalb des Portfolios
Assist and oversee the quarterly valuation process	Unterstützung und Beaufsichtigung des vierteljährlichen Bewertungsprozesses

11 Job Applications

Investment Agent	
Responsible for acquisitions and disposals of commercial property on behalf of both existing and new clients	Zuständigkeit für Akquisitionen und Veräußerungen von Gewerbeimmobilien im Namen von bestehenden und neuen Klienten
Deal with office, warehouse and retail disposals and acquisitions and general agency consultancy throughout Southern Germany	Bearbeitung von Büro-, Logistik-, und Einzelhandelsveräußerungen und -akquisitionen sowie allgemeine Investmentberatung innerhalb Süddeutschlands.
Deal with extremely high profile clients	Zusammenarbeit mit namhaften Klienten
Provide advice on acquisitions and disposals	Beratung im Hinblick auf Akquisitionen und Veräußerungen
Build client relationships and provide professional advice	Aufbau und Pflege von Klientenkontakten und professionelle Beratung

Land Surveyor	
Survey works from field to finish	Vermessung von Grundstücken bis zur Erstellung von Abschlussberichten
Manage field team of 5 working on all aspects of geomatics	Beaufsichtigung des 5-köpfigen Vermessungsteams in Bezug auf alle Aspekte der Geomatik
Completion of topographical surveys	Durchführung von topografischen Vermessungsprojekten
Prepare and maintain sketches, maps, reports and legal descriptions of surveys	Vorbereitung und Erstellung von Skizzen, Karten, Berichten und rechtlich verbindlichen Abschlussberichten
Verify the accuracy of survey reports, including measurements and calculations	Verifizierung der Genauigkeit von Vemessungsberichten einschließlich Vermessungs- und Berechnungsdaten

11 Job Applications

Lettings Agent	
Work with high profile retail clients	Zusammenarbeit mit namhaften Einzelhändlern
Liaise with landlords and tenants	Zusammenarbeit mit Vermietern und Mietern
Canvass new lettings business	Akquise von Vermietern als Geschäftspartner
Build and maintain relations with landlords	Aufbau und Pflege von Kontakten mit Vermietern
Arrange and attend lettings viewing	Organisation von und Teilnahme an Besichtigungsterminen
Closing of lease agreements	Abschluss von Mietverträgen

Planning Consultant / Planning Officer	
Negotiate development proposals with local authorities	Verhandeln von Bauvorhaben mit den örtlichen Behörden
Assess planning applications and enforce and monitor regulations	Bewertung von Bauanträgen sowie Durchsetzung und Kontrolle von relevanten Vorschriften
Compile reports and make recommendations for local councils	Berichterstellung und Empfehlungen für Gemeinderäte
Present proposals at public meetings and planning committees	Präsentation von Bauanträgen bei öffentlichen Tagungen und Planungsausschüssen

11 Job Applications

Project Manager	
Management of multiple real estate projects throughout the EMEA region	Leitung von vielfältigen EMEA-Immobilienprojekte
Responsible for delivery of projects (construction and fit-out)	Verantwortung für die Projektausführung (Bau und Ausstattung)
Close liaison with local business teams, service providers	Enge Zusammenarbeit mit lokalen Businessteams und Dienstleistern
Develop project briefs, manage consultant and contractor teams, acting as the client's representative on all parts of the project life cycle for major infrastructure and building projects	Entwicklung der Projektaufträge und Leitung der Berater- und Bauunternehmerteams sowie Vertretung des Klienten in allen Projektphasen für größere Einrichtungs- und Bauprojekte
Responsible for managing a range of planned maintenance and refurbishment projects	Zuständigkeit für die Leitung einer Reihe von geplanten Instandhaltungs- und Sanierungsprojekten
Provide technical advice and undertake inspections of properties	Ansprechpartner für technische Fragen und Durchführung von Objektbesichtigungen
Liaise with tenants and monitor contractor work	Zusammenarbeit mit Mietern und Beaufsichtigung der Bauarbeiten

Residential Agent	
Liaise with vendors and buyers	Zusammenarbeit mit Anbietern und Käufern
Canvass new business	Kundenakquise
Build and maintain relationships with vendors	Aufbau und Pflege von Kontakten mit Verkäufern
Arrange and attend viewings	Organisation von und Teilnahme an Besichtigungen
Responsible for marketing and promotion of properties	Verantwortung für Marketing und Werbung für Wohnimmobilien
Representation of sellers in negotiations with prospective buyers	Vertretung von Verkäufern in Verhandlungen mit Kaufinteressenten
Advise clients and assist buyers in the search for properties	Beratung von Klienten bei der Immobiliensuche

11 Job Applications

Shopping Centre Manager	
Full responsibility for running the centre	Volle Verantwortung der Führung des Einkaufszentrums
Maintain relations with tenants, customers and other stakeholders	Pflege von Kontakten zu Mietern und Kunden sowie anderen Geschäftsinteressenten
Devise leasing strategy and tenant mix strategies	Ausarbeitung von Vermietungs- und Mietermix-Strategien
Responsible for defining target prospective tenants	Zuständigkeit für potenzielle Einzelhandelsmieter
Presentations to local, national and international retailers	Präsentationen vor örtlichen, nationalen und internationalen Einzelhandelsfirmen
Negotiate lease agreements with prospective tenants	Verhandlung von Mietverträgen mit Mietinteressenten
Provide input for marketing strategies and budgets	Input für Marketingstrategien und Budgets
Implement and manage marketing plans	Durchführung und Leitung von Marketingplänen
Assist with the organisation and execution of marketing materials and events	Unterstützung bei der Erstellung von Marketingunterlagen und der Organisation und Durchführung von Marketing-Events

11 Job Applications

Valuer / Valuations Surveyor	
Preparation of valuation reports	Erstellung von Gutachten
Valuation of a diverse range of commercial real estate on behalf of major institutions	Gutachten über verschiedene gewerbliche Immobilien für größere Institutionen
Source and undertake valuations	Akquise und Erstellung von Gutachten
Work in close partnership with local, national and international developers, investors and private buyers carrying out formal valuations for major lending institutions	Enge Zusammenarbeit mit örtlichen, nationalen und internationalen Projektentwicklern, Investoren und privaten Käufern einschließlich Durchführung von offiziellen Bewertungen für große Kreditinstitute
Carry out valuation work for a mixed range of properties including hotels and restaurants	Durchführung von Bewertungen für verschiedene Immobilienarten einschließlich Hotels und Restaurants
Inspection of properties and provision of commercial valuation reports, provision of supporting comparable data, dealing with post valuation/survey queries	Immobilienbesichtigungen und Bereitstellung von gewerblichen Gutachten, unterstützenden vergleichbaren Daten, Bearbeitung von Anfragen nach Gutachtenerstellung

11 Job Applications

> **TIP!**
> The words **"vacancy"**, **"opening"**, **"appointment"**, **"position"** and **"post"** are synonyms for the word job.

Thank you for the interview

Dear Mrs Matthews

Thank you for taking the time to discuss the opening for the position of (Asset Manager). It was a pleasure meeting you on 15 February and learning more about the **opening** and (name of company).

I was particularly interested to hear about (the success of your recent tenant marketing programme). As I mentioned in the interview, I feel that my experience and academic background make me an ideal candidate for this position.

Thank you again for your consideration for this opportunity. Should you wish to contact me, I am available on 0132 289 989.

I look forward to hearing from you.

Yours sincerely

Simon Watts

Accepting a job offer

Dear Mrs Matthews

Thank you for your letter of 10 March offering me the position of (Asset Manager) in your company.

I am pleased to accept the position and have enclosed a signed copy of the contract.

I very much look forward to commencing work on 1 July 2012.

Yours sincerely

Simon Watts

11 Job Applications

Declining a job offer

Dear Mr Morris

Thank you of your letter of 10 March offering a position as (Asset Manager) in your company.

After much careful thought, I have decided to decline your offer and accept a position at another company. This was a most difficult decision to make as I was very impressed with the new business strategy plans for the European portfolio.

I sincerely appreciate the time you have taken to interview me and thank you for your consideration.

Yours sincerely

Simon Watts

Letter of resignation

resignation
Kündigung

Dear Mr Harper

I regret to inform you that I wish to give 3 months' notice of my intention to resign from my position as (name of position). My last day of work will be on 30 September 2012.

An opportunity has arisen for a position which is of great interest to me.

I have very much enjoyed working at (name of company) for the last 4 years and would like to thank you for having me as part of the team.

Kind regards

Simon Watts

Avoid the real estate mistake

Test your knowledge gained in this unit by identifying the real estate mistakes.

1. I have five years experience in the service *sector / branch*.
2. I have *made / given* a lot of presentations.
3. I have nine months *practice / work experience* in the property and asset management field.
4. I am applying for a position as a *static engineer / structural engineer*.

Improve your style

Exchange the word/phrase in brackets with a more appropriate expression from this unit.

5. I have a proven (history of experience) _____ in a range of different property sectors.
6. I (did) _____ a range of duties in mid to large-scale office and retail schemes.
7. I (helped) _____ with the preparation of sales details for the office investment department.
8. I am writing to (ask) _____ whether you have a vacancy in your company for a Property Manager.

Test your real estate vocabulary

9. I have experience in the (Vergabeverfahren) _____ , from the tendering stage to final account settlement.
10. Responsible for all requisite documentation related to acquisitions and (Veräußerungen) _____.
11. Arrange and attend (Besichtigungen) _____.
12. Responsible for (Wohnimmobilien) _____ properties.

1. sector | 2. given | 3. work experience | 4. structural engineer | 5. track record | 6. undertook | 7. assisted | 8. enquire | 9. procurement process | 10. disposals/sales | 11. viewings | 12. residential

Glossary

Term	Unit
acceptance Abnahme	9
access control system *(tech.)* Zugangskontrolle	8
accessibility Erreichbarkeit, Zugang	8
accommodation Räumlichkeiten, Unterkunft	3
acknowledge *(verb)* bestätigen	7
acquisition Ankauf, Erwerb	11
acquisition costs Grunderwerbskosten	9
actual costs tatsächliche Kosten	9
addendum *(law)* Nachtrag, Zusatz	7
administration fee *(finan.)* Bearbeitungsgebühr	9
administrative building Verwaltungsgebäude	3
advance payment *(finan.)* Vorauszahlung	9
advice Beratung	7
affiliation Mitgliedschaft	11
agenda Tagesordnung	2
air conditioning *(tech.)* Klimaanlage, Kühlungssystem	8
alteration, amendment, modification Änderung	8
amenities Nahversorgung, Geschäfte mit Waren des täglichen Bedarfs	8
anchor store, magnet store Anker, Magnetbetrieb	4
anchor tenant Ankermieter	4
ancillary areas Nebenflächen	4
ancillary space Nebennutzfläche	4
application *(job)* Bewerbung	11
appoint *(verb)* beauftragen	6
appointment, opening, position, post Stelle, Arbeitsplatz, Anstellung, Termin	11
appraisal Investitionsbewertung	8
approval Genehmigung, Zustimmung	7
aptitude Befähigung, Neigung, Tauglichkeit	11
arcade Passage	4
architect Architekt	9
area of archaeological interest Bodendenkmal	9
arrangement fee Bearbeitungsgebühr	9
arrears (to be in arrears) Verzug	6
articles of association Satzung oder Gesellschaftsvertrag	8
as-built drawings (as-is drawings) *(tech.)* Bestandspläne	9
ascertain *(verb)* bestimmen, feststellen	9
assembly Zusammenbau, Montage	5
asset deal Grundstückskauf	7
asset value Sachwert	9
assignment Vertragsübernahme, Vertragsübergang	8
apprenticeship Ausbildung	11
Automated Storage and Retrieval System (AS/RS) *(tech.)* automatisches Hochregallagersystem	5
bank guarantee Bankbürgschaft	8
bar Bar	4
base lending rate Leitzins	9
basement Untergeschoss	8
bear costs Kosten tragen	7
bespoke maßgefertigt	3
bid Gebot	7
blockage Verstopfung	6
bookseller, bookshop Buchhandlung	4
borrower Kreditnehmer, Darlehensnehmer	9
breach of contract *(law)* Vertragsverletzung	7
break option, break clause *(law)* Sonderkündigungsrecht	8
break-out areas/zones Rückzugsräume	3
breakdown *(tech.)* Störung	6
break-even point Gewinnschwelle, Rentabilitätsgrenze	9
bricklayer Maurer	6
brickwork Mauerwerk	6
bridal wear Brautbekleidung	4
brief Anweisung, Projektauftrag	7

Glossary

Term	Unit
brownfield site Brache, Industriebrache	9
buffer Zeitpuffer	9
building control Bauaufsicht	9
Building Management System (BMS) *(tech.)* Gebäudeleittechnik, Gebäudemanagementsystem	8
building regulations Bauordnung	9
building services *(tech.)* technischen Einrichtungen, Gebäudetechnik, Haustechnik	8
building services engineer Ingenieur für Gebäudetechnik	11
building specification *(tech.)* Gebäudequalität, Baubeschreibung	8
building surveyor Bausachverständiger	11
business park Gewerbepark	3
cadastral map Flurkarte	8
cadastral plan Katasterplan	8
cancel *(verb)* absagen	2
canvass *(verb)* um Kunden werben, Kunden akquirieren	11
capital expenditure *(capex)* Investitionsaufwand	8
capital gains tax Kapitalertragsteuer	8
capitalised income value Ertragswert	9
carpenter Zimmermann	6
carpet fitter Teppichleger	6
cash and carry Abholgroßhandelsmarkt	4
catchment area Einzugsgebiet	3
CBD (central business district) Hauptgeschäftsviertel	3
CCTV (closed circuit television) *(tech.)* Videoüberwachung	3
cellular office Einzel-/Zellenbüro, Kombibüro	3
centrality index Zentralitätskennziffer	4

Term	Unit
CEO (Chief Executive Officer) Vorsitzender der Geschäftsführung, Vorstandssprecher, Vorstandsvorsitzender	11
Certificate of Making Good Defects Bauabnahmeprotokoll zur Bestätigung der Mängelbeseitigung bzw. Restmängelfreiheit	9
Certificate of Partial Completion Teilabnahmebescheinigung	9
Certificate of Practical Completion Abnahmebescheinigung	9
checkout Kasse	4
circulation areas Verkehrsflächen	4
cladding *(tech.)* Verkleidung	3
clause *(law)* Klausel, Ziffer	7
clerk of works Bauaufseher	9
client (principal) Bauherr, Auftraggeber	9
collateral Kreditsicherheit, zusätzliche Sicherheit	9
collateral warranty (UK) Ausfallbürgschaft, Gewährleistung	8,9
column *(tech.)* Säule	3
column grid *(tech.)* Stützenraster	3
commence *(verb)* anfangen, beginnen	11
commercial property Gewerbliche-, Geschäftsimmobilien	11
commission *(verb, noun)* jmdn. beauftragen, Provision	11
commitment Einsatz, Engagement	10
commitment fee Zusageprovision	9
common areas Gemeinschaftsflächen	3
commonhold *(law)* Teileigentum, Wohnungseigentum	8

Term	Unit
communications, transport infrastructure Verkehrsanbindungen	3
compensation *(law)* Schaden(s)ersatz	7
competing properties Konkurrenzobjekte	8
competition clause *(law)* Wettbewerbsklausel	8
competitive tender Ausschreibung	9
compilation Erfassung, Zusammenstellung	11
complaint Beschwerde	2
completion Erfüllung	7
completion date Fertigstellungszeitpunkt	9
compliance (with regulations) Übereinstimmung (mit gesetzlichen Vorschriften)	6
compulsory auction Zwangsversteigerung	9
concrete Beton	5
condensation *(tech.)* Kondenswasser	6
confidentiality agreement *(law)* Vertraulichkeitserklärung	7
confirm *(verb)* bestätigen	2
consent Genehmigung	6
conservation area Schutzgebiet	9
consideration (price) *(law)* Kaufpreis, Gegenleistung	7
consolidating Konsolidierung	5
construction manager Bauleiter	11
consulting Beratung	8
consumer spending Verbraucherausgaben	4
contamination *(tech.)* Kontaminierung, Altlasten	7
contingency sum Rücklage für Unvorhergesehenes	9

Glossary

English	German	Unit
contingency time	Zeitreserve, Zeitpuffer	9
contract award	Auftragsvergabe/-erteilung	9
contractor	Auftragnehmer, Bauunternehmen	9
contractual defects liability period	Gewährleistungsdauer	9
conurbation	Ballungsgebiet	7
convenience store	kleiner Lebensmittelladen, Tante-Emma-Laden	4
conversion	Umbau, bauliche Veränderung	9
conversion of footfall to spend	Anzahl der konsumierende Passanten	4
convey *(verb)*	übermitteln	10
conveyance *(law)*	Auflassung	7
conveyor belt *(tech.)*	Förderband	5
core catchment area	Unmittelbares Einzugsgebiet	4
corporate income tax	Körperschaftsteuer	8
corridors, hallways	Flure, Gänge	3
corrosion *(tech.)*	Korrosion	6
cost estimate	Kostenschätzung	9
cost plan	Kostenaufstellung	9
countersign *(verb, law)*	gegenzeichnen	7
courtyard	Innenhof	3
covenant (good/poor covenant)	Mieter mit guter/schlechter Bonität	6
covenant information	Information über den Mieter	8
covering letter	Bewerbungsschreiben	11
crack *(tech.)*	Riss	6
craftsperson	Handwerker	6
credit standing	Bonität	8
cross docking	Direktumschlag, Kreuzverkupplung	5
cross section	Querschnitt	9
current rent	aktuelle Miete	8
curriculum vitae (CV), US: résumé	Lebenslauf	11
curtain wall *(tech.)*	vorgehängte Fassade	3
customer profile	Kundenprofil	4
damp *(tech.)*	feucht	6
debt	Fremdkapital	9
debt service cover ratio (DSCR)	Kapitaldienstdeckungsgrad	9
dedication	Engagement, Einsatz	10
default *(law)*	Verzug, Versäumnis	8
default interest	Verzugszinsen	8
defect	Mangel	9
Defect Rectification Period	Gewährleistungsfrist	9
defect rectification, remedial work, making good defects	Mängelbeseitigung, Nachbesserungsarbeiten	9
defects in quality *(law)*	Sachmängel	7
defects in title *(law)*	Rechtsmängel	7
Defects Liability Period	Mängelhaftungszeitraum	9
Defects Notification Period	Mängelanzeigefrist	9
deferment of possession	Verzögerung der Übergabe an den Auftragnehmer	9
deferred maintenance	aufgeschobene Instandhaltung	6
delay	Verzögerung	9
deleterious material *(tech.)*	schädliche Stoffe	8
delivery entrance	Liefereingang	8
demise	Mietflächen, Mietsache	6
demised premises, rental space	Mietfläche	8
demolition	Abriss	9
department store	Warenhaus, Kaufhaus	4
deposit account	Sperrkonto, Kautionskonto	8
detailed (full) planning application	Bauanfrage	9
details	Detailzeichnungen	9
developer	Projektentwickler	11
developers' profit	Entwicklergewinn	9
developers' return	Projektentwicklersgewinn	9
developers' yield	Projektentwicklerrendite	9
development (property development)	Projektentwicklung	9
development charges, utility diversion and connection costs	Erschließungskosten	9
development plan (detailed local)	Bebauungsplan	9
devise *(verb)*	ausarbeiten	11
diagrams	Strangschema (Wasser- oder Heizungsleitungen)	9
disclose *(verb)*	offenlegen	7
discolouring *(tech.)*	Verfärbung	6
display window	Schaufenster	4
disposable income	verfügbares Einkommen	4
disposal	Verkauf, Veräußerung, Entsorgung	11
disruption (to building users)	Beeinträchtigung (für die Nutzer)	6

Glossary

Term	Unit
dissatisfaction Unzufriedenheit	2
distribution centre Verteilzentrum	5
DIY (Do It Yourself) store / (US) home improvement center Baumarkt	4
dock leveller *(tech.)* Überladebrücke	5
downtime Ausfallzeit	6
draft Entwurf, Fassung	7
drainage *(tech.)* Oberflächenentwässerung	6
drainage system *(tech.)* Entwässerungssystem	8
draw up a contract *(law)* einen Vertrag aufsetzen	7
drawdown Auszahlung, Inanspruchnahme (bei Krediten)	9
drive time Fahrzeit	4
drop dead fee, abortive fee vorvertragliche Bearbeitungsgebühr	9
dry liner *(tech.)* Trockenbauer	6
Duty of Care Letter Sorgfaltspflichterklärung	9
dwell times Verweildauer	4
easement (US: servitude) *(law)* Grunddienstbarkeit	8
economic climate Wirtschaftsdaten	8
effective rent Effektivmiete	6
efflorescence *(tech.)* Ausblühung	6
electrician Elektriker	6
electronics retailer (also electricals) Elektrohandel, Elektrofachhandel	4
elevation *(tech.)* Aufriss	9
elevator, lift Aufzug	8
elevator/lift lobby Aufzugsvorraum	3
emergency exit, fire exit *(tech.)* Notausgang	3

Term	Unit
employment structure Beschäftigungsstruktur	4
encumbrance *(law)* Grundstücksbelastung	8
envelope *(tech.)* Gebäudehülle	9
environment Umwelt	8
equity Eigenkapital	9
erect *(verb)* aufstellen, errichten	9
escalator clause *(law)* Indexklausel, Wertsicherungsklausel	6
escalator *(tech.)* Rolltreppe	8
escrow account *(law)* Notaranderkonto	7
estoppel certificate *(law)* Bestätigung vorhandener Rechte und Pflichten	8
excerpt from the commercial register *(law)* Handelsregisterauszug	8
execution, to sign a contract, to complete the terms of a contract *(law)* Durchführung, einen Vertrag unterschreiben, Ausführung	7
expansion land Erweiterungsflächen	5
expenditure forecast Ausgabenprognose	9
expense budget Kostenplan	9
expenses Ausgaben	9
expiry Vertragsablauf	6
extension of time Bauzeitverlängerung	9
external grounds Außenanlagen	3
façade *(tech.)* Fassade	6
factory outlet centre Fabrikverkaufszentrum	4
fast food chain Fastfoodkette	4
fault Fehler, Störung	6
feasibility study Machbarkeitsstudie	11
fee Gebühr, Provision	9

Term	Unit
fee calculation Honorarberechnung	9
final statement Schlussrechnung, Endabrechnung	9
financial covenants Finanzskennziffern, -zahlen	9
fire alarm system *(tech.)* Brandmeldesystem	8
fire extinguisher *(tech.)* Feuerlöscher	8
fire officer Feuerwehrmann	6
fire protection Brandschutz	8
fit-out *(tech.)* Ausbau	8
fittings, chattels Zubehör	7
fixtures wesentliche Bestandteile	7
flashing Abdeckblech	6
flood plain Aue, Talaue, Überschwemmungsgebiet	9
floor area Grundfläche	8
floor box Fußbodentank	3
floor covering Bodenbelag	8
floor plan Grundriss, Raumaufteilung, Flächengrundriss	3
floorlayer Bodenleger	6
floorplate Geschossgrundriss, Grundrissgestaltung, Etagengrundriss	3
food discounter Lebensmitteldiscounter	4
footfall Passantenfrequenz	4
footprint Grundfläche	3
force majeure *(law)* höhere Gewalt	7
foreclosure Zwangsvollstreckung	9
forklift truck Gabelstapler	5
forward *(verb)* weiterleiten	2
franchise restaurant Franchiserestaurant	4
freehold *(law)* Eigentum	8
frontage Schaufensterfront, Länge der Straßenfront	4

Glossary

Term	Unit
Full Repairing and Insuring Lease (FRI Lease) *(law)* see page 120	6
full table-service restaurant gehobene Küche	4
furniture retailer (also home furnishing) Möbelgeschäft, Möbelmarkt	4
gantt chart Gantt-Diagramm, Balkendiagramm	9
general contractor Generalunternehmer	9
goodwill Wohlwollen	10
government Regierung, öffentliche Hand	8
graduate Hochschulabsolvent	11
greenfield site Neubauland, Rohbauland, Grundstück auf der grünen Wiese	9
grocery (store) Lebensmittel(-laden)	4
gross capital value Bruttokapitalwert	9
gross development value Bruttoentwicklungswert	9
gross rent Bruttomiete	6
guarantee Garantie, Bürgschaft	8
gutter *(tech.)* Abflussrinne, Dachrinne	6
handling equipment *(tech.)* Hebetechnik	5
handover Übergabe, Abnahme	11
Hard Services Technik (FM-Dienste)	6
hazard Gefährdung	6
headlease *(law)* Hauptmietvertrag	7
headline rent Nominalmiete	6
headquarters building Firmenzentrale	3
heads of terms (HoTs) Grundsatzvereinbarung	6
health & beauty retailer Drogeriemarkt	4

Term	Unit
health food shop Reformhaus	4
Heavy Goods Vehicle (HGV) LKW	5
hedging Zinssicherung	9
high bay warehouse Hochregallager	5
high street shop / town centre (in-town sector) Geschäft in der Fußgängerzone / Innenstadt	4
high-class restaurant Nobelrestaurant	4
home furnishing (also furniture retailer) Möbelgeschäft, Möbelmarkt	4
hoomewares Haushaltswaren	4
hourly fees Stundensätze	9
HVAC Engineer (Heating Ventilation & Air Conditioning) *(tech.)* Ingenieur für Klimatechnik	6
implement *(verb)* durchsetzen	11
incidental building costs, on-costs Baunebenkosten	9
incoming shipments Wareneingang	5
indemnity *(law)* Ausfallhaftung, Schadloshaltung, Entschädigung	9
independent retail outlet privat oder familiengeführtes Geschäft (nicht einer Kette angehörendes Geschäft)	4
inspection for final completion Besichtigung zur Endabnahme	9
instalment *(finan.)* Abschlagszahlung	9
insurance Versicherung	6
interest *(finan.)* Zinsen	6
interest cover ratio (ICR) *(finan.)* Zinsdeckungsgrad	9
interest on default *(finan.)* Verzugszinsen	9
interim accounts *(finan.)* Zwischenabrechnung	9

Term	Unit
internal rate of return (IRR) *(finan.)* interner Zinsfuß	9
international brands internationale bekannte Einzelhändler	4
investment agent Immobilienmakler An- und Verkauf	9
investment memoranda Exposé	7
invitation to tender Angebotsaufforderung	9
invoice *(finan.)* Rechnung, Abrechnung; *(verb)* in Rechnung stellen	6
ITZA (in terms of zone A) see page 68	4
joiner Tischler	6
kitting Bereitstellung, körperliche Bereitstellung	5
land charge *(law, finan.)* Grundpfandrecht, Grundschuld	8
land register Grundbuch	8
land tax, UK: rates *(finan.)* Grundsteuer	8
land use permission Nutzungsgenehmigung	8
land use plan (US: zoning ordinance) Flächennutzungsplan	9
land value *(finan.)* Bodenwert	8
landlord Vermieter	6
landscape architect Landschaftsarchitekt	9
landscape gardener Landschaftsgärtner	6
landscaping Gärtnerdienste, Grünflächengestaltung	6
land register *(law)* Grundbuch	7
latent defect *(tech.)* versteckter Mangel	9
latent defects insurance (UK) Versicherung gegen versteckte Mängel	9

Glossary

Term	Unit
latent value *(finan.)* Wert, potenzieller Wert	9
layout Flächenaufteilung, Raumplan	3
leak *(tech.)* Leck	6
lease (contract) *(law)* Mietvertrag	6
lease expiry Ende des Mietvertrages, Mietvertragsende	8
lease renewal, lease extension Mietvertragsverlängerung	6
leasehold *(law)* (ähnlich wie) Erbbaurecht	8
leasing flexibility flexible Vermietungsgestaltung, Vermietungsmöglichkeiten	8
lease-up (US) *(verb)* neu vermieten	6
leisure Freizeit (Freizeitimmobilien, z.B. Kinos, Theater oder Ferienhäuser)	7
lender Darlehensgeber	9
lessee (tenant) Mieter	6
lessor (landlord, owner) *(law)* Vermieter	6
letter of acknowledgement Empfangsbestätigung	9
Letter of Intent (LOI) Absichtserklärung	7
letting costs Vermietungskosten	8
lettings agent Vermietungsmakler	9
leverage (UK: gearing) Fremdkapitalaufnahme	9
liability Haftung	6
liaise *(verb)* mit jmdm. zusammenarbeiten, Verbindung aufnehmen	11
lien *(finan.)* Grundpfandrecht	9
lightning protection *(tech.)* Blitzschutz	8

Term	Unit
limited recourse loan *(finan.)* Finanzierung mit eingeschränktem Rückgriffsrecht der Fremdkapitalgeber auf die Projektträger	9
liquidated and ascertained damages *(law, finan.)* vertraglich festgesetzte Schadensumme, Verzögerungsschadenersatz	9
listed building (US: landmark property) denkmalgeschütztes Gebäude, Baudenkmal	8
live load *(tech.)* Nutzlast	3
load bearing wall, structural wall *(tech.)* tragende Wand	3
loading dock *(tech.)* Ladetür	5
loan amount *(finan.)* Kreditbetrag, Darlehensbetrag	9
loan to cost (LTC) *(finan.)* Kostenquote	9
loan to value ratio (LTV) *(finan.)* Beleihungsquote, Beleihungssatz	9
lobby Eingangshalle	3
local/neighbourhood shopping centre Nahversorgungszentrum	4
local land charge *(law)* Baulasten	8
Local Planning Authorities (LPA) regionale und kommunale Planungsbehörde	9
local shopping parade Haupteinkaufsstraße in einem kleinen Ort, vorgelagerte Ladenzeile	4
location Standort, Makrolage	7
lump sum *(finan.)* Pauschale	7
lump sum contract *(finan.)* Pauschalvertrag	9

Term	Unit
luxury retailer (also high-end retailer or upmarket brand) Einzelhändler im Luxussegment/im Nobelsegment	4
magnet store, anchor store Magnetbetrieb, Anker	4
main contractor Hauptunternehmer	9
maintenance Instandhaltung, Wartung	6
maintenance backlog *(tech.)* Instandhaltungsstau	8
maintenance planning *(tech.)* Instandhaltungsplanung	6
maintenance schedule *(tech.)* Instandhaltungsplan	6
major space unit (MSU) großflächiger Einzelhandel	4
make good *(tech.)* beheben	7
manoeuvring area Rangierflächen	5
manufacturing Fertigung, Produktion	5
margin *(finan.)* Marge	9
market flex clause *(finan.)* Marktanpassungsklausel	9
market rent Marktmiete	8
market value Marktwert, Verkehrswert	8
masonry, brickwork *(tech.)* Mauerwerk	6
master programme *(tech.)* Bauzeitplan	9
materials handling Materialfluss	5
matter Angelegenheit	6
maturity *(finan.)* Laufzeitende	9
measured survey Flächenaufmaß	7
meter *(tech.)* Zähler	8
mid-market clothing retailer Modegeschäft im mittleren Preissegment	4
milestone Meilenstein	9

Glossary

Term	Unit
minutes (meeting minutes) Besprechungsprotokoll	6
mobile telephone shop (also telecommunications) Handyladen / Mobilfunkgeschäft	4
modification, amendment Änderung	7
monitor *(verb)*, **supervise** *(verb)* beaufsichtigen, betreuen, leiten, überwachen	11
monitoring surveyor Sachverständiger, Bauleiter	9
mortgage *(finan.)* Hypothek	8
mortgage lending value *(finan.)* Beleihungswert	9
mould Schimmel	6
multiple Filialist	4
national multiple Filialist (bundesweit)	4
negotiated tender freihändige Vergabe	9
negotiation Verhandlung	6
neighbourhood Nachbarschaft	8
net asset value (NAV) *(finan.)* Nettovermögenswert	9
net initial yield *(finan.)* Nettoanfangsrendite	8
net rent Nettomieteinnahmen	6
new-build Neubau	8
newsagent Zeitungsgeschäft (kein Kiosk)	4
noise sources Schallemissionsquellen	8
non-recoverable costs nicht umlegbare Kosten	8
non-utilization fee *(finan.)* Nichtabnahmeprovision	9
notary *(law)* Notar	7
notice Mitteilung	6
obligation Verpflichtung	7
occupancy Belegung, Besitz, Gebäudenutzung, Nutzungsart	11

Term	Unit
occupier Nutzer	3
open tender öffentliche Ausschreibung	9
opening, appointment, position, post Stelle, Arbeitsplatz	11
open-plan *(office)* Großraumbüro	3
operating costs *(finan.)* Betriebskosten	6
order picking Kommissionierung, Kommissionieren	5
outgoing shipments Warenausgang	5
outgoings *(finan.)* Ausgaben	9
outline planning application/permission Bauvoranfrage / Bauvorbescheid	9
out-of-town shopping centre/mall Einkaufszentrum auf der grünen Wiese	4
overage *(finan.)* Überschuss	9
overrun Terminüberschreitung	9
owner Eigentümer	8
painter Maler	6
pallet Palette	5
pan-European retailers europäische Einzelhändler	4
pantry, kitchenette Teeküche	3
paragraph *(law)* Absatz	7
partition wall *(tech.)* Trennwand	3
passing rent *(finan.)* aktuelle Miete	6
patrol (of a security guard) Runde	6
payment certificate *(finan.)* Zahlungsbescheinigung, Zwischenabnahme	9
payment conditions *(finan.)* Zahlungsbedingungen	9
payment schedule *(finan.)* Zahlungsplan	9

Term	Unit
pedestrian flow (also shopper flow) Passantenströme	4
per annum pro anno, jährlich	7
performance *(law)* Ausführung, Erfüllung	7
perimeter *(tech.)* Umfang, Umriss eines Gebäudes	3
perimeter trunking *(tech.)* Fensterbankkabelkanäle	3
periphery Peripherie, Umland	8
permitted use Art und Maß der baulichen Nutzung	8
pest control Ungezieferbekämpfung	6
pest controller Kammerjäger	6
pharmacy Apotheke	4
pipework *(tech.)* Rohrleitungssystem	8
pitch Einschätzung der Lage einer Einzelhandelsimmobilie im Bezug auf potenziellen Umsatz und Gewinn.	4
planned maintenance *(tech.)* vorbeugende Instandhaltung, Wartung	6
planning appeal Planungsrevision	9
planning application Bauantrag	8
planning authority Planungsbehörde	9
planning consultant Bauingenieur	9
planning grid *(tech.)* Ausbauraster	8
planning permission (US: building permit) Baugenehmigung	8
plans Grundriss-, Aufrissplan	9
plant *(tech.)* Anlage	xx
plant room *(tech.)* Haustechnikraum	3
plaster *(tech.)* Putz, Verputz	6

Glossary

	Unit
plasterboard *(tech.)* Gipskartonwand, Gipsplatte	6
plasterer Gipser / Verputzer	6
plot ratio (US: floor to area ratio) Geschossflächenzahl (GFZ)	9
plumber Klempner	6
point of sale (POS) Verkaufsort	4
point of sale terminal *(tech.)* POS-Kassensystem	4
population Einwohner(zahl)	8
position, post, opening appointment Stelle, Arbeitsplatz	11
possession Besitz	7
power of attorney, authority to act *(law)* Vollmacht	7
preamble *(law)* Präambel	7
pre-letting *(law)* Vorvermietung	9
preliminary building application Bauvoranfrage	8
preliminary building notice Bauvorbescheid	8
preliminary enquiries Voruntersuchungen	9
premises Gebäude	4
premium clothing retailer Modegeschäft im oberen Preissegment	4
prepayment *(finan.)* Vorauszahlung, vorzeitige Rückzahlung	9
prepayment fee *(finan.)* vorzeitige Rückzahlungsgebühr	9
prestigious repräsentativ	6
preventative maintenance *(tech.)* vorsorgliche/vorbeugende Instandhaltung	6
previous vorherig	2
prime pitch Ia-Handelslage	4
prime rent Spitzenmiete	8
prime trading location Ia-Handelslage	4

	Unit
principal Kapital, Darlehensbetrag	9
principal *(client)* Bauherr, Auftraggeber	9
priority notice *(law)* Auflassungsvormerkung	7
procurement Beschaffung, Besorgung, Einkauf	11
procurement procedure Vergabeverfahren	9
production information Projektanforderungen	9
profit *(finan.)* Gewinn, Ertrag	9
progress payment, interim payment *(finan.)* Abschlagszahlung, Zahlung nach Leistungsabschnitten/ Bautenstand	9
project manager Projektleiter	9
projector Beamer	10
prominent hervorstechend	3
propose *(verb)* vorschlagen	2
prospective Interessent	6
provisions, terms of the contract *(law)* Bestimmungen, Vertragsklausel	7
proximity Umgebung	3
public house Kneipe, Gaststätte, Wirtshaus	4
purchase Kauf	8
purchaser Käufer	7
purchasing power Kaufkraft	4
pursuant gemäß	7
pursue *(verb)* weiterfolgen	7
quantity surveyor (UK) Architekt / Kosten- und Abrechnungsingenieur	9
query Anfrage, Frage	6
quotation Kostenvoranschlag	6
rack rent (UK) höchstmögliche erzielbare Miete / Marktmiete	6
racks Regale	5
raised floor *(tech.)* Doppelboden, Hohlraumboden	3

	Unit
rates (UK) / property tax (US) *(finan.)* Grundsteuer	6
Real Estate Transfer Tax (RETT) (UK: Stamp Duty Land Tax) *(finan.)* Grunderwerbsteuer	8
rear entrance Hintereingang	8
reception Empfangsbereich	3
recommendation Empfehlung	2
reconcile *(verb)* abgleichen, abstimmen	7
recoverable costs *(finan.)* Umlegbare Nebenkosten	8
rectify *(verb)* beheben	6
redecorate *(verb)* renovieren	8
redevelopment area Sanierungsgebiet	8
refurbishment Renovierung, Sanierung	3
refuse, waste Abfall	8
regarding, concerning bezüglich, betreffend	2
re-gear a lease Mietvertrag neu verhandeln	6
regional, city centre scheme regionales Einkaufszentrum	4
regional multiple Filialist (regional)	4
regret *(verb)* etw. bedauern	2
remediate *(verb)* beseitigen	6
remediation (of contamination) Altlastensanierung	9
reminder Mahnung, Zahlungserinnerung	2
rent Miete	3
rent guarantee *(law)* Mietgarantie	8
rent review Überprüfung und Anpassung bzw. Neufestsetzung der Miethöhe	6
rent roll Mieterliste, Mieterbestandsliste	6
rental income Mieterträge	9
repairs Reparaturen, Instandsetzung	6

Glossary

Term	Unit
representations and warranties *(law)* Zusicherungen und Gewährleistungen	7
request Anfrage	2
reschedule *(verb)* neu ansetzen, verlegen	2
residential property Wohnimmobilien	11
residual method *(finan.)* Residualverfahren	9
resignation Kündigung (Arbeitsstelle)	11
resolve *(verb)* beheben, beseitigen, klären	6
respond *(verb)* antworten, beantworten	2
response Antwort	2
restaurant chain Systemgastronomie	4
restricted tender beschränkte Vergabe	9
restriction Beschränkung	8
restrictive covenant *(law)* dingliche Nutzungsbeschränkung	8
retail area Verkaufsfläche, Einzelhandelsfläche	4
retail chain Einzelhandelskette	4
retail turnover Einzelhandelsumsatz	4
retail warehouse (also: big-box store, solus unit) Fachmarkt	4
retail warehouse centre/park Fachmarktzentrum	4
retention *(finan.)* Einbehalt	9
retirement Pensionierung	10
return frontage eine Schaufensterfront auf der Seite oder Rückseite des Gebäudes	4
revise *(verb)* überarbeiten	7
grid *(tech.)* Raster	3
right of pre-emption *(law)* Vorkaufsrecht	7
right of way *(law)* Wegerecht	8

Term	Unit
right of withdrawal *(law)* Rücktrittsrecht	7
roofer Dachdecker	6
rumour Gerücht	7
rust *(tech.)* Rost	6
shaft *(tech.)* Schacht	3
salutation Anrede	2
schedule Verzeichnis, Tabelle, Aufstellung	7
schedule *(verb)* einen Termin ansetzen	2
schedule of areas Flächenaufstellung	7
schedule of defects, snagging list, schedule of dilapidations (UK) *(tech.)* Mängelliste	9
schedule of quantities *(tech.)* Leistungsverzeichniss	9
schedule of work *(tech.)* Bauablaufplan	9
schedules Aufstellungen / Übersichten zu den verwendeten Materialen, Produkten und Ausstattungen	9
scuffing *(tech.)* Abscheuern	6
seal *(tech.)* Abdichung	6
secondary catchment area sekundäres Einzugsgebiet	4
section *(law)* Abschnitt, Paragraf	7
sectional completion *(tech.)* Fertigstellung in Bauabschnitten	9
sections *(tech.)* Schnitte	9
security Sicherheit	9
security, deposit Mietkaution	8
service charges Nebenkosten	6
service core *(tech.)* Gebäudekern	3
service riser *(tech.)* Versorgungsschacht	3
service sector Dienstleistung	8
service yard *(tech.)* Andienungszone	5

Term	Unit
servicing fee *(finan.)* Bearbeitungsgebühr	9
sewage *(tech.)* Abwasser	6
share deal Anteilskauf	7
shoe repair Schuhreparatur	4
shoe shop (also footwear) Schuhgeschäft	4
shopfitter Ladenausbauer	6
shopping basket Warenkorb	4
shopping centre visitors Kundenfrequenz in einem Einkaufszentrum	4
shopping trolley (US: shopping cart) Einkaufswagen	4
side letter Nebenabrede	7
sign *(verb)* unterschreiben	7
signage Beschilderung	8
site Grundstück	3
site agent Bauleiter des Auftragnehmers	9
site bearing capacity *(tech.)* Baugrundbeschaffenheit, Tragfähigkeit	9
site boundary *(tech.)* Grundstücksgrenze	3
site conditions Bodenbeschaffenheit	9
site coverage (ratio) *(tech.)* Grundflächenzahl (GRZ)	9
situation Mikrolage	7
socio-economic profile sozioökonomisches Profil	4
soft services Infrastruktur (FM Dienste)	6
soil analysis Bodenanalyse	
solar shading *(tech.)* Sonnenschutz	3
solicitor, lawyer Anwalt	7
solus unit Fachmarkt (alleinstehend und nicht Teil eines Fachmarktzentrums)	4
sorting Sortierung	5
sought-after gefragt, begehrt	3
space Flächen	8

Glossary

Term	Unit
space planner and interior designer Innenarchitekt	9
speciality retailer Fachmarkt	4
specification *(tech.)* Spezifikation, Leistungsbeschreibung, Baubeschreibung	3
staff rooms Sozialräume	4
staging area *(tech.)* Bereitstellungszone	5
staircase Treppenhaus	3
standard shop unit (SSU) Standard-Ladenlokal	4
stand-by fee *(finan.)* Bereitstellungsprovision	9
statutory *(law)* gesetzlich	6
statutory regulations, provisions *(law)* gesetzlichen Vorschriften	8
stock (Immobilien-)Bestand	8
stonemason Steinmetz	6
storage areas Lagerfläche	4
structural engineer Statiker	11
structural grid *(tech.)* Gebäuderaster, Konstruktionsraster	3
structural wall, load bearing wall *(tech.)* Konstruktionswand	3
subcontractor *(tech.)* Subunternehmen	9
subject to contract see page 150	7
sublease, underlease *(law)* Untermiete, Untermietvertrag	6
sublessee, underlessee *(law)* Untermieter	6
sublessor, underlessor *(law)* Untervermieter	6
sublet *(verb)* untervermieten	8
substructure *(tech.)* Unterbauten	9
suite Büro, Büroeinheit	3
supermarket Supermarkt	4
superstore (also hypermarket) Verbrauchermarkt	4
superstructure *(tech.)* Überbauten	9
supervise *(verb)*, **monitor** *(verb)* beaufsichtigen, betreuen, leiten, überwachen	11
supplier Hersteller, Versorger, Lieferant	6
surrounding developments unmittelbar angrenzende Liegenschaften	8
survey Messung	7
suspended ceiling *(tech.)* abgehängte Decke	3
tail-end fee (exit fee, end fee) Exit-Gebühr	9
takeaway Schnellrestaurant, Imbissbude	4
take-up Flächenumsatz	8
tax Steuer	8
tenancy agreement *(law)* kurzfristiger Mietvertrag	6
tenancy schedule Mieterliste	9
tenant Mieter	3
tenant's improvements (TIs) Mietereinbauten, vom Mieter bezahlte Verbesserungen	6
tenanted areas Miterfläche	3
tender Ausschreibung, Angebot	11
tendering Angebotseinholung	9
tenure *(law)* Eigentumsverhältnisse	8
term (lease term) Laufzeit des Mietverhältnisses	6
terminate (the lease contract) Mietvertrag kündigen	6
termination Kündigung	8
terms Bedingungen, Allgemeine Geschäftsbedingungen	7
tertiary catchment area tertiäres Einzugsgebiet	4
tile *(tech.)* Fliese, Ziegel, Platte	3
title deed *(law)* Eigentumserwerbsurkunde, Eigentumsnachweis	7
town planning Stadtplanung	8
tradesperson Handwerker	6
traineeship Lehre	11
transfer of possession *(law)* Besitzübergang	7
transfer of title *(law)* Eigentumsübergang	7
transformer *(tech.)* Trafostation	8
travel agent Reisebüro	4
turnover rent *(finan.)* Umsatzmiete	6
types of use Nutzungsarten	8
undergraduate Student vor dem ersten akademischen Grad	11
underlease, sublease *(law)* Untermiete, Untermietvertrag	6
underlessee, sublessee *(law)* Untermieter	6
underlessor, sublessor *(law)* Untervermieter	6
undertake *(verb)* ausführen, durchführen	11
unemployment levels, rate Arbeitslosigkeit, Arbeitslosenquote	8
unforeseen unvorhergesehen	6
unit Einheit, Bauteil, Bauelement	11
uplift (rent uplift) Hebung	7
urgent dringend, eilig	2
use Nutzung(sarten)	8
use class Art der Flächennutzung	9
usufruct *(law)* Nießbrauch	8
utilities Versorgungseinrichtungen, Versorgungsbetriebe, Stadtwerke	11

Glossary

	Unit
utility easement *(law)* Kabelrechte, Grunddienstbarkeit für Versorgungsunternehmen	8
vacancy, void Leerstand	8
vacant leer stehend	6
vacate *(verb)* räumen	6
valuation Bewertung	8
value clothing, fashion discounter Textildiscounter	4
value retailer, discount retailer Discounter	4
valuer, valuations surveyor Sachverständiger, Gutachter	11
vendor Verkäufer	8
ventilation *(tech.)* Lüftung	3
vet *(verb)* überprüfen	6
vetting Sicherheitsüberprüfung	6

	Unit
vicinity Umfeld	8
viewing Besichtigung	11
visible sichtbar	5
void *(tech.)* Leerstand (tech. Hohlraum)	3
void (allowance) Abschlag für Mietausfall	9
waiver *(law)* Verzicht	7
warehousing Lagerung, Einlagerung	5
warranty *(law)* Garantie, Gewährleistung, Zusicherung	7
warranty bond *(law)* Gewährleistungsbürgschaft	9
waste management Müllbeseitigung	6
wayfinding system Gebäudeleitsystem	8

	Unit
wear and tear *(tech.)* Abnutzung	7
weathering *(tech.)* Wetter bedingte Alterung	6
witholding tax *(finan.)* Quellensteuer	8
women's clothing / women's fashion Damenbekleidung / Damenmode	4
work stages *(tech.)* Leistungsphasen	9
workmanship *(tech.)* Ausführungsqualität	9
workstation, work space Arbeitsplatz	3
yield *(finan.)* Rendite	9
yielding up *(law)* Verpflichtungen bei der Rückgabe der Mietsache	8
young fashion junge Mode	4